Aquinas, Feminism, and the Common Good

MORAL TRADITIONS SERIES
James F. Keenan, S.J., Editor

American Protestant Ethics and the Legacy of H. Richard Niebuhr
William Werpehowski

Aquinas and Empowerment: Classical Ethics for Ordinary Lives
G. Simon Harak, S.J., Editor

The Banality of Good and Evil: Moral Lessons from the Shoah and Jewish Tradition
David R. Blumenthal

Bridging the Sacred and the Secular: Selected Writings of John Courtney Murray
John Courtney Murray, S.J.
J. Leon Hooper, S.J., Editor

A Call to Fidelity: On the Moral Theology of Charles E. Curran
James J. Walter, Timothy E. O'Connell, and Thomas A. Shannon, Editors

The Catholic Moral Tradition Today: A Synthesis
Charles E. Curran

Catholic Social Teaching, 1891–Present
Charles E. Curran

The Christian Case for Virtue Ethics
Joseph J. Kotva, Jr.

The Context of Casuistry
James F. Keenan, S.J., and Thomas A. Shannon, Editors

Democracy on Purpose: Justice and the Reality of God
Franklin I. Gamwell

Ethics and Economics of Assisted Reproduction
Maura A. Ryan

The Ethics of Aquinas
Stephen J. Pope, Editor

The Evolution of Altruism and the Ordering of Love
Stephen J. Pope

The Fellowship of Life: Virtue Ethics and Orthodox Christianity
Joseph Woodill

Feminist Ethics and Natural Law: The End of the Anathemas
Cristina L. H. Traina

The Global Face of Public Faith: Politics, Human Rights, and Christian Ethics
David Hollenbach, S.J.

Heroes, Saints, and Ordinary Morality
Andrew Michael Flescher

Introduction to Jewish and Catholic Bioethics: A Comparative Analysis
Aaron L. Mackler

Jewish and Catholic Bioethics: An Ecumenical Dialogue
Edmund D. Pellegrino and Alan I. Faden, Editors

John Paul II and the Legacy of Dignitatis Humanae
Hermínio Rico, S.J.

Josef Fuchs on Natural Law
Mark Graham

Love, Human and Divine: The Heart of Christian Ethics
Edward Collins Vacek, S.J.

Medicine and the Ethics of Care
Diana Fritz Cates and Paul Lauritzen, Editors

The Origins of Moral Theology in the United States: Three Different Approaches
Charles E. Curran

Shaping the Moral Life: An Approach to Moral Theology
Klaus Demmer, M.S.C.
Translated by Roberto Dell'Oro
James F. Keenan, S.J., Editor

Who Count as Persons? Human Identity and the Ethics of Killing
John F. Kavanaugh, S.J.

Aquinas, Feminism, and the Common Good

Susanne M. DeCrane

GEORGETOWN UNIVERSITY PRESS/WASHINGTON, D.C.

Georgetown University Press, Washington, D.C.
© 2004 by Georgetown University Press. All rights reserved.
Printed in the United States of America

10 9 8 7 6 5 4 3 2 1   2004

This book is printed on acid-free paper meeting
the requirements of the American National Standard
for Permanence in Paper for Printed Library Materials.

Library of Congress Cataloging-in-Publication Data

DeCrane, Susanne M. (Susanne Marie), 1949–
    Aquinas, feminism, and the common good / Susanne M. DeCrane.
        p.   cm. — (Moral traditions series)
    Includes bibliographical references and index.
    ISBN 0-87840-349-3 (alk. paper)
    1. Peace (Philosophy) 2. Common good.   3. Thomas, Aquinas, Saint,
1225?–1274.   4. Women—Medical care—United States.
    5. Feminism—Religious aspects—Christianity. I. Title. II. Series.
B105.P4D43   2004
230′.2′082—dc22   2003019457

If any among us in the human community are not equally welcomed at the center; if any among us is dying because they have been displaced from the community and denied its goods; if any among us has been subjugated by the community, enslaved by it or exploited, with their heritage stolen or their access to it closed off; if any of us have been thought to be less "human" than others, humiliated or ignored, then these are to be given some priority in our commitments to all. These are the "poor," the disadvantaged or unprotected, theirs are the voices least likely to be heard, theirs is the pain least likely to be seen; theirs is the participation least likely to be allowed. A "preferential option for the poor" is, therefore, a recognition of, and a granting of strategic priority to, the just claims of those whom the human community has heretofore excluded, deprived, or unfairly burdened.

—MARGARET FARLEY, RSM

Contents

◌

Acknowledgments

THE EXISTENCE OF THIS BOOK is due to the support and encouragement of many people. Many thanks are due to Ellen Leonard,
C.S.J., who helped it reach fulfillment. Lisa Cahill, Jean Porter, Ronald
Mercier, S.J., Steven Dunn, and Roger Hutchinson read this work
when it was in the stage of a dissertation, and their comments have
strengthened it immeasurably. I am blessed to have good friends who
are also wonderful moral theologians in Patricia Lamoureux and Diane
Caplan. They read an early draft and encouraged me to believe that the
project had merit and should be pursued. Their enthusiasm was a wonderful gift! James Keenan, S.J., editor of the Moral Traditions series,
and Richard Brown, director of Georgetown University Press, gave me
the opportunity to express myself as a scholar and an ethicist, which was
more than I dared hope for when this project began. Students, col-
leagues, and administrative staff members of Mercy High School, the
Ecumenical Institute of Theology, and St. Mary's Seminary and University in Baltimore all contributed interest and encouragement, which
helped my work.

I am particularly mindful of the support of two special men. I am
grateful for the steadfast encouragement of my father, William J. De-
Crane. While he himself never graduated from high school and worked
all his life as a meat cutter, Dad knew this labor was very important to
me, and he was immensely proud of both it and me. Dad died in 1995,
but I still clearly hear his voice telling me how proud he is of me, and I
cherish this as a priceless legacy.

My husband, Brian D. Berry, is also an ethicist. He, more than
any other person, has helped this book reach fulfillment through many

years of stop-and-start work. His love and encouragement of me and my work have been unfailing. He read endless drafts and revisions of this work in all its forms, always offering the gift of cogent critiques, valuable suggestions, and needed criticism. He has endured endless conversations about hermeneutics and Aquinas over breakfast and dinner. His questions and insights have been those of a friend who at times believes in your project more than you do and holds the vision safe until you can pick it up again. To him it is dedicated—Brian, best colleague, best editor, best friend.

Introduction

IT IS WIDELY RECOGNIZED that postmodernism has shaped contemporary approaches to theology and ethics.[1] Given this fact, a writer must make clear at the outset the ways in which she responds to the postmodern challenge regarding the use of classic texts and universal claims. However, the issue is not as simple as responding to a *singular* postmodern challenge.[2] Rather, the postmodern critique of modern, liberal, Enlightenment-based convictions holds within it a range of orientations toward purported universal truths. This book is a response to these postmodern positions. At the same time, it offers a constructive method for retrieving a classic text from the Christian tradition—Thomas Aquinas's principle of the common good—from a feminist, liberationist perspective, and applying this text to contemporary issues in women's health care in the United States.

Some postmodern positions reject many, most, or sometimes all classic texts as no longer relevant or usable because they bear the enduring (some would say imprisoning) presumptions of the contexts in which they developed and which render the texts otiose, having little or no cultural, philosophical, scientific, sociological, religious, or ethical bearing on the current situation. From a feminist perspective, the misogyny identified in many classic texts—or the negative presumptions about women (and nonwhite persons) embedded in universal claims—appears so blatant and/or pervasive, that it seems impossible to find in these texts any contribution to the human project. This is also true for most feminist scholars in the Christian tradition who find in the classic texts—especially, but not limited to, the Scriptures—and in many

Christian doctrines judgments about women presented as universal truth claims that in themselves are denigrating and untrue, and which have functioned historically to justify social, economic, and religious relationships of power that are extremely harmful to women. In the face of this critique, some Christian feminist scholars withdraw the designations "canonical,"[3] "authoritative," or "revelatory"[4] from Christian texts or from parts of texts that reveal insupportable presumptions and judgments about women. Rosemary Radford Ruether's now classic statement represents this position:

> Whatever denies, diminishes, or distorts the full humanity of women is, therefore, appraised as not redemptive. Theologically speaking, whatever diminishes or denies the full humanity of women must be presumed not to reflect the divine or an authentic relation to the divine, or to reflect the authentic nature of things, or to be the message or work of an authentic redeemer or a community of redemption.[5]

Other Christian feminist scholars have responded to the scriptural and doctrinal aspects of the Christian tradition that denigrate the dignity of women by withdrawing from the Christian tradition altogether, judging it to be irredeemably misogynistic.[6]

Postmodernity has given rise to another trajectory. Here, efforts to find rapprochement between diverse views—such as Hans-Georg Gadamer's notion of the "to and fro" of conversation as a model of interpretation, and David Tracy's effort to bring the wisdom and values of a theological tradition into the public arena—are rejected. Rather, the classic texts and traditional doctrines (and traditional interpretations of the doctrines) of the community are given pride of place by the community or person. This approach finds expression in the Christian tradition in the writings of George Lindbeck.[7] In his framework, priority is given to the Scriptures among the various sources for Christian theology, and reason and experience are given less weight.

My argument is that many of the postmodern critiques regarding the oppressive, crippling presumptions identified in many classic texts (as well as in traditional formulations of many Christian doctrines) *are* deeply needed in order to argue effectively against the texts, interpretations, and doctrines judged by women to be facile, erroneous, oppressive, and reductionistic. This critique is not simply a worthy intellectual exercise, but extends to a critique of systems, institutions, and policies that are based on these texts and doctrines and which have harmed women in particular. At the same time, however, a feminist, liberation-ist retrieval of the principle of the common good not only contributes to the project of feminist ethics but makes the Christian moral tradition richer by exposing the relevance and significance of the classic principle in a venue very different from its historical origins.

The more radical forms of postmodern relativism, which reject the possibility of virtually any universal claims, are a shortsighted response to the abuses of universal claims in the past. In fact, classic texts of a tradition may serve as sources of insight and wisdom if retrieved through a rigorous, critical process. To reject classic texts leaves the human community stripped of enduring sources of human wisdom and moral insight. In order to defend this claim, however, one must demonstrate a critical way to adjudicate and retrieve both classic texts and traditions that have been part of sustaining the oppressive social and religious systems against women. This is essential if one is to prevent merely cosmetic realignments of the same oppressive insights and conclusions.

In order to accomplish this, I will retrieve Thomas Aquinas's principle of the common good—a fundamental ethical proposition in the Christian (and particularly the Roman Catholic) tradition—and apply it to two issues in health care in the United States: women's health in general, and black women and breast cancer in particular. Retrieving this principle is significant in that it will demonstrate that a feminist, liberationist approach to ethics can accommodate and appropriate a universal claim that has seemed, for centuries, to oppress—not liberate—women.

CHAPTER 1

Feminist Theological Hermeneutics

Hermeneutical theology is a distinct approach to theology. Hermeneutics itself is the science of interpretation.[1] Since Christianity is a textually based religion shaped by and oriented around a particular set of symbols, Christian theology needs to reinterpret its significant doctrines, texts,[2] and symbols for each new generation and within each new culture in which it emerges. Such interpretation is necessary for several reasons: on anthropological grounds, in light of the principle of analogy, because of the nature of foundational documents themselves, and, finally, in light of the hermeneutics of suspicion.[3]

Anthropologically, human existence and human knowledge are closely bound to the historical, material, concrete world. For symbols and texts which emerged in specific settings to be meaningful in new contexts, they must be reinterpreted, taking account of the changed meanings of words, new symbols, a different sociological setting than was the context of the original text, etc. This leads to the principle of analogy, which points to the fact that all new knowledge is in some way linked to experiences and knowledge we have already had. As theologian Roger Haight notes: "This principle postulates a certain consistency and homogeneity of human experience across history, so that data and meaning which falls completely outside current experience really has no basis for being comprehended or affirmed."[4] In other words, new experiences and new perceptions are possible, but they are acquired as they are linked in some way and are given meaning in relation to past experience and knowledge.[5] Foundational documents in themselves (authentic classic texts)[6] by their nature emerge from particular contexts and historical moments and address particular realities using symbols, images, linguistic structures, and language belonging to a particular time, place, and people. Texts that are not reinterpreted are merely repeated, without attention to the intelligibility of the text to a new audience or what it *can* mean in a new setting. Repetition in itself does not produce insight and understanding of the essential truth offered by the documents or the tradition, any more than repeatedly shouting at a deaf person produces hearing of the voice. Finally, the hermeneutics of suspicion is a legacy of the Enlightenment—most particularly of Nietzsche, Freud, and Marx—who argued that religion alienated people from life in this world by discounting their life reality now.

The task of hermeneutics requires the interpreter to establish several things at the outset which orient the interpretive work in a fundamental way: What significance does the interpreter give to tradition and to the received text? Is it a norming significance? What role do critical reflection and the social sciences play in the interpreter's hermeneutics? How does the interpreter engage tools of literary analysis? How does the interpreter deal with the contextual nature of the text and the effect of historical consciousness on the interpretation of the text? For whom does the interpreter carry out the task of hermeneutics? For the community that subscribes to the text as a norming reality? Or does the interpreter carry out the hermeneutic task in order to make the text meaningful for those outside the community?

Feminist hermeneutical theology is premised on the need of any theological tradition to be reinterpreted. However, its distinguishing character and many of its distinctive methodological procedures stem from its being a form of liberation theology. As with other liberation theologies, it uses the suffering of a particular constituency as the starting point for its work. Such use of suffering as the point of departure for theological investigation also guides the selection of methodological tools. Liberation theology gives particular priority to the experience of the constituency at issue; it requires social analysis of the situation faced by members of the constituency, in order to expose oppressive structures that contribute to their suffering; and it engages a hermeneutics of suspicion toward received texts and traditions in light of the relationship between the larger context or tradition and the constituency that suffers. This is especially necessary when a social context marked by systemic injustice and suffering of an identifiable constituency invokes the texts and traditions themselves as a justification for the situation. In feminist theology it is the experience of *women's* suffering that is the starting point for the theological investigation and a critical factor in the principle of analogy.

Feminist hermeneutical theology is frequently attractive to women who desire to remain within a particular religious/faith tradition, even though their experiences have convinced them that significant aspects of the tradition are directly connected to and responsible for their experience of injustice and suffering. At the same time, they are convinced that the tradition holds more than the constructions of God and humanity that women have experienced as oppressive and denigrating. Even more, they are convinced that *the tradition itself* contains resources (previously repressed, unseen, or unexplored) to support their demand for full and equal dignity and just treatment of women within the community. Given this, feminist hermeneutical theology proceeds similarly to other liberation theologies; it uses experiences of women's suffering as the starting point, and employs social analysis and ideology critique to investigate the intellectual, religious, social, and political systems that the tradition endorses and which diminish the status of women; and it investigates the texts and doctrines through a hermeneutics of suspicion as *part of* a hermeneutics of retrieval.

In this chapter, I will develop a feminist hermeneutics of retrieval. In order to develop a feminist hermeneutics suitable for the work of retrieval and mutually critical correlation,[7] I will examine the hermeneutical method of Sandra Schneiders and (to a lesser degree) that of Rosemary Radford Ruether, identifying key elements of their feminist hermeneutics. I will also use the work of Aristotelian philosopher Martha Nussbaum to identify a set of "anthropological markers" that will serve a crucial role in developing a reinterpretation of the common good from a feminist perspective. Making universal anthropological claims is often suspect in the current, highly postmodern environment. While I am aware of the concerns of postmodernism to avoid the oppressive identification of the human with characteristics of one set of persons, I still believe that a key component in any hermeneutical or ethical method is its anthropological presumptions. The way one conceives of the human person and the phenomena that mark the human reality as distinctly, unequivocally human—and the way one correlatively understands the human good and the relationship between the individual and the community—profoundly and directly affect the ethical character of the theological method itself and the resulting theology, as well as the issues that are addressed and the responses that are possible to the issues. By engaging Nussbaum's work, I will consider a proposed set of "anthropological constants"[8] based on the thought of Aristotle (particularly Aristotle's conception of human virtues), which Nussbaum suggests offer a dependable if minimal set of "constants" for understanding the phenomena of human personhood.

I have made use of the work of these three women because each uses a hermeneutical approach in her discipline and because they represent three disciplines that are considered central to the task of constructing a feminist hermeneutics. Other scholars might have been invoked here, but Schneiders, Ruether, and Nussbaum offer significant methodological guidelines for a feminist hermeneutics.

TEXTUAL HERMENEUTICS: SANDRA SCHNEIDERS

As a feminist scripture scholar, Sandra Schneiders offers a hermeneutical response to the fact that the classic text[9] of the Judeo-Christian scriptures contains material judged by many to be oppressive to and denigrating of women.[10] Schneiders addresses the issue of whether such texts could have meaning or authority for the community whose members judge the contents of the texts to be oppressive. She concludes that such texts can, indeed, offer women and the entire community a liberating word, but only to the extent that the texts are retrieved through a carefully designed feminist hermeneutics. In order to appreciate more fully the issues accompanying feminist scripture scholarship and hermeneutics, and the dimensions of the hermeneutical issues particularly within the Roman Catholic perspective, it is important to recall the history of the relationship between the scriptural texts and the community.

Dogmatic and positivistic conceptions of tradition, truth, and meaning of texts marked the Roman Catholic approach to the Scriptures before the promulgation of the encyclical *Divino Afflante Spiritu* in 1943. This positivistic approach to truth claims and the meaning of scripture developed out of the struggles of the Counter-Reformation as the Roman church offered definitive responses to the emerging Protestant position of *sola scriptura* with its sanction of individual interpretation of scripture. The Roman magisterium attempted to defend the traditional position that God, through revelation, inspired the church in its development of dogma, and the dogmatic positions the Roman church defended were permanently fixed, divinely revealed truths, not open to further development or interpretation since the church also held that revelation per se no longer occurred.[11] Scripture was invoked primarily in an apologetic manner for the dogmas that the church defended. These dogmatic truths were understood as unchanging propositions, which could be delivered to the present exactly as they had existed in the past—a nonhermeneutical, ahistorical approach to the truth claims of the tradition as well as scripture.

A positivistic approach to texts, including scripture, typically associated with the early period of the Enlightenment,[12] understands a text ultimately as "a semantic container whose meaning content was definitively established by its author."[13] The belief in the ability of the scientific method to identify the singular "true" meaning of a text left the believing community with a "flat" or "thin" text. All that could be known of and through the text was essentially already known. Using this approach, as Schneiders observes, "[o]ne cannot, finally, get out of the text itself anything more than or anything different from what was put into it."[14] The possible meanings and interpretations of a text were limited to accurate translation, and an attempt to get into the author's mind to deduce what the author intended by writing the text. Pastoral and eisegetical engagement of scripture constituted the ways in which creative engagement of scripture could occur.

This approach to texts became particularly problematic after the late 1800s in light of developments in philosophical hermeneutics, anthropology, linguistic analysis, semantics, rhetorical criticism, the natural sciences, psychology, historical consciousness, critical sociology, and a heightened appreciation of the contextual nature of knowledge. How is the critically insightful and discerning contemporary community to understand and employ scripture when the apparent meaning of a text sanctions or calls for the diminishment of some people or groups, most notably women and slaves, and attributes this treatment to God's designs, invoking the authority of God to justify the oppressive social situation that results? Since the 1960s, feminism in Western Europe and North America has frequently challenged scripture as a foundational text to which any truth claims or revelatory status are connected.[15] In addition, critical feminist scholarship by women in non-Western countries brought together the instincts of liberation theology with feminist textual scholarship. While in some cases linguistic analysis offers the possibility of an alternative reading of problematic texts, too often such analysis confirms that, indeed, the best meaning of the text is still one that creates and justifies grave injustice in the treatment of women. Is the only response to such a text, which serves a foundational role in the community, one of complete rejection? If such texts are not rejected, how shall the community deal with them and the history engendered by them? Is the community left with no recourse other than ignoring sections of the text as anachronistic embarrassments? Should we attempt to develop alternative readings of the text or pastoral accommodations to a text that is problematic?[16] Schneiders herself frames the question as follows:

> My hypothesis is that the question raised by feminist Second Testament criticism is finally a hermeneutical question with theological implications. The ultimate question is not what ideal object the structures of the text generate, what the authors of the text intended to say about women, or how the early church thought about or behaved toward women (although the answers to all of these questions have instrumental roles to play in interpretation); it is whether the meaning of the Second Testament as it is decontextualized and recontextualized in the interpretation of successive generations is irredeemably and necessarily oppressive of women or whether and how it can offer liberating possibilities to the very people whose oppression it has legitimated.[17]

Effective History—Effective Historical Consciousness

In response to this situation, Schneiders suggests a methodology based on the theory of effective history and effective historical consciousness developed by Hans-Georg Gadamer and on the theory of text and interpretation developed by Paul Ricoeur.[18] She also employs the insights of Jürgen Habermas, particularly those concerning ideology critique. The work of Hans-Georg Gadamer regarding effective history and effective historical consciousness[19] challenges the Enlightenment's positivistic concept of history as freestanding, autonomous information packages concerning an original occurrence. In a positivistic understanding, one accesses history and the meaning of texts as if by looking back through a long tunnel to the past. Obviously there is, in fact, a temporal distance between the moment a particular event occurred and the current moment, or between the generation of a text and the current moment. Gadamer sought to overcome the distance that seemingly separates the contemporary audience from the past by viewing the temporal distance between the past event or text and the contemporary receiver as a useful matrix for interpretation rather than as an impediment to interpretation. In essence, Gadamer denied the fact that the separation or distance between the past and the contemporary moment was a problem.[20]

Gadamer held that by sharing language with the author of the text, the reader shares a tradition with the text from which she or he develops prejudgments that facilitate understanding, in addition to the general pre-understanding the interpreter brings to a text. Since the reader is unavoidably part of the tradition that the text itself has generated, the conceptual horizon of the author and that of the contemporary interpreter become, in a sense, fused or joined in the effective history the text has created.[21] The text no longer exists as an item to be observed in the past through a long tunnel of time; it exists with all the effects that have been generated through time by its invocation, interpretation, and application. David Tracy comments on this phenomena when he notes that texts do not come to us "clean"; they all come bearing the mixed history that their existence has produced.[22] Schneiders observes:

> History, then, as it really exists, is always the past as integrated into and influencing what succeeded it, that is, as effective or productive. . . . Effective history is composed of events recognized to be not free-standing or fixed but generative of consequences that then enter constitutively into the reality of those events and help to determine their historical significance.[23]

Meaningful engagement with a text from the past occurs, then, through the awareness and appreciation that the text is a dynamic reality, not a static item. The way in which a text or event is interpreted evolves as time passes, and the significance or meaning of the text or event is understood in light of further developments that are connected to the initial incident or the origination of the text.[24] Schneiders, drawing on Gadamer, notes:

> The sense in which the event "does not change," namely, materially or in its facticity, is insignificant in comparison with the very real sense in which it is transformed, namely historically or in its meaning. In fact, it is not even really correct to say that it has not changed materially, because what we experienced in the past did not, at the time, have the character it now actually has.[25]

The reader/interpreter is necessarily in the midst of what Schneiders identifies as a double movement, "forward in time from an event and backward toward the originating event. The event generates a history which becomes part of the event by, as it were, flowing back into it and influencing its meaning and significance, that is, its present reality."[26] This produces in the reader/interpreter an effective historical consciousness; that is, one brings to the interpretation of an event or text a consciousness that is not only influenced by the existence of the originating text or event, but that views and evaluates the originating text or event through the consequences that earlier interpretations of the text or event produced.

Schneiders identifies three characteristics of language that are particularly relevant to the discussion of effective historical consciousness and the possibility that texts containing oppressive material might still serve a function within a community. Texts, while they are more than "conversation writ down," share the characteristics of language that Schneiders outlines.[27]

First, while something specific is said through language, what is said stands against the backdrop of all that is left unsaid and to which it is connected.[28] "Thus, there is no such thing as the final and complete expression of something in language, of the expressed as an isolated and totally self-sufficient monad of meaning. . . . [A]ll language not only says something, means something, but evokes an entire range of meaning beyond itself that can be made explicit under different circumstances."[29] This meaning, which can be recontextualized in different circumstances,[30] offers possibilities for interpretation of, and perhaps even more importantly, possibilities for relating to texts deemed oppressive. The yet-developing effective history of a text holds the possibility, if not the promise, at least of refinements in interpretation as the text is brought into play with new circumstances.

Second, language is essentially a symbolic system for communication. Because of its symbolic nature, language exists much more as a porous membrane through which meaning emerges rather than as a solid, impenetrable mass of dicta. As with the first characteristic, the symbolic nature of language means that it is at the same time constantly revealing *and* concealing the very thing it attempts to communicate. As a symbol system, language is ambiguous, subject to misinterpretation and misappropriation. (Consider how frequently in conversation one party responds, "Oh, I didn't know *that* was what you meant." Or again, one partner in a conversation must ask the other, "What do you mean by that?") In many ways a symbol is at the mercy of those who receive it, as they project onto the symbol aspects of their own bias, their own psyche and all its conflicts, their own fears, and their own best hopes. Texts share this character of language as symbolic communication. Valid interpretations and meanings of texts emerge rather than a single meaning or interpretation of a text standing as a solid, fixed, unrefinable reality to be assimilated. If the latter were so, the text would not share the symbolic characteristic of language.

Finally, language is essentially metaphoric.[31] Metaphor functions through the tension of "saying" that something is and at the same time is not like something; it affirms a likeness and at the same time reminds us of a dissimilarity in order to provoke the mind to creative perception. The mind intuits its way through metaphor; it does not conquer the proposition of a metaphor through linear logic. To say, "I love you," in spite of the sincerity with which it is said, realistically contains within it the truth that, "I do not love you perfectly or with perfect constancy." Metaphor produces a surplus of meaning in the deliberate engagement of the metaphoric form; and language, as a metaphoric system of communication, similarly produces a possibility of more than one valid meaning of a spoken or written word. Texts function metaphorically, not as perfect one-for-one correlates with reality.

These considerations about the characteristics of language are germane to the discussion of the text producing an effective history and effective historical consciousness. As we understand language and text in this way, we see that a text exists as a symbolic vehicle of communication that has a dynamic, yet-emerging quality with a range of possible meanings and implications available in the living engagement between the text and the reader.

Distanciation

Gadamer viewed the temporal distance between the production of the text and the contemporary reader as a problem resolved by the "fusion of horizons" of the text and the reader. For Paul Ricoeur, the distance in question is not between the origination of the text and the contemporary reader, but between the oral discourse and the resulting written text which, Ricoeur holds, is rich with interpretive opportunity.[32] This is the basis of Ricoeur's theory of distanciation, which Schneiders employs to construct the possibility of the community's relationship to scriptural texts judged oppressive by women.

According to Ricoeur, three changes occur when oral discourse becomes written. First, and most obviously, the discourse is preserved

in some manner from being lost and forgotten. Second, and importantly, "the text attains a relative semantic autonomy in relation to the
author's intentions," or, as Ricoeur states, "What the text signifies no
longer coincides with what the author meant; henceforth, textual
meaning and psychological meaning have different destinies." The author of the text had an intention when composing the text. But once
the text exists in its own right, the intention of the author no longer
rules the meanings that are possible from the text. "The text now
means what it means and all that it can mean regardless of whether that
meaning was intended by the author or understood by the original audience."[33] However, the autonomy gained by the text is not an absolute autonomy; the criteria of the dialectic between the sense and
reference of the text provide parameters of interpretation.[34]

The inscription of a text produces a third effect, the transcending
of the particular psychosocial conditions that formed the context of its
origination. Once written, the text can be decontextualized and recontextualized in very different contexts, releasing possibilities and necessities for interpretation that were never imagined by the author.[35] This
effect of inscription is particularly important for Schneiders's hermeneutical method of retrieval. It produces what Ricoeur refers to as the
world of the text,[36] a reality that the text projects by its reference to an
experience or a truth that is larger than any one moment in time, larger
than any specific culture. Ricoeur suggests that the text does not refer
the reader to itself and to the particularities of context reflected in the
text; rather, the effect of distanciation and inscription is to provoke the
reader to transcend the specific contours and limitations of the text by
entering into the world that it projects.[37]

Considering the Christian scriptures as an example of the effects
of an oral story becoming a written text, Schneiders observes: "[T]he
real referent of the text, that which is normative for the Christian community of all time, is not the experience of those first Christians but the
experience that is made possible for the reader by the text."[38] The textual reality of the Christian scriptures does not orient the contemporary
reader to the limits of first-century Christianity, or to the behaviors,
choices, and actions of Christians of that time, as the norm to be observed and reproduced in the current situation. Rather, the Christian
scriptures invite the reader to an experience the text can mediate, to go
behind or beyond the particularity of first-century Christians, to find
and engage an interpretation of the text that is not coterminous with
the data of the text. It is the integrity and sense of the text as a whole

that should be used to understand and norm the world before the text, not the use of excerpts excised from the context of the whole. This is consistent with Ricoeur's understanding of meaning as event, a dynamic engagement with continuously new possibilities for interpretation because of the ever-new audience that receives the text in new circumstances, and the effects of distanciation that free the text from the authorial intent. For Schneiders, this understanding of the interpretive possibilities inherent in the text is critical for feminist hermeneutics if it is to deal adequately with the oppressive contents found throughout the Scripture: "If in fact the meaning of texts is actually fixed, limited to what the author intended, then the dilemma is truly insoluble: Either we live by a text which is increasingly irrelevant, dead, and in places immoral, i.e., deadly, or we abandon the text in favor of later insights and thereby slip our historical moorings in the apostolic tradition."[39]

Hermeneutics of Suspicion—Ideology Critique

While Gadamer's contribution is important in Schneiders's hermeneutical method, it is not sufficient in itself. His work has been criticized for lacking an adequate or sufficient critique of the tradition or text.[40] His model of interpretation as conversation is judged, particularly by some feminist scholars, as too benign a model of engagement with the text or tradition, especially with respect to highly patriarchal texts or their use as justifications for discrimination and oppression. Rebecca Chopp, for example, suggests the model of struggle to describe the process of feminist interpretation of text and tradition.[41]

The development of critical theory by the Frankfurt philosophical school has played a major role in the hermeneutics of many postmodern interpreters, particularly feminists and liberation theologians.[42] Based on the challenges of Marx, Freud, and Nietzsche to established conceptions of social-political or interpersonal power relationships, the critical theory of the Frankfurt school leads the interpreter to approach all texts (and traditions) through a "hermeneutics of suspicion" in order to expose the distortions of the text.[43] These distortions are understood as systemic, not simply isolated errors of thought, and as such they fashion through the text or tradition a skewed version of reality which favors or advantages particular groups within the community to the detriment of others. A hermeneutics of suspicion uses disciplines such as psychoanalytic theory, sociology, and cultural anthropology to expose the frames of reference, presumptions, power structures, and social relationships in which the text or tradition developed.

A hermeneutics of suspicion demands that the interpreter engage in ideology critique of the text. Tracy identifies ideologies as "unconscious but systemically functioning attitudes, values, and beliefs produced by and in the material conditions of all ages of language, all analyses of truth, and all claims to knowledge."[44] Schneiders holds that ideology critique and the use of a hermeneutics of suspicion is demanded when approaching the text of scripture because of the presence of material in the Bible which legitimates the oppression of women in family, society, and the church.[45] This is not an optional approach to the text, and it is not a critique to be undertaken by women or feminists alone. It is, in Schneiders's assessment, a step that is necessary to allow the text to transcend the oppressive material it contains—material which, if accepted as normative, corrupts the integrity of the text for anyone who would engage it.

Schneiders identifies two forms of ideology criticism that must be brought to the scriptural text. In its first form, ideology criticism addresses the distortions found in the text itself that present women and minorities as inferior, marginal, or expendable.[46] In its second form, such criticism addresses the way in which a text may be ideologically damaged by the work of its interpreters, "who have used the biblical material to legitimate the economic and political status quo from which the dispossessed suffer."[47] Here it is the effective history that is reviewed through ideology critique. Both forms of ideology criticism must be engaged in the hermeneutical method she proposes.

Interpretation, Appropriation—Hermeneutics of Transformation

Drawing on the work of Paul Ricoeur, Schneiders identifies interpretation as a dialectic between explanation and understanding, both a process and a product.[48] The final goal of interpretation is meaning, and understanding constitutes the grasp of the meaning of a text, an event, or a dogmatic statement.[49]

The first step in interpretation of a text (or an event, or a dogmatic statement) requires the use of analytical tools such as historical, literary, rhetorical, and other forms of textual criticism in order to establish the otherness of the text. The text exists on its own terms before it is an interpreted reality, and the distinct dimensions of the text must be exposed for an interpretation to be more than a projection of the interpreter on the text.

The use of analytical tools provokes further questions for the reader/interpreter. "Explanation offers to the reader of the text a possibility of understanding that is usually partial and inadequate. This, in turn, raises further questions to be investigated methodically until the dialectical alternation between explanation and understanding comes to rest in the experience of meaning that is satisfactory."[50] Meaning, as Ricoeur understands the term, involves the dialectic between sense and reference of a text.[51] It is most fully achieved in appropriation, and exists as both content and event (of understanding).

Schneiders suggests that rather than a concern for the "literal meaning" of a text, the goal of interpretation is the textual meaning of the material. Textual meaning is composed of both the ideal meaning of the text (i.e., what it actually says about its immanent referent) and the liberated and reconstituted meaning of a text (i.e., the text, through its semantic autonomy and surplus of meaning, available to all it can mean). Such a textual meaning accommodates the need for the reconstitution of the meaning of the text in new circumstances without constricting the meaning to one that was appropriate given the operative referents at a particular time and in particular circumstances.[52]

An obvious and important issue is that of criteria for assessing the validity of an interpretation of a text (or an event, etc.). Schneiders offers seven criteria, identifying the first two as global criteria: First, that which cannot be left undone in the process of developing an interpretation serves as a negative global criterion; that is, an interpretive process that did not include the use of appropriate analytical tools would not be deemed valid. A failure to use appropriate analytical tools would be a failure to sufficiently scrutinize the text. Second, as a positive global criterion, the fruitfulness of the interpretation must be examined. "If an interpretation renders the text meaningless or banal, especially if the text has a history of significance, one suspects the validity of the interpretation."[53] In light of this criterion, questions should be raised about interpretations that judge a text to be patriarchal and denigrating of women. What must be looked at in such a situation, at the very least, are the first two global criteria. If the proposed interpretation emerges from the use of social analysis, linguistic analysis, and other analytical tools not previously brought to bear on a text, the proposed interpretation gains credibility and a right to serious consideration. If a feminist interpretation of the text, using the appropriate disciplines (including ideology critique), offers an interpretation that women experience as particularly fruitful, that honors the dignity of women, then the interpretation gains credibility.

After identifying these two global criteria, Schneiders describes five general criteria by which to judge the validity of an interpretation. She reminds us that a judgment of validity is always a logic of probability rather than a logic of verification: the validity of the interpretation will never be proven like a mathematical equation, but will involve a convergence of indices.[54] First, an interpretation accounts for the text as its stands. The interpretation does not require convoluted emendation in order to fit the text. Second, the interpretation is usable for the text as a whole and is not applicable only to selected phrases. Third, the interpretation is more successful at explaining anomalies within the text rather than explaining them away as an interpolation in the text that cannot be accounted for. Fourth, a valid interpretation is compatible with what is known from other sources, both biblical and extra-biblical. Finally, valid interpretations use responsibly all methods of analysis and interpretation that are appropriate to the framework of the particular interpretation.

Schneiders reminds us that the ultimate goal of interpretation is appropriation, which she understands as "a kind of deconstitution of the self and reconstitution of the self according to the coordinates of the world of the text. It involves a new self-understanding, a new self-appropriation, a further engagement in what Ricoeur calls the ongoing effort to be."[55] This is what she understands as a hermeneutics of transformation: in the process of dealing with the text on these many levels, the interpreter is changed through the encounter with the challenge of the authentic truth the text reveals. The hermeneutical process is accomplished when the interpreter is affected in some way by what he or she has encountered. The goal for the reader/interpreter, Schneiders holds, is not simply to arrive finally at an application of the text in a utilitarian sense. Rather, the reader/interpreter is in relation to the text as one is in relation to a work of art in an aesthetic surrender to the text:[56]

> We are not asking what conclusions for contemporary Christian life one might draw from the foregoing interpretive work. . . . We are asking about the transforming effect on the reader of the interpretation process itself. This effect is not some willed change in attitude or behavior brought about by an extrinsic process that follows from

exegesis and criticism but rather the effect of interpreting on the interpreter. It is analogous to the effect on the audience of participation in the play. Watching the play participatively is an act of interpretation that terminates in the transformation of the viewer through the aesthetic experience itself. This transformation can be made explicit afterward and can even result in some decisions or actions to be carried out later, but it is itself not something added on to interpretation but the terminating moment of the interpretation itself.[57]

Appropriation, as Schneiders envisions it (and which is based on the "fusion of horizons" suggested by Gadamer), is not accomplished by ignoring the problems of the texts for contemporary readers, particularly women. Rather, Schneiders describes a relationship to the text that subverts the literal reading of the text and the traditional interpretations of it. This "subversive" possibility, which might appropriately be seen as a work of liberation of meaning and a liberation of the text, is based on the belief in the capacity of the text to transcend the distortions that are endemic to it and are parts of its effective history. The liberation of the text from distortion occurs in the living engagement between the reader/interpreter and the text itself, as the reader allows herself to be engaged by the fundamental experience the text mediates, enabling the exposure of the distortions and allowing the text itself to serve as part of the ground of its own critique. This appropriation, Schneiders contends, is not accomplished by the use of traditional tools of interpretation alone; it requires the engagement of the text by the reader/interpreter through a hermeneutics of transformation.[58]

The final judgment on the text (or sections of the text) judged as not offering to the community the authentic message of the tradition is not its exclusion from the canon of the Scripture because of its distortion. Nor, Schneiders maintains, is it the withdrawal of authoritative or revelatory status from the text for individuals and the community. Schneiders proposes that the text is indeed revelatory, even in the midst of its distortions. The issue in one sense is not the distortions in themselves, as bad as they are. Rather, the issue is that the text is able to reveal to the reader/interpreter the disjunctures between the liberating experience into which it has invited the reader/interpreter and the text in itself. What is revealed is the ability of the text, as it is appropriated, to serve as a source of liberating power for women and marginal groups. To put the text and its distortions outside the community withdraws from the community the opportunity to embrace the full effective history of the text that includes the liberation of the fundamental energy or trajectory of the text from distortion. A great measure of the text's effective history is comprised, as Schneiders notes, in the distortions of the text and the distortions that are part of its interpretations. But the full appropriation of the text allows the reader/interpreter to encounter the authoritative revelation of the text and its interpretations that include the indictment of the distortions in the text.

For the person who approaches the text from a faith perspective, this ability of the text to critique itself and reveal its own distortions may be attributed to a transcendent reality, to God who is believed both to reveal God's self through the text and to accompany the reader/interpreter in the reading/interpreting. For the person who does not approach the text from the perspective of faith, the text still retains its ability to engage the reader/interpreter by its sheer power and, in many places, beauty. The appropriation of the text by a nonbelieving reader/interpreter does not mean the text no longer has the ability to reveal its own distortions and to critique the distortions of interpretation. Nor does it mean that the nonbelieving reader/interpreter must come to subscribe to the particular religious tradition that uses the text as an originating source. Schneiders speaks to this facet of appropriation:

> Many biblical scholars regard this kind of engagement with the text as non-scholarly devotionalism. In fact, *experiencing* the text as text is as integral to the work of biblical interpretation as hearing a Mozart symphony played in concert is integral to the work of the music critic or seeing Hamlet in the theater is to the work of the literary scholar. It is assuredly not the whole of scholarly work, but unless the critic's work both begins in appreciation and ends in appropriation, it remains peculiarly sterile and lifeless. I would question whether someone who has never felt the religious power of the gospel text, no matter how learned her or his biblical scholarship might be and regardless of whether she or he actually comes to share Christian faith, is competent for New Testament research. . . . For literature to "work," that is, for it to have a truly transformative effect on its interlocutors, the reader must surrender to its dynamics at least long enough to be caught up in its existential horizon.[59]

Summary

Sandra Schneiders's hermeneutical method has as its starting point the question of how scriptural texts that contain patriarchal, misogynistic distortions are to be understood by the community of believers. Her method for approaching scriptural texts has been shown to be heavily reliant on the work of Hans-Georg Gadamer and Paul Ricoeur, as well as engaging the thought of Jürgen Habermas. She uses the following six steps in her feminist hermeneutics of transformation:

First, a consciousness exists of suffering and oppression of women, due to denigration of women or the absence of women in the scriptural texts or through the way they have been interpreted, that is, their effective history. Second, scriptural texts are approached through a hermeneutics of suspicion to identify clearly the texts that endorse a derivative, marginal, dispensable attitude toward women, or in which the presence and experience of women have been totally suppressed. Third, the text and its effective history are submitted to an ideology critique to expose the power systems and relationships that it presupposes as normative, and to expose the beneficiaries of this power structure and the victims of it. Fourth, through distanciation of the text from its inscription, the text obtains a semantic autonomy that liberates new interpretive possibilities for the text. The interpreter can now place the text in conversation with the experience of women, knowing that a new liberating meaning can emerge from the text, even if it is the liberation that comes through awareness of the enduring energy of the original experience between humanity and its encounter with God, which became so subverted, as evidenced in the text. The text allows the fact of the sinful history of the community to be exposed in and through the text itself. Now the text may reaffirm what the community holds as the initiating, comprehensively liberating trajectory of the original experience of God with women as its focus. The scale of the distortion of the text and its traditional interpretation is exposed and in being exposed affirms the original experience of liberation that engendered the text or tradition, and offers that to the reader/interpreter in her own context today. Fifth, an interpretation is developed using the two global criteria suggested, and the five supplemental criteria, to adjudicate the validity of the interpretation. Finally, appropriation occurs as the reader/interpreter allows her self-understanding and her understanding of herself in relation to the human community and the text to be affected by the engagement with the sheer liberated dynamics of the text. The issue is not one of faith assent, but of availability to the power of the classic text set free from the distortions that are found in the text itself or that have accrued to the text over time.

A FEMINIST ETHIC:
ROSEMARY RADFORD RUETHER

Rosemary Radford Ruether's work focuses primarily on the retrieval of dimensions of the Christian/Catholic tradition of systematic theology and ethics.[60] She argues that critical retrieval and mutually critical correlation place an ethical demand on the community of believers to create a new and just social order. This ethical demand emerges as critical retrieval and mutually critical correlation free the text and tradition from the ideological distortions that have become confused with the authentic sense of the retrieved elements. Her feminist methodology involves a process of identifying aspects of the Christian tradition deemed corrupted and distorted when judged by their effects on the lives of women. At the same time, her work includes strategies to identify and employ usable dimensions of the tradition in a hermeneutical process of critical retrieval and correlation. Ruether is committed to retrieval as the only hope for women to remain with integrity within the Christian tradition.[61] The following section will examine some of the hallmarks of her methodology that can contribute to a feminist hermeneutics.

Women's Experience

Since all theological articulations are symbolic language by which we attempt to speak a true word about the divine, about ourselves (including our relationships to the world and other people), and about our relation to the divine, the symbols of language and ritual must constantly be assessed to determine whether and to what degree they succeed in their descriptive and revelatory task:

> Received symbols, formulas, and laws are either authenticated or not through their ability to illuminate and interpret existence in a way that is experienced as meaningful. Systems of authority try to reverse this relationship and make received tradition dictate both what may be experienced and how it may be interpreted. But the relationship is the opposite. If the symbol does not speak authentically to experience, it becomes dead and is discarded or altered to provide new meaning.[62]

As an element of feminist hermeneutics, the experience of *women* is sought and used as a criterion of adequacy on received texts, symbols, rituals, and traditions.[63] In the process of critical retrieval and correlation, the lived experience of women, particularly the ways they have been excluded and diminished (with an appeal to the "received symbols, formulas, and laws" as a justification for this reality) is used as a correlate and criterion of assessment on the text and tradition and the social structures that are justified by them. Essentially, the experience of women is used to reveal how the texts and traditions have affected women negatively, and been used against them. While this may be seen as part of the effective history of the text or tradition, it is the effective history specifically as it has impacted the lives of women. When a text or tradition has an effective history of continually being used to diminish women, it must be considered highly suspect and, Ruether and others would argue, not capable in itself of revealing the liberating truth of God. It may, as Schneiders shows, function as a mediation of the prophetic-liberating principle as the community acknowledges it as a *countersign* of that tradition. In such a moment, the text or tradition is seen as having betrayed or distorted but not absolutely destroyed the fundamental liberating truth of the original revelatory experience. It is revelatory now in that it exhibits the capacity of the original revelatory truth to endure and now explode against the distortions exposed through the experience of women.

Background

Ruether attributes the directions of her theological work to the influence of two major social-religious movements which occurred at the time she finished her advanced studies and was teaching at Howard University in Washington, D.C. (1965–1976): the civil rights and peace movements in the United States, and the Second Vatican Council. "From my first writings I became concerned with the interconnection between theological ideas and social practice."[64] This interconnection between theology and social practice is most clearly evident in the utopian vision she proposes, which reflects her stance as a socialist feminist. She draws on Friedrich Engels's *The Origin and History of the Family, Private Property, and the State* to criticize the structures of family and private property, which, she holds, have been the major contributors to patriarchy; and she believes that "feminists today who seek to go beyond reformist strategies and to envision a reconstructed society and family as the basis of women's liberation, must still go back to it as a primary text."[65]

Ruether rejects a Marxist-Leninist orientation for what she judges to be its regrettable rejection of the Freudian psychoanalytical revolution and its confusion of feminist consciousness-raising with bourgeois feminism and sexual promiscuity, its exaltation of repressed sexuality in the name of avoiding "bourgeois degeneracy," its extreme glorification of the work ethic, and its acceptance of class conflict as an ultimate value. She asks: "Is the endless prolongation of models of life drawn from warfare and industrial labor the best we can do in envisioning a liberated society?"[66]

Dualism

Ruether describes her own work as an examination of social issues of domination and oppression and a tracing of "the ideological patterns in Christian thought which have served to justify violence and oppression. These ideologies are variants on a single root pattern":[67] a fundamental dualism expressed as a hierarchy, i.e., spirit/body, intellect/intuition, male/female, etc. One form of this hierarchical dualism is seen in racism, sexism, and other construals of people that establish one group as more able, more naturally suited or gifted for leadership of the other segment. The incapacity of the other segment of the population for leadership exists because of a supposed or presumed inherent incapacity, such as a lack of rational capacity, not being suited for leadership because of their "nature," or a lack of abilities or talents needed for leadership which the dominant group claims to possess. The other form of hierarchical dualism she identifies is that in which the dominated are understood to have "sinned" at a previous time, earning the punishment of being subjugated to the dominant class. Both forms of justification of a dualistic conception of humanity are applied to women.[68]

According to Ruether, dualism produces three types of alienation: (1) alienation from one's self and one's body; (2) alienation from others (making the "other" the enemy); and (3) alienation from the created reality of the earth.[69] Ruether's emphasis on dualism as the foundation of patriarchy is indeed a hermeneutical issue. A searching critique of embedded ideology is necessary to expose the incorporation of dualism at every level of every social, religious, and theological structure, because it has functioned as a "truth." In addition, the degree to which dualistic conceptions of humanity and creation are seen as normative will greatly affect what is *imaginable* as a reconstruction, interpretation, and application of texts and tradition toward more just social and religious structures and systems. Identification of the dualistic construction of human existence that has penalized women will also accurately flag the areas in which members of the dominant group who have enjoyed these benefits as a matter of course will resist extension of the benefits of full and equal status.

The Prophetic Liberating Tradition

Just as Sandra Schneiders points to the existence of elements and trajectories within the tradition which—when released through the use of the text's semantic autonomy, ideology critique, and the reconstruction of texts and tradition in new circumstances—can provide a critique of the oppressive dimensions of the tradition and texts themselves, Ruether identifies the "prophetic liberating tradition" of the Hebrew and Christian scriptures as such a principle of critique:[70]

> [B]oth Testaments contain resources for the critique of patriarchy and of the religious sanctification of patriarchy. We make it clear from the start that feminism must not use the critical prophetic principles in Biblical religion to apologize for or cover up patriarchal ideology. Rather, the prophetic liberating traditions can be appropriated by feminism only as normative principles of Biblical faith, which, in turn, criticize and reject patriarchal ideology. . . . Feminist theology that draws on Biblical principles is possible only if the prophetic principles, more fully understood, imply a rejection of every elevation of one social group against others as image and agent of God, every use of God to justify social domination and subjugation. . . . Feminist readings of the Bible can discern a norm within Biblical faith by which the Biblical texts themselves can be criticized. To the extent to which Biblical texts reflect this normative principle, they are regarded as authoritative. On this basis, many aspects of the Bible are to be frankly set aside and rejected.[71]

Ruether does not overtly subscribe to the proposition of a canon within a canon, and she does not suggest that the text or tradition may be revelatory for the community in the retrieval of the originating experience that has survived in spite of the betrayals of the text itself or the interpretations of it. Her relationship to the Scripture does not extend to a retrieval such as Schneiders suggests is possible. Ruether appears to accept the inability of certain texts or traditions to function for the community in an authentically revelatory way at all.

Ruether identifies four themes that constitute the basis of the prophetic liberating tradition, and also constitute the criteria to be used in the assessment of texts and traditions for the degree to which they reflect the authentic, enduring tradition of the community:

> 1) God's defense and vindication of the oppressed; 2) the critique of the dominant systems of power and their power holders; 3) the vision of a new age to come in which the present system of injustice is overcome and God's intended reign of peace and justice is installed in history; and 4) the critique of ideology, or of religion, since ideology in this context is primarily religious.[72]

This prophetic liberating tradition of biblical faith is political; it addresses the social order in the public and private spheres. Wherever the order is based on the subjugation of one group of people to a dominant group, it is judged immoral on theological grounds. It is also political for another reason:

> The prophetic liberating tradition creates a shift in the social location of religion. Instead of religion being socially located on the side of the ruling class, race, and gender, justifying their power as divinely ordained, the prophetic tradition speaks through prophets, male and female, located on the side of the poor and marginalized people of the society.[73]

Apocalypticism

Ruether's vision is apocalyptic as well as social—it looks to created reality as the locus for the anticipated experience of embodied redemption. This is similar to Edward Schillebeeckx's notion of salvation having to be (to a genuine degree) a "this world" experience that addresses and redresses actual experiences of deprivation, oppression, and suffering, not salvation with only an eschatological orientation.[74] Her apocalypticism is not based on the expectation of divine intervention to create the envisioned reality of justice in this world. Rather, it is based in the belief that the changes that are required to bring about communities of justice and full human flourishing will occur as social structures and systems are made more just and mutual through human choices. Social structures so changed will be characterized by genuine equality and by divisions of labor that enable women and other marginalized groups traditionally consigned to support tasks (leaving the dominant, usually male constituency free to pursue their interests) to exercise their talents in creative and professional pursuits. This activity will be carried out with the guidance of the Spirit. Fundamentally, the utopian social vision of Ruether is one in which the dualisms which she believes generate "the very world of alienation from which we seek liberation"[75] are overcome.

Ruether expects that the degree of change required to establish such an altered social reality is possible only through *metanoia*, reminiscent of Schneiders's hermeneutics of transformation. Consonant with her emphasis on the earth and creation as ethical partners with women and all humanity in the response to the God revealed in the Hebrew and Christian traditions, Ruether's apocalypticism challenges the devaluing of created reality that has occurred since the sixteenth century in Renaissance Europe. "The concept of social change as conversion to the center, conversion to the earth and to each other, rather than flight into the unrealizable future, is a model of change more in keeping with the realities of temporal existence."[76] Her apocalypticism is a dimension of the ethical implications of her work of critical retrieval and mutually critical correlation. Ruether's apocalypticism is also a natural consequence of her identification and use of the prophetic liberating tradition that is held in a text and endures in the community, even if at times as a subversive knowledge.[77] As a basic principle of her hermeneutics of critique, retrieval, and correlation, the prophetic liberating (or prophetic-messianic) tradition noted above is not finished in its task merely by identifying textual deformations and interpretations. The one who would speak a retrieved and liberating word to the community of faith and to society "points toward an alternative social order, an alternative era of human history, when these wrongs will be righted and a new time of God's peace and justice will reign."[78]

Summary

Ruether's hermeneutical method of retrieval for correlation shares many characteristics with that of Schneiders. Her hermeneutics, however, is more explicitly ethical than that of Schneiders and may be summarized in the following four moments: First, the experience of women, particularly their experiences of systemic oppression and denigration, functions as a principle of adjudication on received texts, dogmas, and traditions. When the content or subject of a text, dogma, or tradition, traditionally viewed as a classic of the community, is virtually foreign to the experience of women, or when it has been experienced by them primarily as a justification of their oppression, the status of the classic is suspect, since it does not reflect the experienced life reality of a major segment of the community and cannot function in a revelatory manner for them. The "revelation" the classic offers is of their diminished status. Second, the "prophetic liberating tradition" of the Scripture functions as a principle of critique on the text itself. Third, hierarchical dualism is a primary source of oppression of women and is evident in anthropologies that grant greater status in the community to one group, justifying the "necessity" of leadership by the advantaged group. This must be identified and rejected in text, tradition, and society. Finally, Ruether joins an apocalyptic expectation with a socialist perspective. The envisioned just society, which will bring redress to those who have been marginalized and have suffered injustice, will emerge as a response to the Spirit's demand for *metanoia*. A hermeneutical experience is complete only when the demands of the retrieved text or tradition, freed for God's own justice from the distortions of patriarchy, are responded to in effective structure- and system-changing ways.

ANTHROPOLOGY: MARTHA NUSSBAUM

To suggest that an anthropology is a necessary component of a theological method could be to risk the intense debates that have developed in the last thirty years in an intellectual climate marked by postmodern, countermodern, and postliberal[79] perspectives on one hand, and liberal, revisionist, hermeneutical, and correlational perspectives on the other.[80] It is beyond the scope and purpose of this book to explore in depth the methodological concerns of the postmodern, postliberal deconstructionist approach, as significant as those concerns are. I suggest a methodology that walks between the more extreme expressions of a postmodern methodology, using a critical hermeneutical, correlational approach. I will outline the reasons I believe the use of an anthropology and accompanying minimal claims about the human person are necessary for theological ethics and will draw particularly on the contributions of the Aristotelian philosopher Martha Nussbaum (and other resources) to develop the anthropology I propose to use in the hermeneutical method of retrieval being developed here.

Postmodern and Hermeneutical Methodologies

Postmodern and postliberal orientations are distinct from one another, but come to similar conclusions about the impossibility of positing anything resembling a universal claim, including any universal anthropological claim. Usually postliberal and postmodern theologies propose abandoning altogether attempts to articulate truth claims applicable outside the community of origin. This includes general anthropological and sociological claims, ethical and moral claims, and religious claims. In fact, the argument runs, such claims are simply not applicable or even valid outside the community from which they emerge, and to try to insist that they are is an expression of cultural imperialism. Any claims of normativity that are endorsed by the community and order the life of the community are not applicable outside the community. The work of Ludwig Wittgenstein, Hans Frei, and George Lindbeck[81] suggests that religious language functions primarily, if not exclusively, for the service of the community itself, not for the purpose of engaging in public conversation. From a postliberal perspective, universal truth claims distort the beliefs of the community for the sake of engaging in an apologetic dialogue with those outside the community, when in fact the Christian community is understood to exist primarily as a witness of Christian life to the surrounding culture, not as a partner in the larger religious and secular conversation. From a highly postmodern perspective, universal claims violate the uniqueness of distinct cultures and groups by imposing on them agreement with irrelevant and oppressive conceptions of normativity.

The liberal, hermeneutical or revisionist methodological position understands the challenge to the Christian community as that of providing reasonable warrants in the public arena for its truth claims, so that it may participate in and influence the dialogue between Christian traditions and different faiths, and between the Christian tradition and the secular society, helping shape the social fabric through its credible, if not explicitly religious, truth claims.[82] The revisionist position pursues a process of retrieval and correlation between the tradition and the contemporary situation because of the contextuality and cultural locatedness of the origins of the text or classic element. The classic elements of the tradition are believed to offer an enduring truth that is capable of being apprehended through a process of analogy by rational people who are not part of the tradition itself, but who perceive in the tradition a valuable dimension of truth.

In the revisionist, hermeneutical model, the Christian community seeks to develop rational forms of argument to explain the positions it holds about fundamental and systematic theological truth claims, as well as its ethical and moral claims. Its strength lies in valuing the larger, global community as people to whom truth has also been revealed and as partners in the pursuit of greater justice. Yet it is possible, as its critics charge, that the attempt to speak a word that is intelligible to the inter-faith, intercommunity conversation, as well as to speak to secular society, can result in a distortion of the basic Christian claims. But this is not inevitable any more than it is necessarily inevitable that a biblically based community become sectarian.

The position maintained here is that both the postmodern and postliberal communities and the revisionist, hermeneutical communities of conversation offer important perspectives that should not be lost to the Christian theological project. The postliberal theological perspective values the development of communities shaped by the Christian story in which character and virtue are fostered in the members by exposure to the foundational narratives of the community and through the influence of members whose lives embody faithful response to the Gospel. This fostering of "people of character" is a valuable and worthy concern for the Christian community.[83] However, the tendency to see the focus of the community as *only* the community itself can tend to blunt the influence that the Christian message and tradition could bring to the larger community, particularly to issues of ethics, morality, and practical justice. The postmodern orientation reminds us of the all-too-real dangers that are at hand when universal conceptions are presumed possible (even easily possible) premised on features of a segment of the community or on a particular incarnation of social life.

Anthropology as a Methodological Issue

The anthropologies developed and used in the past are judged by many to be deeply flawed. They privileged a small group who met certain anthropological criteria, and at the same time served to justify the exclusion of many people from full participation in and benefit from the community, because their status was judged beneath the anthropological norm. One can point to the treatment of the indigenous peoples of the Americas by missionaries and conquerors, the fate of black men, women, and children taken from Africa for slavery in the Americas and their treatment here, the fact of the Jewish Holocaust of the late 1930s and 1940s, and the reality of women globally and historically. These and countless other examples point to the grave abuses that are possible on anthropological grounds. Strong objections have been raised by feminists,[84] racial/ethnic minority groups, and groups that make up a statistical minority in their sexual orientation to the entire project of making general anthropological claims. They argue that they, in particular, suffered from the use of anthropological descriptions that did not include them, and that this experience documents the inevitably oppressive nature of all anthropological claims. At the same time, other scholars maintain that the complete rejection of any normative description of the human leaves the community with no basis from which to make moral decisions and from which to adjudicate ethical alternatives.[85] They further argue that having no general description of the human person (even minimally) leaves the global human community without recourse for condemning human rights abuses.

Feminist theology shares the moment in which careful, ongoing work is required to develop an anthropology that provides a resource for condemning the denigration of women in any context in which it occurs, and at the same time allows for the great variety of ways in which women experience their lives *as* women in particular cultures. Rather than retreating from the task because it is daunting and concluding from the abuses of the past that it is futile and arrogant even to pursue a theological anthropology using the lives and experience of women, "[f]eminist theological anthropology (and feminist theology in general) must remain ever vigilant lest multiplicity tumble into such fragmentation that it plays into the hands of those who benefit from keeping patriarchal/kyriarchal patterns of repression in place."[86] The problem is not multiplicity. The conclusion that multiplicity leaves us with nothing but fragmentation is the potential danger in the awareness of difference.

While the anthropology traditionally used in theology and ethics was, indeed, oppressive of the many people who did not meet the standards of "normativity" developed by a dominant group, the position proposed here is that it is still important and possible to identify some few constitutive elements that are universally dependable as truth statements about what it means to be human and to enjoy the circumstances that foster a relatively authentic (good) human life. This most likely will mean that the anthropological constants[87] that are proposed as universally true (for men as well as women) must always have a conditionality to them, even as they are proposed as universally true. The awareness of the conditionality of such anthropological claims is a needed humility and indicates a willingness to understand the human being and the claims we make about human beings as always in a process of evolution to a certain degree. Even if such anthropological claims stand the test of time and critical reflection, the humility that is part of a conditional claim of universality is a needed protection against the tendency to arrogance in the use of anthropological presumptions.

Anthropology must be developed inductively; that is, minimal statements about the phenomenon of being human are based on the experience of many people over time. While an inductive anthropological method uses human experience as its foundation (in contrast with a deductive method, which postulates theoretical universals by which human beings are subsequently judged and to which they must correspond), it is important that what is proposed as a universal human phenomenon should reference what it is reasonable to believe may be common to people generally (women and men). It would be short-sighted and unfortunate if the *way* or the form in which a particular culture or group lived out an anthropological element was confused with the element itself. In other words, we must find a way to refer in our anthropological claims to aspects of the human which are lived out and embodied in many ways in various settings; what is proposed as an anthropological claim has the quality of a formal norm which is materially embodied in the local situation.

Anthropological Universals

The phenomenon of historical consciousness has produced a range of positions on the possibility of any universal truth claims, including any claims about being human. At one end of the spectrum is an embrace of historical consciousness and the radical contextuality of all knowledge to the point of rejecting the possibility of any universal truth claims, including universal claims about the human. Furthermore, some scholars maintain that virtually all anthropological claims, as well as gender identification itself, are social constructions that do not cohere with any objective truth.[88] This extreme of historical consciousness produces a relativism that in theory makes it impossible to posit any objective statements about the human or any critiques of culture and customs. This has the effect of eliminating a basis on which to condemn injustice and human rights abuses cross-culturally. At the other extreme, a genuine lack of (or rejection of) historical consciousness permits the postulation of sweeping claims about the human, the human good, and human communities, delivered as irrevocably factual and true for all times and in all settings. This position allows for no growth in human nature, nor in the ability of the human community to speak about constitutive dimensions of being human that are embodied in various ways. A middle way between these two extremes is needed. I aim to develop such a middle way here, by developing a minimal set of anthropological claims which will be used as part of a critical hermeneutical principle.

The issue of anthropology is critically important in feminist theology, feminist hermeneutics, and feminist ethics. Presumptions about normative humanity and the status of women in regard to the normative description of the human have dramatically shaped the attitudes and ethics of all social and religious systems and structures. These presumptions have shaped the ethical sense of what is due women by virtue of their humanity, or what is not due them. In the West, these presumptions about human nature in relation to women were based originally on Greek biological knowledge (which in itself was quite erroneous) and were joined with deductions about the relationship between physiology, rational capacity, and human status. The resulting philosophical presumptions understood males as more capable of rational activity and closer to the perfection of absolute being/knowledge/truth, unencumbered by physicality. This philosophical tradition was received into the emerging Christian philosophy and theology and formed the basis of attitudes toward women which saw them as derivative from men in their nature, less capable of rational and intellectual activity, captive of carnality, temptations to men, and responsible for the sin of the world, since it was concluded that Adam sinned because of Eve's temptation. This attitude is clearly demonstrated in the writings of many classical writers such as Tertullian, Augustine, Jerome, John Chrysostom, and Thomas Aquinas.[89]

Ruether observes:

> When we examine the theological tradition we see an ambiguity in the way *imago dei*/sin has been correlated with maleness and femaleness. On the one hand, deeply rooted in Christian thought is an affirmation of the equivalence of maleness and femaleness in the image of God . . . but it has tended to be obscured by a second tendency to correlate femaleness with the lower part of human nature in a hierarchical scheme of mind over body, reason over passions. Since this lower part of the self is seen as the source of sin—the falling away of the body from its original unity with the mind and hence into sin and death—femaleness becomes linked with the sin-prone part of the self.[90]

This anthropological tradition has endured to the current time, even though the biological knowledge that formed its original basis has changed.

Feminist scholars hold a range of opinions on the relationship between the normatively human and women; some argue that women and men share an identical human nature; others argue that there exist differences between male and female at the level of nature but that this difference cannot be used as the basis for lesser treatment of women. Some argue that there is profound difference between men and women at the level of basic humanity. Margaret Farley suggests that the fact that the supposedly universal anthropologies and common moralities proposed in the past functioned negatively toward women (and some men) does not rule out the possibility of minimal anthropological claims, nor does it automatically mean that some form of common morality is impossible. The criticisms of past anthropologies and their applications highlight the fact that the anthropologies developed so far have been inadequate and have been used badly.[91] But rather than concluding that it is impossible to identify anything that can serve as minimal, shared human phenomena which help describe usable anthropological markers, Farley points to the range of experiences human beings *do* share across cultures and genders:

> These convictions presuppose some commonality in human experience—in the experience of what it means as a person to rejoice and to be sorrowful, to be protected or violated, nurtured or stifled, understood or misjudged, respected or used. Whatever the differences in human lives, however minimal the actuality of world community, however unique the social arrangements of diverse peoples, it is nonetheless possible for human persons to weep over commonly felt tragedies, laugh over commonly perceived incongruities, yearn for common hopes. And across time and place, it is possible to condemn commonly recognized injustices and act for commonly desired goals.[92]

In similar fashion, Lisa Sowle Cahill and Martha Nussbaum appreciate the well-deserved suspicion of anthropological claims that has led some scholars to eschew all such claims in the name of respect of difference—to the point, however, of withholding judgment on situations in which human welfare is at risk.[93] However, Cahill reminds us that people in the midst of oppression and suffering most often do not reflect on the philosophical dimensions of the situation: "I note that women who are practically involved in the most desperate sorts of struggles for women's very lives do not resort to any rhetoric of the incommensurability of worldviews, but appeal straight to the heart of our common humanity."[94] Nussbaum argues similarly that in actual situations,

> when one sits down at a table with people from other parts of the world and debates with them concerning hunger, or just distribution, or in general the quality of human life, one does find, in spite of evident conceptual differences, that it is possible to proceed as if we were all talking about the same human problem; and it is usually only in a context in which one or more of the parties is intellectually committed to a theoretical relativist position that this discourse proves impossible to sustain.[95]

Nussbaum, Cahill, Farley, and others suggest that we must take very seriously the criticisms of postmodernism against the oppressive, paternalistic presumption of easily identifiable human universals that advantaged the already fortunate. In particular, these anthropologies repeatedly judged women as less than human in the same way men were human, and by subtle extension, less worthy of the same dignity due men, less capable of exercising judgment on their own behalf than men (which is a significant dimension of human dignity), and needing less than men in order to have a good life. However, we lose our ability to speak a critical word against injustice under the guise of respect for cultural difference at a great price: "[I]mperialism of class, race, or continent are not the only dead-end for feminist ethics. Another is the self-silencing of social protest by announcement of plurality as ultimate."[96]

Nussbaum argues for the necessity of some minimal anthropological account because to proceed without such an account is to trust that unconstrained social forces will eventually produce an appropriate set of circumstances for human living. However,

> to give up on all evaluation and, in particular, on a normative account of the human being and human functioning [is] to turn things over to the free play of forces in a world situation in which the social forces affecting the lives of women, minorities and the poor are rarely benign.[97]

The pursuit of some form of anthropological claims is not undertaken simply because it is an intellectually possible exercise and an intriguing challenge; minimal anthropological claims of a universal nature are important because they ground our ability to identify injustice and to demand justice, particularly on behalf of women. They are also needed for the project of shaping a more just state of affairs globally. The ability to identify the human, the human good, and those things that destroy human life and dignity are ethical foundations that are needed to address the situations of women whose lives are played out in situations of systemic as well as situational injustice. If, in fact, there are no usable signifiers of commonly shared humanity to serve as touch-stones for identifying human flourishing and, even more importantly, for judging situations unjust and harmful, then on what ground can we stand, from what position can we speak to denounce the injustice?

Where shall we look for resources to identify the anthropological dimensions of this feminist hermeneutics? I suggest that usable tools are available in the general approach of the Roman Catholic moral tradition, in contributions of feminist scholarship, and in philosopher Martha Nussbaum's recommendations regarding the Aristotelian conception of spheres of human life, the correlative virtues, and by extension "human functioning capabilities."

The Roman Catholic Moral Tradition

The Roman Catholic moral tradition (grounded to a great extent on a reinterpretation of Aristotle by Aquinas) is based on a belief in an objective moral order which is knowable, at least in principle and in its basic shape, through rational consideration by reasonable persons. This is consistent with earlier observations that even in the midst of great difference, it is generally possible for people to identify destruction as destruction, and good as good. Further, the Roman Catholic tradition, understood as a "natural law" tradition, pursues (at least theoretically) the good of *all* persons based on the belief of the creation of the human by God.[98] The extensive body of writings that constitute the distinct contribution of Roman Catholic social teaching is also a valuable resource, both in the documents of Catholic social teaching themselves and in the obvious evolution of Catholic social teaching in the last hundred years that the documents reveal. These documents offer a time capsule of sorts, tracing a developing understanding of the person whose social needs are increasingly seen as moral obligations impinging on the community, a growing appreciation of the complexity of the national and international arena in which justice is sought, and an increasing condemnation of systemic injustice in its many forms. Catholic social teaching, including its insistence on a basic "floor" of human rights due all people, is based on a description of the human that produces a set of correlative rights and obligations. This tradition warrants a further investigation of the relationship between the principle of the common good and the situation of women, highlighted by social analysis to reveal previously unappreciated dimensions of systemic injustice as it particularly affects women.

The Experience of Women

One of the contributions of feminism to this process is the use of women's experience and a hermeneutics of suspicion on received definitions of both human flourishing and injustice.[99] Feminist scholarship insists that an adequate anthropology must expose the particular forms of oppression and destruction that frequently are unique to women's lives and are missed by traditional categorizations. Correlatively, feminist scholarship uses these experiences of injustice and suffering unique to women as "negative markers" for the good that is missing and must be sought. In other words, when certain realities exist, women are prevented from achieving their own dignity and flourishing. Feminist writers have discussed the term "women's experience" extensively. I am using it here to point to a particular phenomenon of being a female person, someone who experiences distinct patterns of suffering[100] because she is a woman.[101] In formulating a feminist hermeneutics of retrieval, I will engage these patterns of suffering in women's lives in order to illuminate women's experience.[102]

As theologian Maria Pilar Aquino has observed: "In this theology—as in all liberation theology—the social sciences become vitally important for knowing and transforming the situation, especially that of poor and oppressed women."[103] The social sciences provide an important tool for assessing the lived situation of women. But in addition to social sciences as formal disciplines, another fact must be appreciated to pursue specifically the experience of women: the recognition that women frequently need help to *name* their own experience. Many women are so used to providing the culturally acceptable account of their own lives and have so internalized it that it is unfamiliar for them to speak "in their own voice" about their situation.[104]

Lisa Sowle Cahill comments: "What is most important to a feminist and intercultural retrieval of Aquinas (and Aristotle) is his openness to an inductive objectivity and realism, perhaps better phrased today in terms of shared framing experiences and moral common ground, than of moral 'universals'."[105] If we believe that Aquinas offers an enduring and valuable perspective on the truth of human existence in his teaching on the common good, and if we desire to develop a hermeneutics that will allow a critical retrieval of this truth of the common good, then we should seek to develop such "shared framing experiences and moral common ground." To do this, we must identify some type of anthropological claims or constants that can be used to develop a minimal conception of the good for a human person, and the obligations that fall to the larger community (such as the state) to help provide the circumstances in which the human good may be pursued by its members. This presupposes some measure of objectivity in describing the human good, and therefore some minimal moral objectivity regarding the common good.

The Human Good, Human Functioning Capabilities

The "human functioning capabilities" developed by Martha Nussbaum are a valuable resource in constructing a minimal description of the human good. Her project is one of identifying the experiences and needs that human beings have in common, and by extension, the values and rights they have in common. Her starting point is the pursuit of those distinguishing characteristics of the *human* good that then may be used as a basis for making moral claims on behalf of women. The goods that are denied to women, she argues, are goods that *all* human beings need for a full human life. To seek the establishment of these goods is not to ask for justice in regard to needs that only women have, extending to women by exception things they need that men do not need. Rather, if we establish those things that are required for a good human life, and if we show that women (though they are human) do not experience them, then we can develop an unassailable claim on behalf of women for these requirements and for the community to provide appropriate assistance for women to have these needs met. At the same time, this identification of the human good in a minimal way allows us to recognize the unique needs women have, often for things such as prenatal and postnatal care, child care, reproductive counseling and assistance, assistance in caring for sick or elderly family members, educational opportunities that can be shaped to work with women's distinct social role and time constraints.

An Aristotelian philosopher, Nussbaum draws on Aristotle's conception of arenas of human functioning and the virtues that are associated with these spheres.[106] Nussbaum first describes a set of limits and capabilities common to all persons:

- Mortality
- Embodiment
- Hunger and thirst
- Need for shelter
- Sexual desire
- Mobility
- Capacity for pleasure and pain
- Cognitive ability (perceiving, imagining, thinking)
- Early infant development
- Practical reason
- Affiliation with other human beings
- Relatedness to other species and to nature
- Humor and play
- Separateness (singularity)
- Strong separateness (having to do with a whole human life and the experience of uniqueness of one's context, possessions, friends, etc.)[107]

Of these human limits and capabilities, Nussbaum identifies practical reason and affiliation as "architectonic" characteristics of the human person. This description, Nussbaum maintains, is both tentative and open-ended: "We allow explicitly for the possibility that we will learn from our encounters with other human societies to recognize things about ourselves that we had not seen before, or even to change in certain ways, according more importance to something we had thought more peripheral."[108] Therefore, such a list need not be rejected because it is a closed and final set of human characteristics which are used oppressively against those who do not find themselves or their experience within it.

Nussbaum suggests that these human limits and capabilities are of such a basic nature that they describe the minimal features beneath which a human life will be so impoverished that it will not be a truly human life. But Nussbaum delineates a further set of "functional capabilities" (related to the first set) which, she suggests, provide a second threshold for identifying not just a minimally human life, but also a *good* human life. She suggests these are not only anthropological markers,[109] but *functioning* capabilities at which societies should aim for their citizens and which quality of life measurements should address. The basic human functioning capabilities she identifies are:[110]

- Being able to live to the end of a human life of normal length (not dying prematurely)
- Being able to have good health (to have adequate nourishment and shelter, having opportunities for sexual satisfaction and choice in matters of reproduction, being able to move from place to place)
- Being able to avoid unnecessary and non-beneficial pain and to have pleasurable experiences
- Being able to use the senses (to imagine, to think, and to reason and to do these things aided by adequate education, and to enjoy and produce aesthetic and religious materials)
- Being able to have attachments to things and persons outside ourselves (to love those who love and care for us, to grieve at their absence, to experience longing and gratitude)
- Being able to form a conception of the good and to engage in critical reflection about the planning of one's own life (to seek employment outside one's home and to participate in political life)
- Being able to live for and to others, to recognize and show concern for other human beings, to engage in various forms of social interaction (being able to imagine the situation of another and have compassion for that situation, to have the capability for both justice and friendship, protection of freedom of assembly and freedom of speech)
- Being able to live with concern for and in relation to animals, plants and the world of nature
- Being able to laugh, to play, to enjoy recreational activities
- Being able to live one's own life and nobody else's (having certain guarantees of noninterference with certain choices that are especially personal and definitive of selfhood such as choices regarding marriage, childbearing, sexual expression, speech and employment)
- Being able to live one's own life in one's own surroundings and context (this requires freedom of association and freedom from unwarranted search and seizure, a certain sort of guarantee of the integrity of personal property)[111]

Positive human functioning grounds human morality, and these functioning capabilities delineate in a provisional way anthropological markers that are able to ground the development of a critical feminist hermeneutics of retrieval and correlation as an ethical task. They are broad enough to allow interpretation and embodiment in local situations, but they do represent fundamental human markers of the good human life that can be agreed upon interculturally. These are not capabilities that a person *must* actuate in order to live a full life, but a good human life is distinguished by the freedom and ability to engage or not engage these capabilities, sometimes to actuate them, sometimes to forgo them. For example, some people may genuinely embrace celibacy for a variety of reasons (some of them religious), but it is a free choice in regard to the exercise of one's capability for sexual pleasure, made without coercion.

Lisa Sowle Cahill notes that Nussbaum does not include two functioning capabilities that she suggests are equally fundamental to the good human life: kinship and religion.[112] Cahill argues that leaving out kinship and the social structure of marriage and family misses a phenomenon of human functioning through which very important meaning is given to life, no matter how the capability for kinship is structured in a society. Cahill suggests that sexual expression as it manifests itself in the birth of children, is inextricably linked across cultures to family of some form (nuclear family, extended family, or family understood as village or other larger group). This kinship is a fundamental and distinguishing functioning capability of the human person, Cahill suggests. She also notes that Nussbaum does not include religion as a functioning capability, although it appears as a basic element of human life across cultures and across millennia.

While Nussbaum does have the basic category of affiliation, I agree with Cahill on the necessity of including the functioning capability of kinship understood as "being able to participate in reproduction in the context of stable, affiliative relationships of support." I would add a functioning capability of "being able to acknowledge, appreciate, and respond to the transcendent." This capability refers to the essential experience of wonder in the presence of that which is other than what I am, in whatever form it occurs, as well as referring to the capacity and the need to live one's life in relation to ultimate reality, no matter how one conceives of that ultimate reality. I further would include a distinct functioning capability of "being able to pursue meaningful work for which one is remunerated adequately and appropriately." While Nussbaum includes this as a dimension of being able to form a conception of the good and pursue it, including it as a distinct functioning capability acknowledges that virtually all human beings engage in some form of labor, and that human life is enhanced in a fundamental manner by a person's having meaningful, appropriately remunerative work.

As Nussbaum sets them out, and as I have appropriated them here, these functioning capabilities do not appear specifically feminist. However, I suggest that they are comprehensive and useful anthropological markers that must be pursued in any setting from an explicitly feminist perspective, that is, with particular, specific attention to the way in which women in the situation are able to live them out. For instance, considered from the perspective of women, these functioning capabilities ask how well *women* in a given situation are able to live what could reasonably be considered a "human life of normal length." Is the mortality rate for women (and female infants) different from that of men in this situation? If so, why? What is the situation of *women* here in regard to their health? Are women adequately nourished? Do women have access to the medical services from which they could benefit? Do women have adequate shelter, and do they have opportunity for sexual choice, freedom, and satisfaction, including reproductive choices? In their inclusion and use as components of the proposed anthropology, each of these functioning capabilities would be investigated from the specific perspective of women, rather than allowing generalized statistics, such as data on the gross national product (which may look splendid), to hide the situation of women. These functioning capabilities, used as a set of dynamic anthropological markers, are coherent with feminist concerns regarding anthropology. Feminists offer varying but similar elements that they insist must be included in any anthropology, elements that they contend have been absent from anthropological formulations in the past. The elements of embodiment, an appreciation of the influence of culture on the formation of sexual identity, autonomy and relatedness, critical reflection on praxis, and dynamic possibility of revision are repeatedly identified by many feminist scholars as significant elements in speaking about the human person which have been ignored in the anthropologies of the past.[113] The functioning capabilities that Nussbaum suggests address each of these elements.

Because Nussbaum suggests that these functioning capabilities must remain open to revision when necessary, feminist scholars may well find this approach to identifying anthropological markers fruitful without being restrictive. What this set of anthropological markers does point to are concrete indications of that which constitutes a human life, and a good human life which therefore exerts a moral claim on society:

> The basic intuition from which the capability approach starts . . . is that human capabilities exert a moral claim that they should be devel-

oped. Human beings are creatures such that, provided with the right educational and material support, they can become fully capable of the major human functions. . . . [J]ust as we hold that a child who dies before getting to maturity has died especially tragically . . . so too with capability and functioning more generally: we believe that certain basic and central human endowments have a moral claim to be assisted in developing, and exert a claim on others, and especially . . . on government.[114]

As we will see in the next chapter, this is quite similar to Aquinas's view of the responsibility of society and government to help bring about circumstances that promote the temporal common good of society's members.

A PROPOSED FEMINIST HERMENEUTICAL METHOD

The goal of this chapter has been to develop a feminist-liberationist hermeneutical method that can help the community determine whether and to what extent the Christian tradition is a usable source for the full human flourishing of women, and can provide resources for resistance and hope specifically on behalf of women. There is a significant degree of congruence between the methodology of Schneiders in textual hermeneutics and Ruether's methodology for the critical retrieval of aspects of systematic theology and ethics of the Christian tradition. They each begin with similar convictions: (1) The texts and traditions of the Christian community in themselves function from a conception of women that is erroneous and invalid. This is an anthropological and ethical issue, and is premised on a paradigm of women's secondary and derivative status to men as human beings. Both text and tradition, therefore, are distorted in their perception of normative humanity, a perception based on the experiences of educated, free males who were the historical winners in the time in which they lived. (2) The experience of women is virtually absent from the text and the tradition. (3) The texts and traditions of the Christian community have been used to justify the oppression of women socially, politically, religiously, ecclesially, sexually, and relationally. (4) Neither the text nor the tradition should be totally abandoned. A fundamental, life-engendering truth exists in the midst of the distorted texts and tradition, which ironically has been accessed by many women (and other groups experiencing suffering) and used by them as a source of courage and strength for their own struggle and resistance. By retrieving dimensions of the tradition based on multidisciplinary criteria (to be discussed below), including the experience of women, the effective history of the text, and the judgment of whether it is able to promote the full flourishing and comprehensive salvation of women,[115] it is possible to identify and critique the distortions of texts and tradition for what they are. (5) The distortions in themselves, when identified and rejected as such, bear witness to a purpose and capability of the texts and the tradition that has not been extinguished by the fiercest ideological distorting of a text or its interpretive application. The exposed distortions serve as a vindication of the dignity of women and are a witness to their suffering and their exclusion from full participation and respect within the community formed around the texts and the tradition.

Starting from these five shared convictions of Schneiders and Ruether, I propose a feminist hermeneutical method using the following steps:

First, the situation and experience of women is sought and used as the starting point for theological investigation—particularly their experiences of suffering. Wherever the experience of women is one of systematic exclusion, suppression, oppression, abuse, and rejection, and wherever women are used for economic, political, or sexual ends against their ability to choose, this is judged an evil to be resisted.

Second, the set of human functioning capabilities (developed in this chapter), employed from the perspective of women, is used as a principle of assessment and critique on the situation of women. Since the functioning capabilities propose the contours of a good human life (not good in the sense of morally admirable, but good in the sense of adequate to the human person's needs), situations in which these goods are absent for women are judged morally wrong.

Third, the text is examined using tools of critical analysis. It is approached with a hermeneutics of suspicion and is submitted to appropriate analytical disciplines: literary and historical criticism, philosophy, sociology, etc. Conceptions of and presumptions about women embedded in the text/tradition are identified, and the text is scrutinized to identify ways in which and the degree to which it endorses the dignity and full humanity of women. The human functioning capabilities are used as a principle of critique and assessment on the text. The truth claims of the text itself in regard to women and the interpretations of the text are studied to see if they are supportable in themselves or if they suggest a negative, derivative, or diminished status for women. This investigation particularly seeks to identify dualistic perceptions of humanity, based on a presumed privileged status for men and a presumption of diminished and/or derivative status for women. The effective history of the text is sought in order to determine the ways in which it has served as a principle of resistance against injustice, as well as the ways in which it has been used to justify the oppression of women. The text is examined through ideology critique to expose philosophical, anthropological, or social paradigms of women which subtly endorse social structures that exclude or disadvantage women. The emancipation of women and their full flourishing is used as a criterion for adjudicating the validity of an interpretation of scripture or the coherence of a dogmatic position with the belief that integral salvation is the community's most fundamental experience of God.

Fourth, a reconstructed interpretation of the text/tradition is developed. While the distorted aspects of the text or tradition are acknowledged, it must be considered whether *the text as a whole* still provides a fundamental perspective that is prophetic and liberating. This prophetic liberating tradition that remains in the text may be drawn upon to promote the dignity and salvation of all people, and now particularly of women.

Finally, the ethical and political implications of the reconstructed interpretation are addressed and a strategy of praxis is developed—the short-term and long-term steps that are required to move toward the goal of more adequately embodying the functioning capabilities in the lives of women in a situation where they have been deficient. A design of implementation that includes regular review and assessment of the effects in light of the functioning capabilities of women is constructed.[116]

According to this schema, the next step is to examine the work of Aquinas in regard to the principle of the common good. To do this fairly, we must first expose or bring to light the elements in Aquinas's thought that address the principle of the common good and then move to the stage of critical analysis of it. At this point in any feminist hermeneutical retrieval, we must be attentive to the temptation to let the convictions, pre-understandings, and presumptions we bring concerning the text or doctrine or principle propel us too quickly to judgments and conclusions on its behalf. The classic element must be allowed to speak on its own terms—for weal or woe—before the dynamic of critical retrieval proceeds.

CHAPTER 2

The Common Good in the Thought of Thomas Aquinas

The process of hermeneutical retrieval presupposes that the one who is attempting the retrieval is dealing adequately and fairly with the classic text, doctrine, or principle in question. While this is obvious, it offers a challenge to the one who would engage in a process of retrieval. A worthy process of retrieval demands that the classic element be dealt with in as balanced a manner as possible, without giving up the integrity of the process by highlighting only those aspects of the classic element that one either endorses or reviles. This requires the one retrieving to be aware of her own presuppositions, pre-understandings, and biases in order to avoid (as much as is possible) an unfair representation of the text in itself.

In this chapter I consider Aquinas's understanding of the principle of the common good in his major writings. This requires attention to the anthropology that informed Aquinas's thought, as well as an examination of his overall theory of goodness and human goodness, the place of the common good in his general theory of goodness, the function of the cardinal virtue of justice in relationship to the common good, his understanding of the relationship between the common good and the good of the individual, and examples of the exercise of the common good in his work. While these divisions will hopefully be helpful in examining Aquinas's thought on a specific topic, this approach has definite limitations, because it treats as distinct units material that Aquinas understood and dealt with in an organic and synthetic manner. Distinguishing the good from the human good from the common good introduces an artificial division into the conceptual flow of Aquinas's thought, which depends precisely on the interconnected quality of these concepts for their coherence and intelligibility. However, for the purpose of analysis, it is helpful.

BACKGROUND

Aquinas's writing was prodigious and dealt with a wide range of theological topics. Perhaps his best-known works are two systematic treatises, the *Summa Contra Gentiles* (*A Summary against the Gentiles*) and the *Summa Theologica* (*A Summary of Theology*). The *Summa Contra Gentiles* was written first, and the "Gentiles" whom Aquinas had in mind were probably not so much the Moslems of Spain but those Christians whose outlook had been affected by the naturalistic philosophy that had become popular after the rediscovery of Aristotle's work. One of Aquinas's goals in writing was to demonstrate that Christian faith rests on a rational foundation, and that the principles of philosophy do not necessarily lead to a worldview that excludes Christianity. The *Summa Theologica* was written, as Aquinas tells us, as a systematic summary and exposition of theology for Dominican novices in their study of theology and was unfinished at the time of his death in 1274. Here these works will have particular bearing, as well as his *De Regimine Principum* (*On Kingship*), which Aquinas was asked to write in 1265 for the king of Cyprus. He left it unfinished in 1267 (probably because of the king's death), and someone other than Aquinas later completed it. This treatise is particularly relevant among Aquinas's writing for the purposes of this work because it offers Aquinas's conception of the orienting focus of a good ruler, which was the common good of the community.

The thought of Aristotle became available in the West in a relatively unfiltered manner in the twelfth century and presented Western Christians with a fully integrated system of thought that was very persuasive in its rational structure. Aquinas's use of Aristotle offered a change in the way in which Christianity understood how it could relate to "the world." The view of Christianity toward the creation had generally followed more the Neoplatonic view of Augustine. Here the creation was understood as being in such a state of dereliction, so scarred by sin, that sense perceptions of the world were of minimal service in discerning evidence of God in creation. For Aristotle, however, the world was a place that was able to be studied by the human senses and human reason, and by doing this it was possible to inductively come to know universal truths. Incorporating this orientation into his Christian philosophy, Aquinas viewed the world as a place of potential revelation of divine truth, and he viewed the human senses and reason not as faculties damaged by sin so that they could not be trusted to reveal truth, but as avenues for growth in perception of God and the good.

The works of Aristotle proposed that existence in itself contains an order, a reasonableness and intelligibility, apart from any reliance on religious concepts or the claims of sacred texts. Aquinas used the philosophical arguments of Aristotle in conjunction with traditional Christian beliefs to develop an essentially teleological theology. Every aspect of reality was to be considered in relation to its own true end. The good of every thing is the fulfillment of its *telos*.

Two key and linked concepts for understanding Aquinas's conception of existence and of the created universe are hierarchy and analogy, both of which are seen in his understanding of the common good. For Aquinas, hierarchy is naturally evident in the range of life forms we observe, in which things that are endowed with greater potential for complex existence, and that in fact enjoy the actualization of such potential, are judged to occupy a higher place in the hierarchical continuum of existence. As philosopher Katherine Archibald writes:

> To organize in proper sequence the diversity of the universe, St. Thomas turns to a number of traditional capacities and characteristics presumed to exist in totality and perfection in the Deity and to be more and more partially and imperfectly present in the descending order of creatures. God is pure spirit, pure act, the unmoved mover, the uncaused cause. Hence, the more adulterated with matter, the more weakened with potency a creature is, the less it moves itself and the more it is moved by others, the less it causes and the more it is caused, the lower in the scale the creature stands.[1]

Borrowing from Aristotle's conception of a hierarchically arranged pattern of existence, Aquinas outlines the relationship of things, one to another. For him hierarchy meant that those things possessing closer affinity to God and higher levels of functioning were naturally deserving of the service of the lower order of creation. Logically, then, to attribute any quality or characteristic to something or someone can only be done in an analogous fashion because it is in God alone that one finds the perfection of all that exists. The qualities that things possess are in relation to the ultimate expression of that quality in God. Hence, goodness is an analogous term.[2] At the same time, Aquinas did not conceive of God as the ultimate pole of a continuum in which created reality also is present but as a lower form. God is the absolute Other, the totally transcendent One with whom all else exists referentially. This hierarchy of being, therefore, is not one in which God is given ultimate status among created realities.

Influenced by Aristotle's naturalism, Aquinas approached the subject of "right order" within the political and social community. While Aquinas is indebted to Augustine, with his focus on recognizing in the earthly realm an existence that relates to the vision of the Kingdom of God presented in the Gospels, Aquinas proceeds with an optimism about the possibility of creation revealing something of the divine order. This optimism is consistent with Aristotle's influence on his thinking, along with his use of Aristotle's conviction that created realities reveal a fundamental, inherent goodness of order in which created beings function (or were designed to function) in harmonious, hierarchical cooperation. Aquinas concluded that while creation exhibited many evidences of the effects of sin, the fundamental goodness originally established in creation by God was still discernible.

While Aquinas in no way offers a complete system of political thought, four principles pervade his teaching on the way in which human government, law, and obligations were meant to function. Lisa Sowle Cahill summarizes these principles:

> First, political authority and the law do not exist merely because of original sin, but correspond to needs and purposes inherent in human nature itself. Second, political authority, although flawed by sin, is distinct from and not in principle subordinate to the authority of the church. . . . Third, temporal power is directed to temporal affairs, including the cultivation of social virtue. "The foremost task of government was to establish and maintain those objective conditions, principally matters of justice, which allowed citizens to lead the good life." Finally, political judgment is more like an art than a deductive science. Because they answer to practical and contingent matters, government and legislation can never be deduced strictly from premises, nor legitimated absolutely by any philosophical or theological reasons.[3]

THE ANTHROPOLOGY OF AQUINAS IN RELATION TO THE COMMON GOOD

Until the advent of feminist theology and other liberation theologies, Western Christian theology operated from a model of the human person that was largely dependent upon the anthropology employed by

Aquinas. This conception of the human person was developed by Greek philosophers and amended by the addition of Christian insights about the soul, sin, and grace. It was based on the free, educated male of Greek society as the normative human, and as such offered a very limited perspective on any type of normative human anthropology.

Aquinas's anthropology was foundational to his conception of goodness and justice, and it cannot be ignored because some significant aspects of it are now judged inaccurate. Passages in his writings regarding women that many today find offensive cannot simply be dismissed without examining them, and the larger context in which they occur, for elements that might be retrieved—shaken loose from their medieval anthropological context—and used in the development of a liberating Christian feminist social ethic. The presumption at the heart of this book is that the Christian community would be poorly served if entire classic texts of the tradition were rejected—without any effort to release possibly valuable principles from their original, contextual frameworks—because the texts contain material now judged to be inaccurate or to reflect a cultural perspective that is no longer tenable and in fact is offensive and oppressive. If it is possible to discover valuable principles within these texts, then the community for whom the texts are significant benefits as elements that hold liberating, challenging, empowering, or guiding energy are brought forward to engage the contemporary situation. The outcome of an effort of retrieval is not guaranteed; it could result in a text being judged so fundamentally crippled by elements deemed irretrievable that it must no longer function in an authoritative manner for the community. But to dismiss the labor because it forces one to confront Aquinas's words about women (or the contents of any contested classic material) which one finds offensive is a dereliction of one's duty as a responsible theologian.

In the last twenty-five years, the limits in Aquinas's anthropology have been discussed at great length. While his anthropology was not completely erroneous, it was based on inaccurate biological and physiological information, and the ways in which he extrapolated from that misinformation resulted in a subordinate status for women. Moreover, most feminists judge the aspects of the person considered constitutive by Aquinas inadequate. Late twentieth-century anthropology uses a set of variables considered essential to describe the phenomenon of a person, as well as biological and physiological knowledge, that was unknown in medieval Europe.[4] However, if we change the anthropological description, we also change what is understood as the proximate or naturally attainable good of the person. The social ethics that is dependent on that anthropology must be reconsidered to determine whether the claims on the individual and the community must be reshaped in light of the amended anthropology.

Philosopher Linda Maloney notes that "Aristotle saw it as his task to describe the existing state of things and to explain why it must necessarily be so."[5] His approach was function-focused or function-based, examining the way something did what it was supposed to do, and it was an approach that presumed a hierarchical ordering of existence, in which the end or purpose of the lower functioning entity is to serve the higher.[6] His conception of a hierarchically ordered set of relationships flowed into his conception of the relationships that characterize human existence also. Women were, in his judgment, functionally different from men: they were less capable, Aristotle concluded, of rational reasoning, and they were deficient in their sexual functioning. Although they lacked what he believed to be the "active" principle in procreation, they served a valuable role in the perpetuation of the human race, but in fact were "deficient males."[7] Finally, women were functionally deficient, lacking the physical strength of men.

This conception of creation and humanity was generally adopted by Aquinas, who harmonized it with the creation story of Genesis. For Aquinas, the functional order of creation works for the woman's good, providing her with the guidance and the protection of a man, and it assists the man to have her as helper.[8] The given in this for Aquinas is that woman is subordinate to man as part of the order of creation. The passages in Aquinas where the presumed imperfection of woman is offered as the basis of her subordination to man are scattered throughout his writings because he did not address woman's subjection to man as a problem. That did not need to be proven by him; it was simply a fact to be commented upon insofar as he tried to understand how woman, with such imperfection, could share the fundamental nature of a human person:

> When all things were first formed, it was more suitable for the woman to be made from the man. . . . First, in order thus to give the first man a certain dignity consisting in this, that as God is the principle of the whole universe, so the first man, in likeness of God, was the principle of the whole human race.[9]

This analogy between God as creator of the universe and head of all that exists, and man as the bearer of the image of God and the head of the woman, permeates Aquinas's anthropology. For him, it was a logical extrapolation and fit with the anthropology he had inherited:

> Hence: God's image is found equally in both man and woman as regards that point in which the idea of "image" is principally realized, namely an intelligent nature. . . . But as regards a secondary point, God's image is found in man in a way which is not found in woman: for man is the beginning and the end of woman, just as God is the beginning and end of all creation.[10]

It is important to note that Aquinas understood both women and men to reflect God's image in a primary sense, both bearers of a rational nature, both having the ability to exercise free will and the potential to grow in virtue:

> [W]e must understand that when Scripture had said, to the image of God He created him, it added, male and female He created them, not to imply the image of God came through the distinction of sex, but that the image of God belongs to both sexes, since it is in the mind, wherein there is no sexual distinction. Wherefore the Apostle (Col.iii.10), after saying, According to the image of Him that created him, added, Where there is neither male nor female.[11]

At the same time, Aquinas does view woman in a position of subordination to man, because he views men as more reasonable than women:

> Subjection is twofold. One is servile, by virtue of which a superior makes use of a subject for his own benefit; and this kind of subjection began after sin. There is another kind of subjection, which is called economic or civil, whereby the superior makes use of his subjects for their own benefit and good; and this kind of subjection existed even before sin. For good order would have been wanting in the human family if some were not governed by others wiser than themselves. So by such a kind of subjection woman is naturally subject to man, because in man the discretion of reason predominates.[12]

Aquinas believed that it was the male, by virtue of his fuller intellectual capacity, who was able to most fully reveal the image of God:

> Properly speaking, then, only creatures with intellect are made to God's image. And the point at which such creatures most closely resemble God is when they imitate his self-understanding and love. So

there are three levels to the images of God by man: the very nature of mind gives to all men a natural aptitude for understanding and loving God; grace adds to some men an actual if imperfect understanding and love of God; and the glory of heaven brings this to perfection. The principle constituent of God's image in man, mind, is found in both male and female human beings which is why Genesis says, "To God's image he created him (namely, mankind); male and female he created them." A secondary image of God as beginning and end of creation is however to be found only in male man, the beginning and end of woman.[13]

While Aquinas reflects this belief in the greater reasonableness of men in the exercise of rational discretion, he does not suggest that women are without discretion; he simply holds that men are less controlled by nonrational forces and therefore more able to rule for the good of all. Aquinas maintains the essential equality of men and women because of their shared rational nature and ability to respond to God through it.[14] However, while maintaining that male and female are equal in their ability to reflect the image of God in a primary way, Aquinas contends that only a man reflects God's image in a secondary way, because only a man can fully reflect God's authority:

The image of God, in its principal signification, namely the intellectual nature, is found both in man and woman. . . . But in a secondary sense, the image of God is found in man and not in woman: for man is the beginning and end of woman; as God is the beginning and end of every creature.[15]

For Aquinas, society is the place in which humanity is called to shape communities where the gradual sanctification of the members by the Spirit of Christ takes place. Society is not antithetical to the Spirit for Aquinas; rather, it is a context in which grace operates. Cahill writes: "In Aquinas' ethical writings, the urgency of life in the kingdom is subordinated to the importance of building human communities in the created order. The Christian is at home within this order, and the gradual sanctification by the Spirit in Christ takes place within it, not over against it."[16] This attitude toward the world is distinct from that of Augustine and offers further insight into the type of change in theological understanding of creation, the human person, and society that Aquinas proposed and why his work, along with that of Aristotle, was so provocative.

THE GOOD

To appreciate Aquinas's writing on the common good, it is necessary to examine his understanding of the good generally. In this way, the common good can be seen in the context in which it functions and in light of the role it plays: that is, it can be seen how the common good is an aspect of the good. Since, as Jean Porter advises, Aquinas's entire theory of morality may be understood as a response to the question "What is meant by acting for the good?" the common good is a significant element in his moral theory.[17]

The very term "good" initially seems straightforward, but on examination, and particularly in examining the ways Aquinas understands and uses the term, one finds that it is a multivalent term and must be appreciated for its nuances and complexity. Commonly, the term "good" is an adjective used to describe a positive quality or judgment about something. Examined philosophically, and particularly in investigating the way Aquinas uses the term, it is understood primarily as perfection. In *De Veritate*, Aquinas describes the good in the following manner:

> Since the essence of good consists in this, that something perfects another as an end, whatever is found to have the character of an end also has that of good. Now two things are essential to an end: It must be sought or desired by things which have not attained the end, and it must be loved by things which share the end, and be, as it were, enjoyable to them.[18]

To be "perfective" of something, then, is to assist it in achieving its full potential or to be the cause of its achieving its full potential. The term "good" refers in a primary or fundamental way only to God who perfects all things and is the perfection of all things. The term can be applied only analogically to other things insofar as a thing is perfective of and desired by another and enjoyed by those who participate in the desired end.

In the *Summa Contra Gentiles*, Aquinas writes that the good for each thing is its action and perfection.[19] And in the *Compendium of Theology*, he says that the "perfect signifies what is good, since the perfection of anything is its goodness."[20] Later in the same work he writes: "[T]he term good signifies perfect being. The good finds its definition in the perfect. . . ."[21] That the notion of the good is derived from the notion of the perfect is nowhere more clearly stated than at the beginning of the *Summa Theologica*. Notably, the discussion of God's goodness (question six) follows the discussion of God's perfection (question four). The bridge between these concepts (question five) is Aquinas's discussion of goodness in relation to perfection.[22] Similarly in the *Compendium* Aquinas writes:

> Since the good has the nature of perfection and of an end, the two-fold perfection and end of the creature discloses its two-fold goodness. Certain goodness is observed in the creature inasmuch as it persists in its nature. This perfection is the end of its generation or formation. . . . The form and existence of a thing are its good and perfection when considered from the standpoint of the thing's nature. . . . Likewise, all creatures receive their perfecting goodness from an end extrinsic to them. For the perfection of goodness consists in attainment of an ultimate end. But the ultimate end of a creature is outside the creature. . . . God alone is his own goodness, and he alone is essentially good. All other beings are said to be good according as they participate, to some extent, in him.[23]

And later in the *Compendium* Aquinas writes:

> To every being its own good is naturally desirable. Hence, good is conveniently designed as that which all desire. The proper good of any being is that whereby it is brought to perfection. We say that a thing is good inasmuch as it reaches its proper perfection. Since there are many degrees of human perfection, that good chiefly and primarily comes under man's desire which looks to ultimate perfection. . . . That good which men chiefly and mainly desire must be of such a nature that it is not sought for the sake of something else, and that it satisfies man. This good is commonly called happiness inasmuch as it means the foremost good.[24]

All other things, pursued as ends, are good in an analogical manner because they are not absolute or ultimate ends in themselves, but they are good insofar as they orient something toward its ultimate end. The term "good," then, may also be used to refer to the incomplete perfection of an object in relation to absolute perfection and particularly to the moral quality of a person.

Aquinas understood goodness to be a transcendental—a concept or quality of such ubiquity that it can be applied to all things in some manner:

> To be good is to be of value, where value is consequent on perfection (since we value what makes for perfection) and perfection is a degree of achieved actuality. Good . . . expresses the notion of value and perfection, and thus the notion of completeness. To be called good without qualification a thing must be completely perfect; when its perfection is not as complete as it should be (even though it has some perfection just by existing) we don't call it good without qualification, but only good in respect of that perfection.[25]

The sheer fact of existence, then, endows a thing with a dimension of goodness; for a thing to exist, it must exist *as* something, and existing as something it exists in some approximation of the perfection of its species or it would not be identifiable as a particular thing. Therefore, that which exists possesses some dimension of goodness by the very fact of existing. Aquinas contends that since all creatures tend toward fulfillment or perfection that is proper to their particular nature, it is possible to say that all things tend toward the good.[26] That is, each thing contains a natural dynamism that impels it toward ever fuller actualization of the form of its species. Therefore, goodness is enhanced in a thing as it achieves a closer approximation of the perfection appropriate to it as it actualizes its potential to become what it is.

Aquinas drew on Aristotle's understanding of the good outlined in the *Nicomachean Ethics*, in which Aristotle observed that goodness has to do with a thing being related to its highest good. Similarly, Aquinas comments: "Everything is therefore called good from the divine goodness, as from the first exemplary, effective and final principle of all goodness."[27]

THE HUMAN GOOD

The way Aquinas understands the good that is characteristic of the human person is consistent with his conception of goodness generally, but the human being is ordered toward goodness and perfection in a unique way. Following philosophically the lead of Aristotle, Aquinas understood human nature to be characterized by rationality and free will.[28] Aquinas held that for human beings, the capacity to act well through deliberate choices is a defining characteristic of our humanity and an essential aspect of the goodness and perfection proper to us. Therefore, the person alone, of all creatures, participates in her own growth in goodness and her natural perfection by her deliberate choices and actions. "To sum up: The thing desired as the final end is that which gives substance to happiness and makes a man happy, though happiness itself is desired by the holding of it. The conclusion to be drawn is that happiness is a real condition of the soul yet is found in a thing outside the soul."[29] It is not simply that a person *may* exercise this choice; to pursue her perfection and her good as a person she *must* exercise her capacity for choice in pursuit of the good worthy of her— appropriate to her—as a human being. A person does not grow in goodness passively, but in a significant way through the use of her capacity to choose and to act on that choice. Aquinas advises: "Insofar as man's happiness is a creaturely reality in him the inference must be that it is an activity. For that is the full expression of his being. Each thing is perfect inasmuch as it is actual, for what is potential is still imperfect. Happiness, therefore, must go with man's culminating actuality. Clearly this means his being active."[30]

As I noted earlier, Aquinas discusses goodness in terms of that which perfects. For the human being, this is complete spiritual union with God known directly in the beatific vision. Therefore, a person's complete good—her full actualization or full coming to be as the unique created reality she is—cannot occur in this life.[31] At the same time, the human person is a historical being and *grows* in goodness through the development of virtue.[32] The goodness possible for her in this life includes to a genuine albeit partial degree her choices. This growth in goodness and virtue is not inconsequential or unimportant even though it is not her absolute perfection, which only God can supply as gift:

> [T]he highest perfection of a rational or intellectual nature is two-fold. There is a perfection which can be attained by the power (*virtue*) of such a nature, and this is called happiness or felicity in a certain sense. . . . But beyond this felicity is another felicity which we expect for the future, that is, that "we shall see God as he is" (1 John 3:2). This latter is beyond the nature of every created intellect.[33]

Porter suggests that Aquinas understands the good a person elects through her free choice as the "proximate norm of the moral life."[34] However, since the *telos* or end of the person is a supernatural one, *no* degree of her exercise of a natural capacity to choose good can achieve her supernatural end or cause an increase in the theological virtues of faith, hope, and love. In Aquinas's thought, the natural end or happiness and the supernatural end or happiness of a person do not stand in conflict to each other, but represent a single end of goodness, perfection, and happiness pursued and attained in a twofold manner, natural and supernatural. As theologian Kevin Staley puts it: "Imperfect as well as perfect beatitude both respond to man's desire for goodness as such, though in differing degrees of completeness."[35] All creatures, Aquinas explains, have the capacity to attain happiness to a limited degree by created participation in God's goodness.[36] The participation is appropriate to the creature's nature: an animal's goodness does not include self-consciousness of itself as a distinct entity with preferences and goals that the animal may at times knowingly sacrifice for the sake of another in self-transcending love, which human goodness might at times ask of a person. Union with God, apprehension of God in God's self, is the ultimate goal; it is the ultimate good and happiness of the person, a supernatural end that is beyond full attainment in earthly life and beyond the natural powers of the human person to achieve.[37] Nevertheless, two observations must be made here. First, although a person cannot attain in this life the absolute end or good appropriate to her—union with God—contemplation of God in this life, by using her natural powers, is possible and orients the person to her proper end:

> So if the ultimate felicity of man does not consist in external things which are called the goods of fortune, nor in the goods of the body, nor in the goods of the soul according to its sensitive part, nor as regards the intellective part according to the activity of the moral virtues, nor according to the intellectual virtues that are connected with the action, that is, art and prudence—we are left with the conclusion that the ultimate felicity of man lies in the contemplation of truth.[38]

Aquinas understands this as the true goal or end of the person. While a person can grow and become relatively more oriented to and capable of contemplation of truth (and not simply truth as speculative knowledge, but truth as God), the supernatural end of a person, direct apprehension of God, is not achievable by any perfection of contemplation using one's natural powers:

> Man's natural resources then are enough to gain for him virtue and the partial happiness that follows virtue in this life; but not man's nor any creature's natural resources are enough to gain for him ultimate happiness. Yet just as nature provides for man's needs, though denying him the weapons and covering natural to other animals, by giving

him reason and his hands to make such things for himself, so too nature provides for man's needs, though denying him the resources to win happiness for himself—an impossibility—by giving him free will to turn to God who can make him happy. . . . And a nature that can thus achieve utmost perfection, even though needing external help to do it, is of a nobler constitution than a nature that can only achieve some lesser good, even though without external help.[39]

The second observation that must be made here is that the natural and specific perfection of the human person includes the development of the virtues that render a person available and responsive to God's action and invitation. A life that embodies and manifests true human goodness is not accomplished by simply, as Porter says, "setting ourselves to perform determinate actions of the correct kinds, while avoiding other kinds of actions."[40] It requires a clear and true apprehension of the good, an appreciation of the dimensions of the circumstances in which one finds oneself, the needs that are at hand or at risk, and the exercise of multiple capacities of discernment and judgment to make a choice that coheres with the integrity of the person and pursues the good in specific circumstances.

The good appropriate to the person is a complex phenomenon, involving both the natural dimensions of the person as she participates in created reality, and a transcendental good to which a person must make a deliberative response. Created reality, including the created reality of the person in her embodiment with all its aspects, is a necessary and privileged avenue of growth in virtues that orient the person progressively through her lifetime toward the good. Porter observes: "The natural end of human life, that is, the attainment of specific perfection as a human being, is not rendered otiose or irrelevant by the fact that we are actually directed toward a supernatural end. The specific natural ideal of humanity remains the proximate norm of morality."[41] While Aquinas never addresses the question of what constitutes the natural perfection of the human being in detail, Porter suggests that for Aquinas the ideal relationship between the natural good or end of a person and her ultimate end involves a balance:

[I]t becomes apparent that the ideal, as he sees it, would be a life that strikes an appropriate balance between activity and contemplation, in accordance with the temperament of the individual (II-II.182.4 *ad* 3; cf. I-II.3.5; I-II.4.5; I-II.5.5). In other words, the specific ideal of humanity, as he sees it, is not a life spent in contemplation alone (as if that were possible), but a life that incorporates other sorts of activities as well.[42]

Aquinas instructs us that the person who is good is not merely one who holds truths in her mind. Exercise of the person's free will in choosing those things that are for her greatest good is an essential aspect of human goodness. In the following extended excerpt, we see Aquinas outlining his justification for this belief that human goodness is constituted not only by the perception of the good, but by the person's *choice* of it:

> Just as mind must by nature assent to the first principles of thought, so will must by nature consent to our ultimate goal of happiness. . . . The will does not have to want limited goods that have no necessary connection with happiness and that a person can be happy without; but other things do have a necessary connection with happiness, joining men to God, in whom alone true happiness is to be found. . . . Understanding takes things in and is concerned with their truth in the mind, whereas willing tends toward the goodness of things in themselves. . . . So the will is the overall motive power behind all human activity, save only those vegetative activities that are involuntary and natural. Mind and will can be regarded either as particular abilities with their own distinct activities, or as concerned with all-embracing objects: the mind as an awareness open to all that exists and is true, and the will as attracted towards everything good. . . . The actions and objects of mind and will mutually include each other: the mind understands the will's willing, the will wills the mind's understanding. . . . Freedom is a fundamental capability of the soul, not just a disposition. . . . Freedom is properly an ability to choose, and involves both the mind deciding what is preferable, and the will accepting this decision. But what we choose is what best serves our goal, what is usefully good, and since goods and goals are objects of desire, choice must fundamentally be a sort of desire and freedom an ability to desire. Freedom is nothing other than the will itself. . . . Willing and choosing are actions of the same power: the ability to will and the ability to choose are one and the same ability.[43]

In this regard, Ralph McInerny notes that a truly good and therefore moral person is one who acts well,[44] and acting well involves a conscious, reasoned grasp of and choice for an authentic good. Here we begin to see why the anthropology that informs the conception of the person and of full human flourishing is significant for determining and choosing those actions that *actually* foster human good both on the natural and supernatural level and by whose choice the person may be deemed "good." Porter writes: "[T]hat goodness of action in which human perfection consists cannot be understood in purely formal terms. It requires that a person acts and sustains activities in accordance with a (roughly) correct understanding of what it means to be a good human being (*ST* I-II.2.7; I-II.3.1)."[45] Porter also comments:

> If I am to select those things that will really promote my healthy functioning as a human being, it is first of all necessary for me to know what that means, concretely. Even then I must still bring that knowledge to bear on each particular situation, and choose accordingly. . . . [A] successful human life is spent in acting in accordance with a (roughly) correct concept of the human good. . . . Such a life calls for deliberate activity guided by knowledge of what is truly good for human beings, and what is not. But of course, this raises the questions of what, precisely, "the truly good for the human person" might be, and how we come to know what it is.[46]

Natural human goodness is approximated to the degree a person actively and deliberately chooses those things that move her toward the ideal of a freely knowing and choosing person—in other words, to the extent that a person chooses authentic goods. Aquinas notes that a person may, of course, choose things that in fact are not authentic goods, but that nonetheless are chosen because they are perceived by a person as attractive, i.e., good.

The goodness of the human person is not one that can be pursued by the person in isolation. By the very constitution of the person, her good is one that is authentically pursued in the company of others. Both to have a created, bodily existence and to live in society flow from the nature of the human person. While the soul may enjoy perfect happiness in the contemplation of God, Aquinas argues that the perfection of its specific nature—human nature—cannot be approached apart from the body.[47]

The significant point for the purpose at hand is that Aquinas valued the material and social dimension of the person as important to her growth in perfection and goodness and did not expect a person to transcend or reject her materiality to choose a gnostic type of good. Since the person is fundamentally social and "political,"[48] this characteristic of communality must be well regarded to assist the person in becoming good. Even heaven will not be an enjoyment of God in isolation. Aquinas describes it as "the ordered society of those who enjoy the divine vision."[49] Hence, attention to the perfection of human goodness must address not only the spiritual attributes and qualities of a "good" person as a single creature, but the way a person is aided in growth in goodness by the communality in which she finds herself, the way the society in which she lives assists her in exercising her ability to choose in a fruitful manner that will help her to grow in true goodness, and the way she is a member of that society promoting the common good by her choices.

THE COMMON GOOD

Just as the term "good" appears deceptively simple but is a multivalent term, reference to "the common good" is complex in the meanings that Aquinas ascribed to it, as well as the interpretations of meaning that have become associated with the term over time. Aquinas's considerations of the common good are scattered throughout his writings rather than being located in one particular text.

In Aquinas's thought, the common good is a formal moral norm, a basic aspect of the good, not an optional dimension of it. His consideration of the common good constitutes one of the concentric circles in his carefully developed understanding of the good—circles which at the same time are not distinct from each other, but are interlocked aspects of the good. My discussion of the common good will be aided by acknowledging that the categories to be considered do not offer specific content: they do not, for example, define or state *how* the human good is to be pursued in a particular circumstance or even the precise shape of the common good in a specific situation. Aquinas's particular conception of good government, which given his culture and context he believed was an elected or chosen monarch functioning in relation to a constitution, does not define or limit the form of government that we may entertain as furthering the common good today. Aquinas's own conception of a constitutional monarchy as the best form of government is not the issue in this retrieval of the principle of the common good. The common good is a paradigm of the ideal of the dynamic relationship between the individual and the society, as individual and social choices are made within time and history, in specific contexts. This paradigm can be facilitated by a variety of forms of government, all of which (in Aquinas's mind) have some type of distinct leadership.

The exercise of retrieval raises up characteristics or hallmarks of the common good which may be used as tools of ethical assessment on any form of government and social reality. Pursuing a retrieval of the Thomistic conception of the common good will not automatically yield concrete or material norms; what it will yield is an orientation, a trajectory, a sense of the construction and elements that contribute to justice that must now be concretized in a new situation.

For Aquinas, the common good of all created reality and of humanity is God. God is the universal common good to which human beings are oriented as their end and ultimate fulfillment:

> Now loving God above all things is something connatural to man, and even to any creature, rational and non-rational, and even non-living in accordance with the kind of love which may befit any creature. . . . Even by natural love every particular thing loves its own proper good for the sake of the common good of the whole universe, and this is God.[50]

God is the reality to be experienced and enjoyed uniquely by each person, and at the same time, the good enjoyed by many: "When St. Thomas asserts that God is a common good, he means a good which is numerically one, yet which can be the end of many."[51]

A logical question at this point would be why the common good is such an important issue for Aquinas. Is it not sufficient simply to appreciate as a general principle that God is the ultimate end of all creation, including people, thus constituting God as the "common" good? This would be a truncated understanding of the common good, reducing it to a numerical issue (God simply being the ultimate good of the one and the many at the same time). This conception of the common good would further be inadequate because it fosters a dualism in which the physical dimensions of creation are not valued as vehicles of revelation and encounter with God nor as privileged means by which a person may grow in apprehension of and response to God, thus reducing creation to a type of "platform" from which creation and particularly humanity focuses on God but which in itself is valueless. A relationship must be appreciated between all creation and its analogical goodness, and its service as a mediation of God who desires to be known and to whom people are to respond.

The central importance of the common good in Aquinas's moral thought flows naturally from his anthropology. As intrinsically social beings, we exist and flourish only within the context of a community.[52] Therefore, Aquinas writes that because of our social nature, we are obligated to do "whatever is necessary for the preservation of human society."[53] The issue is not merely the preservation of the sheer existence of the group, but of its flourishing as a necessary, life-promoting reality for all members of the society. What we begin to see is the extension of Aquinas's concept of the human good, which included a natural as well as a supernatural dimension. While God is the ultimate common good of all creation, the common good is also understood by Aquinas as being connected to the practical exigencies of living in society. How we live in society, how we shape our societies and our relationships within societies, is related to the pursuit of God as the highest good.

Aquinas viewed the existence of society and the state differently from Augustine. Augustine saw it is as a necessity in view of the fallen and sinful nature of humanity, which requires coercive, restricting power to restrain the evil tendencies of people and to punish crime. While he believed the pursuit of peace was a common and worthy human endeavor, he considered this quest fairly futile:[54] "The city of man remains in a chronic condition of civil war."[55] Aquinas, on the other hand, saw society as a good in itself: "Man is by nature a social animal. Hence in a state of innocence (if there had been no Fall) men would have lived in society."[56] Aquinas again follows the lead of Aristotle, who saw politics as the *art* by which societies pursue the earthly/social good that is common both to individuals and to the community.

An examination of the common good as it occurs in the writing of Aquinas reveals an interesting set of considerations surrounding this principle. Aquinas did not usually write with an aim to guide or advise in matters of civic governance.[57] Aquinas was a philosopher and a theologian. To the extent that he did write about government and the rule of the civic life, it was because he appreciated that the civic realm is the arena in which a significant dimension of virtue is pursued, and that the well-run society offers a better hope of providing the circumstances necessary for the members of the society to pursue their highest good. Also, a society that functions properly reflects a proper basic order that Aquinas saw as a reflection of God's intention and desire for humanity. A well-run society reflects more fully the order that Aquinas understood as being part of God's own harmony.

Aquinas understood one of the evidences of the social character of the human person to be seen in the person's physical, intellectual, and moral need for assistance to secure her necessities for life. This includes her needs for social formation in a culture and for relationships in which she can love and be loved, and receive the benefits of friendship. All these things are necessary for her full development and flourishing, and point to the fact that the person living in isolation is unable to grow in the goodness appropriate to her. As Michael Sherwin observes: "Of himself, the individual is not able to acquire those things necessary for human fulfillment. Thus, in order to grow and flourish, the human person must live in society."[58] Aquinas himself writes:

> If it is natural for man to live in association with others, there must be some way for them to be governed. For if many men were to live together and each to provide what is convenient for himself, the group would break up unless one of them had the responsibility for the good of the group. . . . This is reasonable since the private good and the common good are not the same. Therefore, besides what moves each person to his own private good there must be something that moves everyone to the common good of the many. Therefore in everything that is ordered to a single end, one thing is found that rules the rest.[59]

Just as, for Aquinas, the society of the family is at its best when "governed" well by the father, so by extension civil society also functions appropriately when governed well. "Or to state it another way, man's nature requires government and politics."[60] Aquinas saw unity and order as basic qualities of social living indispensable for the pursuit of the common good, qualities which could best be protected by the state. The purpose of the state is to provide organization and unity toward a common purpose or goal, since society is a "union of men acting for a common purpose."[61] But how did Aquinas understand that common purpose which the state and those who govern are to safeguard? In *On Kingship* (book 2, chapters 3 and 4), Aquinas discussed the centrality of the common good in the role of the state (what constituted the common good that the state was meant to protect and foster):

> To govern is to direct what is governed to its appropriate end. . . . It seems that the end of organized society is to live a life of virtue. Men gather together so that they may live well which they could not do if they lived by themselves. The good life is one that is lived in accordance with virtue. Therefore the virtuous life is the end of human society. . . . Because the man who lives the life of virtue is destined for a higher end which is, as we have said, the enjoyment of the di-

vine, this must also be the final end of human society. The final end of organized society then is not merely to live the life of virtue but through a life of virtue to attain the enjoyment of God.[62]

Finally in *On Kingship*, Aquinas suggests that three things are necessary for the good life of a social group: "First, the society must be united in peace. Secondly, the society thus united must be directed towards acting well. . . . A third requirement is that the king work to see that there is a sufficient supply of the necessities required to live well."[63] This follows immediately after Aquinas identifies the two things required for an individual person to lead a good life: "The first and most important is to act in accordance with virtue since virtue is what makes one live well. The second—and it is secondary *and a means to the first*—is sufficiency of the material goods that are necessary for virtuous action."[64] Aquinas essentially charges the king with the responsibility of guiding the community so that the common good is pursued: the earthly circumstances are shaped so that the citizens are enabled to pursue their ultimate good in this life—contemplation of God—living in a situation of peace and justice, and having the practical necessities that they need. The state does not exist for itself, nor does any ruler rule for his or her own end, but for the common good of the society. This common good, while it is ultimately union with God in direct communion, is pursued in the ways possible in this life through virtuous living. As philosopher Richard Crofts writes:

> Thomas knew enough of a "social gospel" to realize that it was difficult for a man to progress far along the road to spiritual beatitude without first having his more pressing physical and material needs met. The state acting under the aegis of the common good should take care of man's temporal needs and the Church should take care of his eternal needs. By supplying man's physical needs and the conditions for a good life, the state attempts to establish universal (though imperfect) happiness.[65]

Unity and order are desirable, Aquinas maintained, because in a peaceful society, free of turmoil and strife, a society which operates justly in regard to its citizens, people are more able to attend to the pursuit of their highest good and their perfection in the midst of their life circumstances. This is much less likely when there is war, social unrest, and a social order in which justice is lacking:

Perfect contemplation requires that the body should be disencumbered, and to this effect are directed all the products of art that are necessary for life. Moreover, it requires freedom from the disturbances caused by the passions, which is achieved by means of the moral virtues and prudence; and freedom from external disturbance, to which all the regulations of civil life are directed.[66]

Throughout his writing Aquinas pronounces a limited constitutional monarchy the best form of government, one that offers the best possibility of securing the common good for the community. In the *Summa Theologica* he writes:

Accordingly, the best form of government is in a state or kingdom, where one is given the power to preside over all, while under him are others having governing powers; and yet a government of this kind is shared by all, both because all are eligible to govern, and because the rulers are chosen by all. For this is the best form of policy, being partly kingdom, since there is one at the head of all; partly aristocracy, insofar as a number of persons are set in authority, partly democracy, i.e., government by the people, insofar as the rulers can be chosen from the people and the people have the right to choose their rulers.[67]

He juxtaposes the good government/benevolent monarch/common good model with bad government/tyrannical ruler/private good, and, predictably, the best form of government is recognized by the fact that it works for the common good. Aquinas felt that an oligarchy that departs from the common good and that pursues the advantage of a few is a worse choice than a democracy in which the common good is sought. His conception of a good government in the form of a constitutional monarchy should not render his considerations on the characteristics of good government and the common good unusable today. The main focus for Aquinas is not on the form of government itself. He drew on his context and experience and identified a form that he felt would most facilitate the purpose of any society—the pursuit of the common good.

Two purposes or ends of human society are identified in Aquinas's work. First, humans seek to live in society because of the innate structure of their human nature that tends toward communication. Jacques Maritain explains: "By the very fact that each of us is a person and expresses himself to himself, each of us requires communication with *other* and *the others* in the order of knowledge and love."[68] Similarly, Maritain observes:

> Why is it that the person, as person, seeks to live in society? It does so, first, because of its very perfections, as person, and its inner urge to the communications of knowledge and love which require relationship with others. In its radical generosity, the human person tends to overflow into social communications in response to the law of superabundance inscribed in the depth of being, life, intelligence and love.[69]

Jean Porter observes that Aquinas's theories of knowledge and language imply some sort of social life that is necessary for the exercise of the rational capacities distinctive to the human creature.[70] We grow in knowledge through a process of discursive reasoning, and the ability to reason discursively requires "language and a shared body of knowledge, both of which are cultural artifacts."[71] To be a member of a culture is to benefit from participation in shared history and traditions, symbol systems, constellations of meaning(s), etc.—goods which transcend any one individual but from which the individual benefits and to which she contributes. Sherwin observes: "For Thomas this collectivity of goods is the temporal common good. Specifically, the temporal common good is the totality of all those goods which promote virtuous living and which can be shared by all."[72] Aquinas understood this temporal common good as a complex or constellation of many things: physical goods necessary to maintain life, i.e., food, shelter, clothing;[73] relational social goods such as peace, tranquility, and security of the community; and goods of the heart and soul such as love, delight, and friendship.[74] The truth is a common good to which people have a right and which is vitally important for a person to grow in the goodness possible to her in this life.[75] This is an extremely significant facet of the temporal beatitude that will be picked up later in its implications for women. Aquinas names virtues themselves as part of the common good. When one acts virtuously one gives good example and does good, and this contributes to the good of everyone.[76] Aquinas also understands the state or society to be responsible for fostering the common good in its enactment and application of laws, which, as they are observed, promote virtue.[77] While in contemporary society we would not think of the laws of a country existing for the purpose of promoting virtue, it is possible to appreciate that observance of the laws of the community (this presumes they are worthy and good laws) demands certain behaviors of the members of the society, such as tolerance, honesty, respect for others and their possessions, sharing of wealth through taxes to provide for common needs and for the support of those who need assistance, etc.

While this approach highlights the positive goods that a culture offers its members—the experience of grounding and location that belonging to a culture provides—this is not to suggest that cultures, with their accompanying social phenomena, are beyond criticism. All cultures function in ways that do not work for the good of the members (or some members) of the community; all have biases and prejudices, embody systemic injustices, are blinded by ideologies, etc. However, a culture is a rich matrix of social networks. Occurring in countless forms, culture born of human association is a universal phenomenon, and its universality points to the unavoidability of culture for the living of human life. In many cultures, "excommunication," rejection, shunning, banishment, or ostracism by the community is the ultimate punishment. To be cut off from one's culture or community is traditionally understood as a profound human suffering.

The second end or purpose of living in society for Aquinas involves a need delineated in two forms. First, a person is in need of the help of others to meet her physical requirements. Of herself, the human person is unable to acquire those things that are necessary for her human fulfillment at the natural level—food, shelter, clothing. But the person also needs society for a second reason. Maritain describes this second aspect as "the help which he ought to be given to do the work of reason and virtue, which responds to the specific feature of his being."[78] The person in isolation is unable to acquire and develop the virtues that orient her to her ultimate perfection or ultimate good. She needs education, guidance, and opportunity to grow in her ability to love the good, to identify it, and to pursue it through her choices.[79]

Aquinas offered his understanding of the human need for society in order to grow in virtuous living:

> Man is helped by a multitude of which he is a part, toward acquiring the perfect fullness of his life: namely, that he may not only live but also live well, having all the things which are necessary for the perfection of living. For this reason, man is helped by the civil multitudes of which he is a part. This assistance concerns not only man's corporal needs . . . but also his moral needs.[80]

Aquinas also noted:

> It is, however, clear that the end of a multitude gathered together is to live virtuously. For men form a group for the purpose of living well together, a thing which the individual man living alone could not attain, and good life is virtuous life. Therefore, virtuous life is the end for which men gather together.[81]

For Aquinas then, a "good" human person is a unique individual who yet requires society to come to the full expression of herself and for the full development of her goodness: "There is in all men a certain natural impulse toward civil communion and toward virtue."[82] Aquinas understands these two impulses as connected. Maritain explains:

> [The common good] is the good *human* life of the multitude, of a multitude of persons; it is their communion in good living. It is therefore common to both the whole and the parts into which it flows back and which, in turn, must benefit from it. Unless it would vitiate itself, it implies and requires recognition of the fundamental rights of persons and those of the domestic society in which the persons are more primitively engaged than in the political society. It includes within itself as principal value, the highest access, compatible with the good of the whole, of the persons to their life of person and liberty of expansion, as well as to the communications of generosity consequent upon such expansion.[83]

But in addition to the person needing the community to help her meet her basic physical and intellectual needs, Aquinas contends that the good that a human person is called to through living in society occurs through her contribution of aid and service *to* others.[84] For a person to exercise charity and justice toward another requires an apprehension of the other, an awareness of their needs, a desire to respond that is actualized to the best of the person's ability. Therefore, participating in community offers the individual members the opportunity to grow in the exercise of charity toward others.

Aquinas inherited his understanding of the person from Aristotle. It conceives of the person as a distinct, unique individual who is (at the same time) by nature social. This sense of the person contributes to what Aquinas understood as life in society ordered by natural law.[85] This fundamental sociality occurs first as a person is born into and grows within a family, and it is further demonstrated by what Aquinas saw as the "natural" tendency of people to pursue life together in various forms of community: "It is natural for man to be a social and political animal, living in community; and this is more true of him than of any other animal, a fact which is shown by his natural necessities."[86] The common good for Aquinas presupposed a hierarchy of being in which a thing is oriented to its own specific or individual perfection; however, the perfection proper to each thing is not a self-enclosed "perfection in isolation." A thing's perfection is achieved as it fulfills its purpose of existence in relation to other beings. As Porter notes: "Each creature is oriented toward wider goods in two senses: Lower kinds of creatures exist for the sake of higher kinds of creatures . . . and all creatures are oriented toward the good of the universe as a whole."[87] Human beings are oriented to their own personal perfection, and like all creatures are also oriented toward the good of all creation. However, the human person is unique in that, while not compromising her status as a unique person, she is a constitutively social being and "is oriented toward a wider good of a specifically human sort, namely, the common good of her community."[88] The person is challenged through the sociality of her nature not only to take account of the good of the other and of the community as equal to her own, but in some instances to choose to forgo a good for herself in order to promote the common good.

Just as the term "good" was seen to refer primarily to God as the absolute and perfecting good, as well as validly referring to the imperfect good of something in an analogous manner, so the term "common good" has linked meanings and it is important to identify them distinctly. It is apparent that in Aquinas's usage the term "common good" refers both to God as the ultimate common good of all people, and to the social circumstances necessary for a person to be able to pursue her ultimate good within the circumstances of her life. In addition, Aquinas uses the term "common good" in a correlative way indicated earlier, as he describes God in God's self as the common good of a person and at the same time describes the person's enjoyment of God as the ultimate human common good. Aquinas takes pains to distinguish between God in God's self and the human enjoyment of God—both of which he at times refers to as the common good.

Porter indicates an aspect of Aquinas's construal of the good in her discussion of the relationship between "is" and "ought" in Aquinas's moral theory.[89] She notes that Aquinas's entire moral theory is dependent on his concept of the good. Working from a natural law orientation in which adequate knowledge of what a thing *is* necessarily includes some knowledge of what it *ought* to be,[90] the move from what *is* to a description of what *should* be (or ought to be) makes a moral judgment on the current situation. Since the human person is understood to be fundamentally a person in society, the good or perfection of the person requires that she "ought" to be able to know the support and benefit of participating in the common good of the society as part of the perfection of her own goodness.[91]

But, one might argue, is not this attention to the earthly circumstances of a person truly peripheral and unnecessary for the development of a person in her fullness? "Far from fulfilling the desires of the human heart, the temporal happiness one experiences in one's earthly travels only leads him to long all the more for one's heavenly home where one's happiness will be complete (*SCG*, III, 48).'"[92] Aquinas understands the person as a developing, choosing creature who is able to grow progressively in natural virtue and in orientation toward her ultimate good. Proper use of the goods and happiness available to her in this life are necessary to help orient her sensibilities and instincts and school her desires toward God, the complete common good.

In discussing the purpose of law in the *Summa Theologica*, Aquinas, referencing Aristotle, comments that "we call those legal matters just 'which are adapted to produce and preserve happiness and its part for the body politic' since the political community is a perfect community, as he says in *Politics* I, 1."[93] For Aquinas, the purpose of law is to orient citizens to a life that provides and protects the circumstances in which the common good may flourish. Prohibitions and prescriptions of a specific nature are valid as law insofar as they are coherent with this pursuit of the common good: "Consequently, since the law is chiefly ordained to the common good, any other precept in regard to some individual work must needs be devoid of the nature of law, save insofar as it is ordered to the common good. Therefore, every law is ordained to the common good.'"[94]

Interestingly, Aquinas notes two ways in which laws may be unjust:

> First by being contrary to human good, through being opposed to the things mentioned above—either in respect of the end, as when an authority imposes on his subjects burdensome laws conducive, not to the common good, but rather to his own cupidity or vainglory; or in respect of the author, as when a man makes a law that goes beyond

the power committed to him; *or in respect of the form, as when bur-
dens are imposed unequally on the community, although with a view to
the common good. The like are acts of violence rather than laws. . . .*
Secondly, laws may be unjust through being opposed to the divine
good; such are the laws of tyrants inducing to idolatry or to anything
else contrary to the divine law.[95]

This observation by Aquinas is one that is rich for retrieval by those who
experience themselves as being asked to bear, as a matter of custom or
policy, an unequal or disproportionate measure of suffering—i.e., deprivation of goods or some form of social burden—for the sake of the
good of others in the community. All members of the community experience forms of deprivation at one time or another—rationing during a
time of crisis would be one example. But Aquinas seems to suggest that
a burden that by design (or, I suggest, by custom or tradition) falls constantly and/or more severely on one segment of society is an unjust
law, even to the point of calling it a type of violence.

The family is needed to foster the pursuit of virtue and the temporal common good by guiding children and establishing them in behaviors and customs and habits that contribute to the well-being of the
community.[96] The teaching of the church is also needed to help people
grow in virtues and in contributing to and participating in the common
good of the community.[97] While the specific content that constitutes
the temporal common good of a community will change over time, it
will always consist of those goods which foster full human flourishing
and attainment of virtue among its members.[98]

THE RELATIONSHIP BETWEEN THE INDIVIDUAL
GOOD AND THE COMMON GOOD

The relationship between the individual and the common good has
been a point of considerable argument in the centuries since Aquinas,
arising from the interpretations of the principle of the common good
in varying contexts. Frequently, the concept or principle of the common good has been criticized for what is seen as a preferencing by
Aquinas of the collective, corporate, or common interest over the good
or the interest of the individual. This has caused some to see in his writing on the common good a dangerous principle which can be used to
justify the oppression of individuals or groups for the sake of a supposed
benefit for the larger group.

There is no doubt that Aquinas believed that the common good of the community and the universal common good hold a privileged place in the moral construction of existence. Thomas Eschmann comments on the relationship between the common good and the individual good in Aquinas: "[E]verything else—the whole universe and every social institution—must ultimately minister to this purpose; everything must foster and strengthen and protect the conversation of the soul, every soul, with God."[99] "Conversation with God" is the ultimate good of the person, which is so inviolable that all creation, all political and social constructions, will be judged as good and worthy to the extent that they enable the person to grow in her union with God. At the same time, circumstances that foster in a created context the possibility of people growing in their ultimate good are the common good of the group:

> Therefore, since the beatitude of heaven is the end of that virtuous life which we live at present, it pertains to the king's office to promote the good life of the multitude in such a way as to make it suitable for the attainment of heavenly happiness. . . .[100]

Given the cautions and concerns surrounding the invocation of the "common good" in much of contemporary Western politics and philosophy, is it possible to understand the principle of the common good in a way that does not foster and justify the oppression of individuals? While the answer ultimately is yes, it is a yes that may be offered only after a careful consideration of how Aquinas, historically one of the primary proponents of the common good, characterized the interplay between the individual and common good, and only after noting the limitations in his thought on the common good.

Aquinas argued that the common good of a person and of society is not simply the sum of individual goods. Rather, the common good differs fundamentally from goods particular to individual persons:

> The common good of the realm and the particular good of the individual differ not only in respect of the many and the few, but also under a formal aspect. For the aspect of the common good differs from the aspect of the individual good even as the aspect of whole differs from that of part.[101]

Individual goods differ from the common good in several ways, one being that the common good is in some way communicable,[102] while individual goods are not necessarily communicable. The common good is the good of the whole shared by each of the parts in some manner. Aquinas argues further that the good of the whole is greater than the private good of the individual, and no individual good is to be judged as truly enhancing or perfective of the individual unless it is also directed to the common good.[103] While virtuous living is the highest achievement of a person in her earthly life, it is approached as a person orients her efforts for the good toward the common good of the community and not exclusively toward her own self-interest.[104]

The question remains whether the temporal common good of an individual person should be directed toward the common good. Aquinas argued that it should be, reminding the reader that the temporal common good *is* one's own good; without the temporal common good, one's own good will not be possible. Furthermore, Aquinas claims that the common good is a higher good that should be valued, protected, and if necessary chosen over one's private good. However, rather than using this claim as a justification of a totalitarian state in which the individual, her good, and her dignity is submerged in preference to a corporate good, Aquinas noted that the community only exists as an entity for which one might sacrifice oneself if the individual person is respected and her individual good valued and protected by the community and if the laws of the community are just and truly ordered toward the common good.

As noted, Aquinas's conception of the common good was rooted in his anthropology. While he saw the human person as a unique, inviolable individual who is constitutively social, Aquinas lived before the time of the Enlightenment from which a liberal, rights-based view of the person that is part and parcel of the social and intellectual milieu today emerged, even while this view is highly contested. The participation of individuals in the fabric of the culture itself is a participation in the common good of society, and each person in some manner contributes to or diminishes the common good of the community. The common good, therefore, has extremely high value for Aquinas, because it is the context in which social harmony is promoted for the multitude, in which the individual person may reap the benefits of being connected to the corporate good.

Porter suggests that,

> correctly understood, the well being of individual and community are interrelated in such a way that what promotes one promotes the

other, and what harms one harms the other as well. . . . . [Aquinas] also defines the good of the community in such a way that it is a necessary condition for the human good that individuals be protected in certain ways, and correlatively, he holds that when these protections are absent, the community may cease to have claim on the allegiance of its members.[105]

What is proposed by Aquinas has the quality of a dialectical relationship between the individual and the common good, rather than the "trumping" of one by the other. Aquinas informs us that as a citizen, the individual has the right to receive certain aids from the group. At the same time, Aquinas clearly establishes the responsibility the individual has to promote and sustain the common good, even sometimes to the point of laying down her life for the sake of the group. Aquinas reminds the reader that the temporal common good is one's own good because without it one's individual good is not possible. Since she is part of the whole, the individual cannot seek her own good without considering what is good for all.[106] In many instances Aquinas instructs that the common good must be preserved even at the expense of sacrificing the appropriate and valid individual good:

As the Philosopher declares, the good of the many is more godlike than the good of the individual, wherefore the more a virtue regards the good of many, the better it is.[107]
    Now the common good is always more lovable to the individual than his private good.[108]

Wherefore it is a virtuous action for a man to endanger even his own life, either for the spiritual or for the temporal common good of his country.[109]

Aquinas holds that distinct human *persons*—with their nonnegotiable human dignity, capacity for choice by free will, self-transcendence as a deliberately elected choice, and unique destiny of union with God as a unique human person—are the members of a society.[110] States and governments have, at times, valued their members as individuals, as singular operative units whose value is in their ability to contribute to the corporate purpose. But these states, Aquinas judges, do not respect their members as *persons*, nor do they function for the common good of the society.[111] Maritain suggests:

For St. Thomas, the intelligible value of "whole," "totality," is indissolubly bound to that of person. It is a fundamental thesis of Thomism that the person as such is a whole. The concept of part is opposed to that of person. To say, then, that society is a whole composed of persons is to say that society is a whole composed of wholes. . . . [I]f the person of itself requires "to be part of" society, or "to be a member of society," this in no wise means that it must be in society in the way in which a part is in a whole and treated in society as a part in a whole. On the contrary, the person, as person, requires to be treated as a whole in society.[112]

While Aquinas appears to give the state great latitude in demanding that an individual forgo her own good for the sake of the community, he is not naive regarding the capacity of the state or of particular rulers for governing in unjust, oppressive ways: "As a roaring lion and a hungry bear, so is a wicked prince over the poor people."[113] Aquinas provides a carefully constructed set of criteria the state must meet in order for it to have the right to expect or require the submission of an individual good for the sake of the community. Sherwin writes:

For Aquinas, the individual is part of the community and belongs to it in what he or she is or has *only* if the community is directed to the common good. . . . Thomas makes a critical distinction. The laws of the community are just only if they are well ordered concerning their end, their author and their form. . . . These three requirements are of great import, especially if they are seen in relation to one's conception of human nature. If the beauty and dignity of the individual is properly understood, then, in Aquinas' view, the state is profoundly limited in the use of its power. . . . [A] temporal good is only a common good if it be directed to the ultimate common good: heavenly beatitude (*ST*, I-II, 90, 2; ad 3). A community which prevents even one of its citizens from attaining this ultimate good in any way he or she has been divinely called is not ordering the community's good to the divine good.[114]

Porter acknowledges that the principle of the common good in Aquinas's writing can be and has been interpreted as a justification for privileging the corporate over the individual good: "Aquinas insists, as strongly as any Marxist, that the common good takes precedence over the good of the individual, just as the good of the universe as a whole is a greater good than the good of any one creature, however exalted (II-II.47.10; II-II.58.12; II-II.64.2). And yet, Aquinas is not in fact the one-sided communalist that these remarks, taken alone, would suggest."[115] In Aquinas's moral theory, the fact of community—its givenness and necessity for full human development—frames and shapes his development of justice and his understanding of the relationship between the individual person and the community. The common good is given a privileged place in his moral theory because it is to the degree that the common good (the *bonum communae*) exists that members of the community have an environment that will support their full development. Therefore, the common good in itself is privileged for the sake of promoting and producing the circumstances that will aid the members of the community to grow in their individual goodness and happiness. Porter notes:

> His [Aquinas's] methodological emphasis on the institutional and communal contexts of moral reasoning does not commit him to the substantive moral view that the interests of the community always take precedence over those of the individual. To the contrary, he sets clear limits on what the community can do to the individual, even for the best of reasons. "However, no one must do harm to another unjustly in order to promote the common good," he says (II-II.68.3), and this acknowledgment informs all of Aquinas' remarks on the limits of the power of the community vis-à-vis the individual (see, for example, II-II.10.8, 12; II-II.64.3 *ad* 2; II-II 67–72; II-II.104.4).[116]

Aquinas does maintain that a just society owes its citizens certain protections. Most basically, the state owes it to individual citizens not to harm them in the most basic ways (Aquinas identifies the prohibited harms as those that affect the individual's basic inclinations to live, to procreate, to participate in society, and to seek the truth about God).[117] At the same time, individuals have the same obligation to one another, and society has the obligation of protecting individual members from being harmed in basic ways by other individuals.[118] Aquinas does not say explicitly that society has an obligation to positively promote the well-being of its individual members, but some of his remarks seem to point in that direction.[119]

JUSTICE AND THE COMMON GOOD

Why is it important to consider the virtue of justice as Aquinas understands it in the midst of a study of the common good? To answer this we must remember that Aquinas's understanding of virtue has its roots in the formulations of Aristotle and Augustine. He describes virtue as an operative habit oriented toward good,[120] or as "nothing else than the good use of free choice."[121] Aquinas identifies acquired virtues and infused virtues, and among the acquired virtues he distinguishes between intellectual and moral virtues. Among the moral virtues, Aquinas identifies four principal or cardinal virtues—prudence, justice, temperance, and fortitude. Of these, justice holds a unique role because it is specifically oriented to ordering the relationship between persons and between persons and the community.

For Aquinas, morality emerges from and in a communal context. The inherent sociality of the human person results in some form of society or community being the context in which the person has the best hope of growing in her goodness and happiness. Human society as it occurs in the organized form of the state is not an end in itself; it exists in order to facilitate and promote the common good of the group because in so doing the circumstances and necessities of full human life can be provided for the members.[122] This means, however, that society is ordered toward an equity in the distribution of the goods of the group if it is to fulfill its reason for existence. A society that oppresses some of the members to protect the advantage of other segments of the group is unjust; to the extent that it does this, it is immoral and is failing to be what it is meant to be. The basic institutions of a society should embody, and are presumed by Aquinas to embody, the principles of justice that are meant to guarantee right relations among individuals and between individuals and the community.

If, as Aquinas holds, a person is oriented by her nature to live with others and to shape with others a community that will respect and foster the common good of the group as well as the good of the individual members, then it is necessary to understand what guides and norms the choices that individuals make as well as those made by the society as a corporate reality. Aquinas suggests that the cardinal virtue of justice is precisely the moral norm that addresses this task.

Porter reminds us that Aquinas understood the person as ordained to live within community of varying forms, beginning with the family and extending to various forms of social and civil communities. Justice, then, is always assessed as a matter of right relationships between individuals and between individuals and communities and vice versa.

> As we would expect, institutional contexts, and more generally communal contexts, are centrally important to Aquinas. . . . Even when

moral species of actions are not defined juridically, Aquinas' discussions reveal great awareness of the communal contexts of the moral life, and more specifically, of the ways in which one can injure another through damaging her standing within the community.[123]

The individual and the community are interrelated in such a way that their "goods" are interconnected, and the virtue of justice orders the pursuit of the well-being of each, protecting it from abuse. Aquinas comments that it would be fair to describe justice as "a habit whereby a man renders to each one his due by a constant and perpetual will."[124] So central is this activity of justice that Aquinas notes further in the same point that "the service of God includes rendering to each one his due." Therefore, a person's relationship with God is, to a certain degree, measured or gauged by her exercise of justice with others, which requires giving them their due. Aquinas considers justice to be a general virtue, since it directs the acts of other virtues toward the common good. But not only does he identify justice as a general virtue, he calls it the "one supreme virtue essentially distinct from every other virtue."[125] It appears that he accords it this singular place among the virtues because the virtues of temperance, prudence, and fortitude (the other cardinal virtues) are more oriented toward assisting the person primarily with respect to her relationship with herself, rather than addressing the person's relationship with others. Aquinas notes:

> Man's dealings with himself are sufficiently rectified by the rectification of the passions by the other moral virtues. But his dealings with others need a special rectification, not only in relation to the agent by whom they are directed but also in relation to the person to whom they are directed. Hence about such dealings there is a special virtue, and this is justice.[126]

This is significant in that it suggests the intrinsic relationship Aquinas perceives between justice and the common good.

The realm of justice is not in the intellect or the reason but in the will whose purpose is *choice* and *action*. It is the action of the will that establishes a person as a just person; it is the way in which their volitional capacity is engaged that renders them righteous.[127] The exercise of justice, in which a person renders to another what is their due "according to equality of proportion,"[128] occurs as particular or commutative justice that governs "mutual dealings between two persons,"[129] or as distributive justice addressing "the order of that which belongs to the community in relation to each single person."[130] Aquinas displays a strong sense that the community is, in a sense, the steward of the goods which the individual members of the community hold in common and require to pursue the fullness of their lives. This is such a strong conviction for Aquinas that he states: "[W]hen the goods of the community are distributed among a number of individuals, each one receives that which, in a way, is his own."[131] The person receiving the goods of the community, seen in this light, receives what is justly hers.

Porter, examining the virtue of justice in the *Summa Theologica*, considers Aquinas's understanding of what constitutes harm to both the community and the individual person as a way to understand what justice is to protect both individual and community *from*. The principles that underlie Aquinas's theory of justice are seen most clearly, she suggests, in his analysis of the norms of nonmaleficence and fairness.[132] She notes that justice guides the will of the person and the corporate decisiveness of the community to protect certain rights to which Aquinas maintains the individual has a claim, and to protect the community from disruption and danger.[133] For example, Aquinas acknowledges that while murder is wrong, an individual may take the life of another in an extreme situation of self-defense, or the state may take the life of an individual under carefully defined circumstances for the sake of protecting the security of the community. The situations of capital punishment, killing during war, and the tension between private property and the common good are similar examples of Aquinas's dealing with the dialectical tension of the personal/private and the communal good, and these specific situations will be discussed below.

In the issue of private ownership of property we see in Aquinas's thought the relationship between the common and the individual good. For Aquinas, private property is an extension of the divine intention that all people should be provided for out of the bounty of creation.[134] However, Aquinas holds that under certain circumstances, the state may appropriate private property, by force if necessary, *for the sake of the common good*.[135] At the same time, Aquinas suggests that under situations of dire need, an individual may seize whatever is necessary to maintain her own life or the life of another.[136] In these examples, justice is, as noted previously, not a trumping of one good by the other (either the corporate good or the individual good), but an equitable response to particular and extreme needs for the sake of preserving the good that is in danger.

A constitutive aspect of Aquinas's understanding of justice is equality. This, again, points to the relational nature of justice, in contrast with the other virtues which, as Aquinas notes, relate to the person in herself. Justice expects an appropriateness and rectitude in a person's dealings with others and in the dealings of the community with individuals. In the beginning of his consideration of justice in the *Summa Theologica*, Aquinas observes:

> It is proper to justice, as compared with the other virtues, to direct man in his relations with others, because it denotes a kind of equality, as its very name implies; indeed we are wont to say that things are adjusted when they are made equal, for equality is in reference of one thing to some other. On the other hand, the other virtues perfect man in those matters only which befit him in relation to himself.[137]

But equality is concerned with more than occasions of exchange with another person. Porter points out that Aquinas also understood equality to mean "an equality of immunity from harm and from certain kinds of coercion," such as the immunity shared with others from the harm of "being deprived of his life, or of the material goods necessary to support life and to maintain a family."[138] Equality is an issue of justice because, as Aquinas remarked, anyone who harms someone in these basic ways "dishonors him by depriving him of some excellence on account of which he has honor."[139] Justice is the virtue that demands recognition of and respect for the equality between people, established by their shared human nature. In addition to material goods and exchanges between persons being ordered by the measure of equality and the virtue of justice, a person has "the claim not to be told lies, or to have her standing in the community impaired without grave reason, both of which would interfere with her participation in the common life of her society."[140]

When an individual is harmed in these ways, her basic dignity as a person is violated. Because of her basic "excellence as a human being," a person has, as an issue of equity and justice, a claim on the minimal conditions that are required for her to pursue perfection, which includes life itself, and the means to pursue the natural and supernatural goods of life. Aquinas's commitment to equality as a constitutive dimension of justice is based on a conviction that human beings, while they might share different functional roles (such as masters and slaves), share a basic human nature that establishes a foundational equality between people. He also is committed to equality based on his belief that all people are equal in their capacity to attain moral virtue.[141] And finally, he is committed to equality as a measure of justice because all people are equal before God.[142]

Justice is "exhibited primarily in external actions which embody right relations among individuals, or between the individual and the community."[143] Justice orients the will of the person and the corporate will of the community to attend to the needs of others who have a claim on them, rather than attending only to the needs of the individual herself or the needs of a particular constituency within the larger group. It is inclusive and comprehensive in its focus. One behaves justly not only with one's friends, but with all people. The justice of the state is toward all the members of the community, not only toward particular groups.

What counts as harm for Aquinas, and therefore as a violation of justice, are deeds that violate another on the basis of fundamental inclinations that are part of the person and that orient the person to her fulfillment: the inclination to live, to reproduce oneself, to live in community, to seek the truth about God.[144] The more basic these inclinations are that are thwarted or violated, the more serious the violation of justice and the more forceful the person's claim against the community, because when one is prevented from pursuing these basic inclinations, she will all the more be prevented from seeking the fulfillment of other human inclinations, such as the aesthetic dimension of life.

EXAMPLES OF THE COMMON GOOD IN AQUINAS

It is useful to consider several specific examples of how Aquinas himself understood the common good in practice. To do that, we will consider Aquinas's understanding of capital punishment, war and peace, and private property in order to indicate how he understood the function of the common good in these instances.

Capital Punishment

Aquinas defines the social good in such a way that it is a necessary condition for the pursuit of the human good that individuals of the community be protected from harm. While security from attacks on one's person, and particularly from loss of one's life, is a fundamental security endorsed by Aquinas, he does at the same time allow for the moral possibility—if not necessity, in his mind—of capital punishment. How can this be? Aquinas maintains that there is no moral justification for the killing of an innocent person.[145] He does allow that in the process of self-defense a person is morally justified if their resistance must escalate to the degree of killing their attacker. In this instance, he justifies the taking of the life under the principle of "double effect": a single act that has one intention but two effects. I intend to save my life through this action, but in the process of pursuing the action, the life of my attacker is ended. "Accordingly, the act of self-defense may have two effects: one, the saving of one's own life; the other, the slaying of the aggressor. Therefore, this act, since one's intention is to save one's own life, is not unlawful, seeing that it is natural to everything to keep itself in being as far as possible."[146]

But how does Aquinas justify the execution of a convicted criminal? This person is going to be deprived of life, and his death is hardly a case where the death is unintended; it cannot be sanctioned as an application of the principle of double effect. It is at this point that Aquinas's principle of the common good is of critical importance. Several criteria must be met for the execution of a criminal to be morally just, he tells us.

First, an individual person may not take it on himself to kill someone, even if the other has been convicted of a heinous crime and is awaiting execution:

> [I]t is lawful to kill an evil doer insofar as it is directed to the welfare of the whole community, so that it belongs to him alone who has charge of the community's welfare. . . . Now the care of the common good is entrusted to persons of rank having public authority, wherefore they alone, and not private individuals, can lawfully put evildoers to death.[147]

The only one who has the right to carry out the execution is the official representative of the state, because (presumably) the conviction occurred in court, following all the correct safeguards against conviction of an innocent person. The state, and those who are in positions of authority within the state, have as their solemn responsibility the protection of the citizens from harm. "[T]he victim must have forfeited the immunity from harm guaranteed to all members of a just community through his own free action of grievous aggression against the community or some individual."[148] Aquinas invokes the image of a physician who must amputate a limb that has become diseased and is threatening the life of an individual in order to explain why, as an issue of the common good of the community, such a normally prohibited action is permitted.

Killing during War

The killing that occurs during war requires adherence to strict criteria for Aquinas to consider it morally permissible, and these criteria again relate directly to the common good. Once again, we find that Aquinas allows only those who are valid holders of authority in the state to call citizens to the dangers of war, in which their own lives may be lost, and to call them to attack the enemy with the intention of killing. War is fought to serve the goal of peace,[149] because it is in peace that the common good of the community, and the good of individual members of society, may best be pursued.[150] We go to war because in some grievous manner the concord of our society has been attacked or threatened, and we fight to reestablish or protect the common good of the group. According to Aquinas's conception of a just war, therefore, a ruler could not declare war to pursue a policy of aggression and acquisition, or to pursue a personal vendetta against another ruler or group of people. War is only justified when the goal is the protection of the common good, and the protection of the common good is the special and specific responsibility of the authorities of the community.

Private Property and the Common Good

The issue of private property in relation to the common good is an interesting example of the interplay of the rights of individuals and the rights of the community. Aquinas saw the ownership of property as a human good, but one that is neither an absolute good nor an absolute right. Sheer possession of goods is seen by Aquinas as a natural outgrowth of the biblical injunction for humanity to have dominion over the things of creation. People generally have greater care over the particular thing that is theirs rather than everyone being responsible for everything.[151] At the same time, Aquinas allows that there are some goods better held in common rather than being the property of one person.

While we find, as we would expect, a condemnation of theft in its more common form, Aquinas also names it as theft when something is withheld from a person that is their due. "To keep back what is due to another inflicts the same kind of injury as taking a thing unjustly."[152] Of particular note with regard to private property and the common good, Aquinas addresses the question of whether it is considered theft if a person out of necessity takes something that belongs to another in a time of great need. Aquinas advises: "In cases of need, all things are common property, so that there would seem to be no sin in taking another's property, for need has made it common. . . . [W]hatever goods some have in superabundance are due, by natural law, to the sustenance of the poor."[153] While Aquinas hopes that each person will respond to the needs of the poor willingly out of their excess, he notes:

> Nevertheless, if the need be so manifest and urgent that it is evident that the present need must be remedied by whatever means be at hand, then it is lawful for a man to succor his own need by means of another's property, by taking it either openly or secretly, nor is this properly speaking theft or robbery. . . . It is not theft, properly speaking, to take secretly and use another's property in case of extreme need because that which a man takes for the support of his life becomes his own property by reason of that need.[154]

In addition to the rare but possible situation of a desperate individual taking from the superabundance of another (ordinarily considered an act of theft, but in this instance lawful), Aquinas also states that similarly, in situations where the common good of society is at risk, property owned by an individual may legitimately be appropriated by a representative of the state (using force or threat of force if necessary) acting *on behalf of* the common good.[155]

> Aquinas holds that public authorities can appropriate whatever is necessary to maintain the general welfare of society from anyone whatever, so long as they limit their appropriations to what is genuinely necessary to maintain the life of the community. Aquinas bases these provisions on his belief that when the institution of property threatens its own raison d'être by preventing individuals or the whole community from having access to the necessary means of life, then the institution itself breaks down, or at least, the claims that it guarantees under ordinary circumstances must give way to more exigent claims.[156]

CONCLUSION

We have seen that Aquinas derived the foundation for the ethical principle of the common good in part from the anthropology of Aristotle, who defined the human being as an individual in society, whose destiny is pursued within society, and whose personal good is fundamentally linked to the good of the society. Aquinas understood the human person as necessarily social, but as one who remains distinctly unique and singular, and whose individuality can never be collapsed into the corporate reality. But more than simply the anthropology of Aristotle, Aquinas's treatment of the common good exposes his Christian belief that the human person is created for ultimate joy and perfection, which he understood as occurring after death through union with God. Furthermore, the principle of the common good also displays his belief in an intrinsic relationship between the divine reality and the earthly, human reality, and it underscores the value he places on the contingent, created reality as an avenue through which people individually and collectively could become progressively oriented to their ultimate truth. An evidence of the significance Aquinas accorded sociality as a characteristic of the human person is his belief that government and governance for the good order of the community would have existed even if no fall from grace had occurred.

It has been important to illuminate the synthetic character of Aquinas's thought by focusing on the interrelatedness of his understanding of the good, the human good, the common good, and justice. While the common good is a utopian ideal in Aquinas's thought, it nonetheless functions as a formal ethical norm and is approximated in the dynamic relationship between the individual good and the good of the group. While some commentators on Aquinas have suggested that the common good can only be understood to refer to the ultimate perfection of union with God, this seems unlikely and tends to minimize the attention Aquinas clearly pays to the practical social and personal goods that are required as part of a well-lived earthly life. This temporal common good is not to be confused with the ultimate common good, but it suggests Aquinas's larger belief that grace[157] is a mediated reality requiring human cooperation for its full effectiveness.[158] The person, for Aquinas, is a created reality capable of choice and progressive development in goodness. Society is the necessary situation in which people grow in goodness, and societies have a responsibility to provide the circumstances that will assist their members to live with dignity and grow into the fullness of their humanity, including challenging them to grow in concern for the other, to be just as individuals and as societies. While Aquinas himself believed that a constitutional monarchy offered the best form of governance, he preferred it because of what he believed was its greater utility in achieving the ends of a good society.

Aquinas's understanding of the role and status of women was based on an inaccurate biology and metaphysics, and on a primitive conception of an intrinsic relationship between the reproductive functions of the male and female and the capacity for intellectual reasoning (and therefore fullness of human status). We do not see in Aquinas an animosity toward women; he accords them full human status but he judges them to be less able to reflect the fullness of God in the same way men are, due to what he judges to be their different substance.

While Aquinas's philosophical and theological genius is recognized and revered, there is another aspect of his legacy to the Christian tradition that could be overlooked. This is his methodological creativity and boldness in using the philosophy of Aristotle to further explain Christian theological concepts. Aquinas did not abandon the contributions of Plato and Neoplatonism in Augustinian theology, but his willingness to engage a conceptual framework that had so recently been considered suspect is the choice of a theologian who did not hesitate to use a source from his culture and context which he believed offered a more helpful, more intelligible, more illuminating approach to Christian beliefs. In his theological methodology, as David Tracy has cautioned, Aquinas did not simply repeat the *tradita*, but used the resources of his time to enhance the communication of the *traditio*.[159] Too often the use of nonreligious sources (the natural sciences, social sciences, political theory, etc.) has been judged dangerous to the "truths" of Christianity. Aquinas, in the middle of the thirteenth century, perceived the valuable contribution that Aristotle's philosophical insights could bring to Christianity, and he brought the benefits of Aristotelian philosophy into mainstream theological reasoning.[160]

In the next chapter, I will pursue the retrieval of the content of the principle of the common good from Aquinas's thought using the feminist hermeneutics developed in chapter 1. I will also take up the challenge of responding to Aquinas's methodological spirit by prudentially identifying and using resources from the contemporary situation that offer a promise of more fruitfully interpreting the principle of the common good for a twenty-first–century audience.

CHAPTER 3

A Feminist Retrieval of the Principle of the Common Good

The feminist hermeneutical method proposed in the first chapter is comprehensive and ethical. It includes a consideration of the text or tradition using appropriate analytical tools, as well as the next and necessary step into praxis. When one engages in a critical assessment of significant aspects of Aquinas's principle of the common good, such as his anthropology, one must attend to the contributions that Aquinas's work can make *to* contemporary scholarship: for example, Aquinas's conception of the person contributes to a fuller description of the human person suggested by Martha Nussbaum's functioning capabilities. Without openness to a mutual correlation of elements both from the tradition and from the critiquing sources, the result can again become a self-enclosed set of parameters available to no outside critique.

The retrieval of a text or tradition does not result in a collection of phrases or words that are finally judged adequate to convey the truth of the text or tradition. What emerges from the work of critical retrieval is more a set of principles that may be brought forward and placed in conversation with an existing situation. Sandra Schneiders and Rosemary Radford Ruether have alerted us to this in their understanding of the capacity of the text as a whole to critique particular aspects *of* the text, exposing the elements that cohere with the fundamental orientation of the text as well as judging negatively those that do not. In considering biblical texts, for example, both Schneiders and Ruether suggest that this critiquing principle is the principle of comprehensive liberation and salvation of all people, particularly those who are most at risk, marginal, or oppressed. Similarly, in considering Aquinas's work regarding the principle of the common good, the goal is not a retrieval of particular phrases from his writing; rather, the result of the process of critical retrieval of Aquinas's text will be the identification of central principles of the common good in his writing—principles that cohere with the fundamental aspects of the Christian tradition and the Scriptures (particularly regarding justice), and very importantly, principles that are faithful to the internal logic and overarching convictions of Aquinas's own writing.

The five presuppositions identified by Schneiders and Ruether are affirmed regarding the retrieval of the common good.[1] When these presuppositions are specified in relation to Aquinas's text and tradition of the common good, the following elements are seen: Aquinas's biological knowledge and anthropology were flawed both in terms of scientific accuracy and in terms of the metaphysical conclusions that he drew based on this faulty biology. Therefore, the anthropology (or aspects of the anthropology) that is dependent on these elements is similarly flawed. (This will be addressed in greater detail below.) The experience of women is virtually absent from Aquinas's text. The principle of the common good has historically often been invoked in ways that have been detrimental to women. Social systems that are predicated on women's corporate *inability* to name their experiences on their own terms (an inability developed over generations through familial and social relationships) are most often the norm. Social relationships and policies based on such incomplete self-definition or self-expression of a major constituency institutionalize unjust patterns of participation and relationships for women. The faulty anthropology of most traditional theology encouraged women to suppress their own full personhood and flourishing for the sake of the "common good" of a group (whether the community of the family, the church, the village, etc.).

The retrieved principle of the common good offers important correctives to any culture based on personal gratification, hierarchy, gender (or other) discrimination, and class stratification. Moreover, there are important principles embedded in Aquinas's development of the common good that can function on behalf of the full flourishing of women, but only if the text and its underlying presumptions are rigorously critiqued. The distortions that are associated with the principle of the common good do not obliterate the contours of a valuable contribution this principle holds for relational justice and communal as well as individual well-being.

In this chapter, the structure of chapter 2 will serve as the template through which to consider a retrieval of Aquinas's principle of the common good. The topics addressed in chapter 2 will be addressed in the same order here. However, this chapter will not address the examples discussed at the end of chapter 2 (capital punishment, killing during war, and private property and the common good). These provided examples of the principle of the common good in key social circumstances. Instead, this chapter will develop a contemporary application of the retrieved principle of the common good, which will be used to consider the situation of women.

EXPERIENCE, AND THE EXPERIENCE OF WOMEN

The first step of the proposed hermeneutical method is the pursuit of the situation or experience of women, particularly their experience of suffering. It is the *suffering* of women that is appealed to as "the experience of women," because it is verifiable that across cultures, around the world, the situation of women consistently holds multiple and intersecting realities of gender-specific patterns of suffering. Suffering is a general term that can include a wide variety of realities. Wendy Farley offers a description of radical suffering, which will be presumed here:

> Radical suffering is present when the negativity of a situation is experienced as an assault on one's personhood as such. . . . This assault reduces the capacity of the sufferer to exercise freedom, to feel affection, to hope, to love God. . . . In radical suffering the soul itself has been so crippled that it can no longer defy evil. The destruction of the human being is so complete that even the shred of dignity that might demand vindication is extinguished.[2]

Such "radical suffering" raises a specter of something horrendous, something that violates the very status of the person as a person.

The appeal to the suffering of women is attentive to the dialectic between, on the one hand, the fact that both men and women possess the same human nature and, on the other hand, the fact that men and women are embodied differently. That women are differently embodied than men has given rise to various cultural, social, and religious attitudes, customs, and legislation that cause (directly or indirectly) suffering in women's lives.

One way to expose and verify something of the reality of the suffering that is characteristic of women's lives globally is through reports from United Nations agencies that specifically focus on gender issues and women's realities. The United Nations Division for the Advancement of Women sponsored a seminar in Vienna in 1992 during which two documents were considered by the participants—the *United Nations Human Development Report, 1993*, and the *World Bank World Development Report on Poverty, 1990*. Seminar consultants Diane Elson[3] and Naila Kabeer[4] offered analyses of these reports and of other papers presented at the seminar, offering also their own perspectives on patterns of women's poverty. The excerpts offered here do not substantiate the entire weight of the claim that for most women in the world, their experience is of gender-associated patterns of suffering that exist cross-culturally, but they do offer a thoughtful analysis of the reality of a great number of the world's women. First, the World Bank assessment:

> The weight of poverty falls most heavily on certain groups. Women in general are disadvantaged. In poor households, they often shoulder more of the workload than men, are less educated, and have less access to remunerative activities.[5]

The *United Nations Human Development Report* noted:

> [P]overty has a decided gender bias. A large proportion of poor households are headed by women, especially in rural Africa and the urban slums of Latin America. Female members of a poor household are often worse off than male members because of gender-based differences in the distribution of food and other entitlements within the family.[6]

Elson critiqued both reports for stopping at the level of observation and not addressing the *roots* of women's poverty:

> A surprising omission [in the *United Nations Human Development Report*] is recognition of the role in human development of women's unpaid work of care for children, the old and sick, and, what is often forgotten, able-bodied adult males too. . . . [There is] no mention that a major input is women's unpaid domestic labour. . . . It is not simply lack of employment opportunities that constrains women to endure intra-household inequality; in many cases it is also the threat or actuality of violence or losing their children. Women's poverty is

deeper than that of men because women are not able to exercise rights of ownership and use of resources, including labour, to the same degree as men.[7]

Kabeer offered similar analyses of the two reports:

> Despite the complexities of collecting and interpreting data on women's poverty in the different contexts, the analysis of its causes is relatively simple. Women are poor because they are disadvantaged, in relation to their male family members, in the satisfaction of their basic needs, and in their access to independent means for satisfying these needs.[8]

The final report of the Vienna Seminar concluded:

> There is a growing awareness that poverty in general, and extreme poverty in particular, has a significant gender dimension. This gender dimension helps to explain why and how women and men experience poverty differently and unequally and become impoverished through processes that may differ. . . . Women are in a more disadvantaged position because of their dual need to make a living and to provide care for family members, tasks that are not equitably shared. Demands on time and energy are particularly constrictive for women living in poverty, as their labour is the single most important resource at their disposal.[9]

These excerpts focus on social patterns and economic realities as forces shaping the lives of women into patterns of suffering. The United Nations document *Women: Challenge to the Year 2000* discussed six areas judged crucial for improving the situation of women globally—areas of impoverishment that contribute to the suffering of women.[10] They are: (1) the need for women to know their legal right to equality of treatment (which includes the establishment of specific legal protections for women in individual countries); (2) women's health (including reproductive issues, nutrition patterns, female infanticide, female genital mutilation, etc.); (3) the education of girls and women (including basic literacy); (4) work issues (including the ability to own and dispose of property, own and run a business, and obtain credit and technical support); (5) women as participants in the political processes; and (6) violence against women.[11]

Women regularly and frequently endure violations of their physical and social rights that constitute gendered patterns of human rights violations that are often not recognized as distinct, widespread, gender-related suffering. The 1948 United Nations Universal Declaration of Human Rights proclaimed: "All human beings are born free and equal in dignity and in rights." However, human rights legislation has not until recently been shaped with a recognition that traditional human rights language generally does not include experiences unique to women and therefore leaves women with no protection under human rights conventions. A major reason human rights documents (such as those prepared by the United Nations) have not addressed the violations of human rights that are experienced primarily by women is the separation between the public and private spheres: it is *states* (or agents of the state) as perpetrators that are traditionally understood as the focus of the human rights documents and the descriptions of what constitutes a violation of human rights and individuals acting on behalf of governments in the public sector.[12] While women *do* experience violations of their human rights by the state for ideological and political reasons, many of the ways in which women's lives and rights are violated occur in private—sanctioned by religious, social, cultural, or familial customs generally considered outside the focus of human rights documents:

> Human rights work has traditionally been concerned with state-sanctioned or condoned oppression, that which takes place in the "public sphere," away from the privacy to which most women are relegated and in which most violations of women's rights take place. This focus has created an artificial legal and perceptual divide between crimes by state actors and those by nonstate actors, whether individuals, organizations, or even unofficial governments. Traditional human rights standards categorize violations in ways that exclude women, eliding critical issues. While men may care about reproductive freedom, their lives are not actually threatened by its absence; for women in areas of high maternal mortality, full reproductive freedom may mean the difference between life and death. Likewise, while asylum law protects those with a "well-founded fear of being persecuted for reasons of race, religion, nationality, membership in a particular social group or political opinion," it rarely protects those persecuted for reasons of gender. While men may be the victims of private violence, such violence is not part of a pattern of gender-based abuse . . . [n]or are they victims of . . . discriminatory family law.[13]

Until very recently, the forms of human rights legislation that have been instituted have reflected the types of violations of rights that men feared, generally excluding much of women's experiences of the types of violence that are distinct to them *because* they are women. But when women are denied their human rights in private, their human rights in the public sphere also suffer, since what takes place in private shapes their ability to participate fully in the public arena. The coming to terms with human rights violations against women is a very slow process, marked by great resistance. In 1979, a treaty addressing the human rights of women (the Convention on the Elimination of All Forms of Discrimination against Women) was ratified by participating nations of the United Nations. However, even though this convention stipulates that "any reservation incompatible with the object and purpose of the present Convention shall not be permitted,"[14] by June 1994, forty of the 133 ratifying states had submitted ninety-one reservations, most of them on religious or cultural grounds, seriously weakening the conceptual framework of the convention.[15]

Finally, the situation of women and women-dependent children among the displaced people of the world is another example of gender-related and systemic forms of suffering which make an already traumatic situation truly horrific or even deadly. At first glance it may seem unjustified to identify the experience of being a refugee as a form of suffering that holds different experiences for women than for men, but when one realizes that between 75 and 80 percent of the refugees of the world (estimated roughly at 18 million) are women and their dependents, the contours of the actual situation become more visible:[16]

> As women, as girls, as mothers, they bear the brunt of the most egregious forms of human rights abuse, from mass rape and torture to the sale of children. . . . In the camps in countries of first asylum, the priority accorded to male refugees means that the needs of rape victims, widows and the handicapped are especially ignored because men do not regard them as valuable or because they lack male protection. Women are often malnourished because they receive less food than male refugees. They are last to receive medical attention, and are among the first to starve to death.[17]

This section has pointed to patterns of suffering experienced by women as the form of women's experience that is referenced here. The proposed feminist hermeneutics, typical of liberationist hermeneutical principles, arises from situations in which the experience of suffering has prompted the search for a resource to address (and redress) the suffering. Not only do these patterns of injustice and suffering themselves cause harm to women, but they also create a "floor" of normativity for women that regularizes a life lived with less respect, opportunity, physical well-being, food, health care, exercise of choice, etc., and more deprivation, suffering, violence, infantilization, disease, etc., than the male members of the society. A difficulty in identifying the experience of women, particularly the ways in which it is an experience of suffering, is underscored by the work of feminist sociologist Dorothy Smith, who observes that women frequently hold very different interpretations and meanings of an event than those held by men for the same event.[18] Her studies point to the inadequacy of simply asking women in particular settings if they find their lives acceptable, or if they are satisfied, as the basis for arriving at a useful understanding of the situation of women and making a judgment about the moral dimensions of their life circumstances. Women internalize the meanings the dominant culture gives to situations that affect them and often, Smith reports, need assistance to reclaim (and risk) their *own* meaning for the situation. One is reminded that in the liberation movements in Latin America, for example, the first task was one of conscientization of the people— introducing them to the idea that they possessed inherent validity as human beings that made them eligible for different/better than was accorded them. This process of conscientization helped people who had been oppressed as a matter of course to discover, often for the first time in their lives, different meanings or interpretations for the situations in which they lived, meanings that rejected the interpretations for their situation that had been given to them by the dominant class and that ultimately demanded change. The situation for women in many settings holds a similar need.[19] Elizabeth Johnson has cogently observed:

> Subordination affects the imagination to the point where, in a dynamic similar to that suffered by other colonialized groups, women internalize the images and notions declared about them by the ruling group and come to believe it of themselves. . . . This process is strongly aided and abetted by male-centered language and symbol systems, key reflections of the dominant group's power to define reality in its own terms and a powerful tool of its rule.[20]

ANTHROPOLOGY

In chapter 1, I outlined a set of human functioning capabilities, drawing on the work of Martha Nussbaum. Nussbaum proposes that it is both possible and necessary to identify a minimal set of characteristics that are universally dependable in describing the human person and the human good. These human functioning capabilities are the foundation of the anthropology being used now, amended through the introduction of the functioning capabilities of kinship, transcendence, and meaningful, remunerative work. When these anthropological markers are used as a lens through which to expose and examine gender-related patterns of suffering, they render a profoundly negative moral assessment on the situation of women's experience of suffering, and on systems which enable it to continue. Anthropology is significant for constructing a social sense of justice; it orients us to examine certain things, and not others (or others to a much lesser degree), depending on how the basic description of the human person is shaped.

The functioning capabilities are *open-ended* (they are available for amendment). They are *minimal* so they may be particularized in any cultural setting, and *universal* because they propose a cross-cultural floor or ground for appeal against the destruction of women in any culture, in any country. They offer a gauge of the person's well-being (particularly women's well-being) that is completely missed when statistical data alone are used, particularly when measurements such as the gross national product of a country are used as a measure of the citizens' well-being. Finally, the human functioning capabilities require creative, narrative engagement with women to establish in fact the degree of well-being they enjoy or are lacking. The answers to the questions raised by these functioning capabilities cannot be obtained simply by sending workers with questionnaires to interview women!

These human functioning capabilities can become even more adequate to the task of functioning as *theological* anthropological constants or markers if we supplement them with certain aspects of Aquinas's anthropology. This will be discussed in the next section considering Aquinas's material.

HISTORICAL CONSCIOUSNESS AND EMBODIMENT

Historical consciousness and embodiment are significant elements of critique in the examination of Aquinas's principle of the common good. These elements are especially appropriate in a feminist-liberationist hermeneutics for pointing out the effects of the original context in shaping the concepts found in the texts, concepts that are no longer tenable in light of developments that have taken place in many disciplines since the texts were produced.

Historical Consciousness

Historical consciousness, while not necessarily easy to define, is a characteristic of contemporary methodology in virtually all disciplines. It refers to the perception of the radical contingency and uniqueness of each person, each event, each culture, each action. "Each word, document, event is historically and culturally conditioned, radically individualized, and understandable as history only insofar as it is unique and the result of man's more or less free action and decision."[21] A significant aspect of historical consciousness in regard to the process of retrieval is the belief that events are the result of *human* causes, not divine interventions:

> What modern historical method enables us to understand more clearly than was ever understood before . . . is that every person, event, and document of the past is the product of very specific and unrepeatable contingencies. These persons, events, and documents are thus contained within very definite historical limits. By refusing to consider them as products of providence or as inevitable links in a preordained chain of historical progress, decline, or development, we deprive them of all absolute character. We relativize them.[22]

No matter how far back one pushes the origins of historical consciousness (some push it back to the Renaissance discovery of discontinuity)[23] Aquinas's intellectual career occurred in an environment *not* subject to its influence. His understanding of the relationship between past and present was of a continuous and homogeneous reality, one in which God was a directly involved and determinative force. To come to his texts today with a historically conscious mentality does not require consigning his texts to the dustbin (it is the aim of this book to disprove precisely this); but to understand them as offering valuable truth requires a critique of the elements of his thought that presumed the givenness and universality of categories and descriptions and the presumption that the divine was (and has been) a directly determinative force in human history.

Strong historical consciousness emphasizes discontinuity with the past and in some of its postmodern forms is expressed as a denial of the possibility of speaking any universal word about phenomena that previously were presumed to be commonly shared. As discussed in chapter 1 relative to the possibility of any universal anthropological characteristics, I proceed here from a historically conscious orientation, but one that, particularly in regard to the phenomena of being human, argues for the existence of some shared characteristics that are embodied in distinct, culturally determined ways.

Embodiment as an Element of Critique

Embodiment points or refers to the experience of existing as beings who know the world, ourselves, and each other through the mediation of materiality—through our bodies, the created world, and the bodies and embodiment of others. Highlighting embodiment as a critical principle acknowledges that it has been disvalued or denied to such a degree that significant aspects of what it means to be a fully flourishing human person have been discounted and that this has been particularly true for women. Embodiment values the uniqueness of each person's experience of themselves and of themselves in relation to others and to the world, and correlatively respects a person's freedom of choice regarding how they will relate to and shape relationships outside of themselves.

A characteristic feature of feminist theology and ethics is a repudiation of anthropological concepts based on a dualism of physicality/materiality/embodiment versus intellect/spirit/reason. The critique brought by embodiment reminds us that virtually all human knowing is embodied knowing: to be human is to be embodied, and *all* human activity presumes embodiment; reasoning occurs in a person who exists as a material creature in specific circumstances. This is a particularly pressing critique for the Western intellectual tradition, which has been strongly marked by such dualism.

Embodiment as an element of feminist critique addresses anthropological constructions, both in theory and as they are lived out, in several important ways. It rejects conceptions of the person that identify the person primarily with intellect and reason or prize intellect and reason so highly that embodiment is only acknowledged as a sidebar dimension of human existence, a "necessary evil" or an inconsequential given of humanity. It rejects any identification of the human with one form of embodiment over another, most specifically, it rejects valuing male embodiment as the fullest expression of the human over female embodiment. It rejects an identification of women with their capacity for reproduction as the most complete expression of the female. It insists on an awareness of cultural influences on the development of a person's understanding of themselves as embodied, sexual, and gendered. It insists on respect for the dialectic of autonomy and relationality as the most adequate way to understand the relational capacity of the human person.

Some critics of feminism associate (or equate) an emphasis on embodiment with the contention that women are more "body-associated" than men because of their experiences of menstruation, pregnancy, and nursing. Such a position, however, is reductionistic and biologistic and is not supported by the conviction of most feminists regarding epistemology, theology, ethics and morality, and the relationship between these issues and the human experience of embodiment. A position that equates women with their reproductive capacity excludes the many women who do not have childbearing as part of their life experience, and makes one form of female physical possibility an overarching, determinative norm for all women.[24]

Embodiment is an issue of anthropology, and anthropology functions as an ethical standard. An anthropology that gives little credence to the feminist insistence on embodiment as a measure of human flourishing for all people risks being blind to various forms of violence against everyone in the community, and against women in particular. It has been the embodiment of women that has most frequently been directly violated in light of the dualistic anthropological models that have dominated much of the Christian tradition. This violation of women's physical selves is not limited to Christian cultures. As human rights organizations point out, gender-related patterns of human rights abuses against women are found in all cultures. Such dualism has permitted blindness to the destruction worked on men as well through reductionistic stereotyping of them[25]—stereotyping that has exacted a terrible price both on the advantaged males of society, and on the lives and bodies of the less advantaged, particularly on marginal, minority people.[26]

AQUINAS AND THE COMMON GOOD

Aquinas's Anthropology

Aquinas's anthropology is often considered a difficult aspect of his theology for contemporary scholars, particularly for feminist scholars. At the same time, it is important to deal with it, since his anthropology is the foundation of his conception of the human good, the common good, and justice. In order to draw on the principles of his ethics it is important to determine how to relate to his anthropology. In keeping with the model of retrieval through a feminist hermeneutics and in light of the proposed human functioning capabilities and the critique of historical consciousness and embodiment, it is necessary to ask which aspects of Aquinas's anthropology should be retrieved and used as a resource for feminist theology and ethics, and which should not, and why the latter must be rejected.

The methodology employed by Aquinas, and by Aristotle before him, should surely be rejected. This methodology involved observations at the level of biological functioning that were used to draw conclusions about a presumably related metaphysical reality. This presumed link between physical function and metaphysical reality is reductionistic: it tends to equate too closely and simply a function with the person and with their social location/value. This has been particularly damaging to women because of Aquinas's presumption that the male was more capable (relatively but significantly) of employing rationality and reasoning.

Aquinas's mistaken judgment that the woman is the passive partner in the process of reproduction, providing the material from which the fetus grows while the male provides the active element, reinforced his judgment that women were naturally subordinate to men and required the oversight of men for their own good. From such biological observations, and from the metaphysical conclusions Aquinas drew from them, the anthropology of women that developed became essentially dogmatized in the Christian tradition and functioned as a justification for what are today considered unjust social relationships and social systems (both secular and ecclesial) that have had highly negative, destructive consequences on the lives of countless women. This anthropology is still invoked (explicitly or implicitly) as a justification for the operatively dualistic anthropology in some forms of Christian theology: that is, there are held to be two distinctly different manifestations of the human person which, while they share basic human "species-making" characteristics, result in two different conceptions of the human.

This is an example of the effective history of Aquinas's anthropology that must be judged negatively. While such anthropological dualism is condemned by the ecclesial community in theory, evidence of it is found at the *operative level* in both secular and ecclesial arenas. Social relationships and systems that offer women a "special" role, suited to

their "nature," which in fact are systems of disenfranchisement and exclusion of women, must be examined to expose what is invoked as justification for such positions.[27] Such arguments are reminiscent of those
raised in the Victorian era as part of the "cult of true womanhood."
During that era, women were given the purportedly honored role as
keepers of the higher qualities of humanity based on a highly dualistic
anthropology. In reality, women were infantilized by this socially embodied anthropology, which justified their exclusion from participation
in decisions that affected them. Similar (perhaps more subtle) expressions of dualistic anthropology can be found today in the attitudes and
doctrines of religious formulations that offer language of respect for the
"special nature" and dignity of women, while withholding from
women full inclusion and participation in all aspects of the community's
life as well as levying disapproval on those women who push past the
conventions of the group to pursue opportunities for meaningful participation in secular and ecclesial venues. Language of "special nature"
must be rejected on the basis of the discrimination against women
which it justifies.[28]

While Aquinas's conception of the human person as an embodied
reality, a unity of body and spirit rather than an antagonistic dualism, is
a valuable element within his anthropology that is worthy of retrieval,
this valuing of embodiment does not work to the benefit of women as
it could. When the fact of embodiment as a woman produces a horizon
of possibility for lived personhood that is different from that produced
by embodiment as a male (and different in a negative way), this conception of the embodied human person actually reinforces the judgment
that while a woman is indeed *homo* (human) it is the one who is *vir*
(male) who enjoys the full benefits of embodiment.[29]

We should also reject Aquinas's literal use of scripture (particularly
Genesis, but other texts as well) to justify unequal relationships of authority between women and men as ordained by God. Aquinas's reliance on a literal reading of the text (and on commentaries that were
also based on literal readings of biblical texts), while common in his
day, is today insupportable as a means of engaging scripture and drawing from it conclusions about human origins and the "proper" relationship between women and men. Aquinas lacked a stance of historical,
critical consciousness toward the text and, faithful to his era, understood the literal reading of the text as offering timeless moral principles.

Aquinas's understanding of the human person as an embodied reality is a much richer resource than the Christian tradition following

Aquinas often appreciated, even given a caveat concerning embodiment conceived in Aquinas's gendered framework. For Aquinas, love is the source of all the passions, and the passions arise from the embodied reality of the person who is drawn by grace to live love out in a concrete manner in the specific context of their life.[30] This is a dimension of Aquinas's anthropology in which feminists will find a resonance with their own insistence on embodiment as a fundamental and critical/critiquing anthropological principle.

Feminist scholars insist that relationality is a fundamental reality of the human person; this stands as a critique to the extraordinary emphasis on the individual as an autonomous reality that has become the normative conception of the person in the West since the Enlightenment. A feminist anthropological perspective rejects the move into extreme individualism by attention to relationality as the context for choice. With this orientation, the exercise of free choice must occur in the midst of high respect for the distinct other (one other, many others, or the creation/cosmos) as one to whom I have an inherent moral relationship and obligation.[31] Feminists can find in Aquinas's thought a valuable resource for this claim in his understanding of the person as indeed a unique individual, but an individual who is also social, political, and who is only able to know the fullness of her personhood in this life in connection with others in society.

Aquinas's emphasis on the common good as the ethical measure of the social dimension of human living draws the relationality of the human person to the forefront in the development of a social ethics reflecting feminist concerns. At the same time, Aquinas's reverence for a person's informed conscience illustrates that it is of the essence of the person to be a deciding, choosing agent on one's own behalf.[32] This aspect of Aquinas's anthropology is a valuable resource for condemning historical, political, and social systems that thwart or altogether deny this capacity of the person—any person. It provides for women an important principle with which to challenge the denial of agency on their own behalf that is characteristic of the lives of many women. Customs, laws, or policies that deny any member of the community—here the attention is on the situations of women—the opportunity to function as a rational deciding agent in decisions that affect her serve to deny that person one of the fundamental ways of expressing her distinct personhood.

Aquinas's setting did not shape his imagination toward democratic participation in government as it is generally understood in the twenty-first century. He envisioned a society divided into decision makers and subjects as simply appropriate (based on his anthropology) and part of the divine will for existence and hierarchically structured order. He insisted that those who are subjects be treated justly, but this did not mean that they should be accorded equal opportunity for participation and decision making. Aquinas's anthropologically based demand for respect for the person as a choosing, deciding individual is a principle of enduring truth and significance, particularly for feminist theological ethics, and should be brought forward as a resource even as it is distinguished from the hierarchical conception of social life envisioned by Aquinas.

One aspect of Aquinas's anthropology that a feminist hermeneutics should seek to retrieve is his conception of the person as a being endowed with rationality, free will, an immortal soul, and an individual relationship with God that she is responsible to live out to the best of her ability. Another aspect that is worthy of retrieval is Aquinas's belief that the person has a destiny of union with God that cannot be fully realized in this life, retaining the transcendent horizon of the person's destiny. Retrieval of this transcendent horizon, however, should not lead to the diminishment of the significance of earthly life as the arena in which a person has the opportunity to make choices that shape her into a certain type of person.[33]

The elements retrieved from Aquinas's writing are not arbitrarily chosen. They are elements that cohere with adequate conceptions of the human person today (for those who would venture such a thing), reflecting enduring philosophical, theological, as well as social scientific understandings of the human person. They are consistent with Schneiders's principle that the text as a whole is able to critique aspects of the text that succumb to distortions of its own trajectory. Aquinas's conception of the person as a unique, embodied being of immense dignity, possessing a capacity and necessity for free and uncoerced choice, who is constituted to find her best reality through living in society with others—these principles of his anthropology allow us to critique and set aside those aspects of his anthropology that are unable to be accommodated by these essential anthropological principles.

The Good

To retrieve through a feminist hermeneutics Aquinas's thought concerning the good returns us to his understanding of the good as ultimate reality: that is, God who *is* good or goodness. Just as God does not *have* existence as a characteristic (God *is* existence), so God does not have goodness as a characteristic: God is the good. At the same time, it is necessary from a human and linguistic perspective to speak about God analogically, using the language of characteristics or attributes. Unspecified, amorphous "goodness" offers a horizon for mystical contemplation, but the ordinary flow of human life and choosing reflects the human need to consider a reality (including God) in terms that allow the historically shaped and limited imagination to apprehend more than a general totality. Human beings need the service of specification of God's goodness—expressed in categories and attributes to help us understand and judge in a more refined manner and to help us make choices in relation to the ways in which we understand goodness as something to be pursued through choice.

It is important here to recall the goal described earlier—the task of hermeneutical retrieval that has been set is *not* one of identifying words and phrases in Aquinas's description of the good that can be retrieved for use by women as a resource for justice. The goal is identification of aspects of his method for understanding and speaking about God as good that can be retrieved for feminist ethics, as well as identification of those aspects of his method regarding the good that are inappropriate for retrieval based on the criteria of critical feminist hermeneutics. While the task is one of methodological retrieval rather than descriptive retrieval, examination of some descriptions of God as good that Aquinas proposes must be considered to better understand his method. This section will develop criteria for understanding and describing God as good, criteria that will be drawn in part from Aquinas, and that also reflect feminist insights on what constitutes an adequate understanding of the good.

Why is the way in which Aquinas describes God as the good an important consideration for feminist ethics? Why shouldn't this be passed over as a question of such a rarified, speculative nature that it may provide an interesting intellectual exercise but is irrelevant to ethics and certainly irrelevant to feminist ethics? The key to the significance of how God is understood as the good is identified by Elizabeth Johnson:

> The symbol of God does not passively float in the air but *functions* in social and personal life to sustain or critique certain structures, values, and ways of acting. Sociologists of religion shed clear light on this power of religions to structure the world. Following Clifford

Geertz's oft repeated formulation, there is an interdependent relation between a religion's symbol system, the moods and motivations it establishes, its concept of the general order of things, and the aura of factuality that surrounds both the moods and the concepts. Since the symbol of God is the focal point of the whole religious system, an entire world order and world view is wrapped up with its character. Specific ideas of God support certain kinds of relationship and not others.[34]

Understanding God as a particular type of reality shapes the way in which the human community correlatively understands the good to which it is related and which it is called to emulate. The way God is understood as good shapes the ethical imagination of the community.

Aquinas followed the lead of Pseudo-Dionysius and Plato in his belief that since no *direct* vision or knowledge of God is possible, what can validly be said about God is more a matter of negation: "Because we cannot know what God is, but rather what God is not, our method has to be mainly negative. . . . What kind of being God is not can be known by eliminating characteristics which cannot apply to Him, like composition, change, and so forth."[35] Aquinas believed that this type of negation applied to God would result in some positive delineations. F. C. Copleston writes:

A point to be noticed is that the application of this method can result in predicating of God attributes which are expressed by apparently positive words. In the case of a word like "immutable" it is obvious that it is equivalent to not-mutable. Similarly, 'infinite' is equivalent to "not-finite".[36]

Aquinas appreciated that there is no other way of speaking a positive word about God except through human experience and knowledge: "Terms signify God to the extent that our intellect knows him. And since our intellect knows God from creatures, it knows him to the extent that creatures represent Him."[37] It is, therefore, necessary and appropriate to attempt to predicate positive reality of God based on the knowledge gained through experience of what it means to live well as human persons (here again the significance of an adequate anthropology is apparent). Aquinas suggests that the objective foundation for predicating terms analogically of God is our own participation in or reflection of these very attributes: "And thus whatever is predicated of God and creatures is predicated in virtue of the latter's relation to God as principle and cause in which all the perfections of things pre-exist in a more excellent manner."[38] Aquinas allows us to reflect on the attributes that describe the person in her best self, in her ideal, and to presume that these attributes are in some way also part of the reality of God. Moreover, Aquinas does not ask us to be content with minimalist language about God, for fear of splitting God into characteristics and attributes that in fact are *our* understanding of what in God is unitary perfection. A variety of concepts are required to speak about God's goodness, even though that goodness is perfectly whole and without "parts." "Although the names attributed to God signify one thing, they signify it under many different aspects, and they are not synonymous."[39] "But although our intellect conceives God under different concepts, it knows that to all its concepts there corresponds one and the same simple being."[40] These positive realities or qualities of God are proposed or used in an analogical sense. As Copleston observes:

> To say that certain terms are predicated analogically of God does not mean, of course, that we have an adequate positive idea of what is objectively signified by the term when it is predicated of God. Our knowledge of perfections is derived from creatures, and this origin necessarily colours our concepts of those perfections. We necessarily think and speak of God in terms which, from a linguistic point of view, refer primarily to creatures, and we can only approximate towards, while never reaching, an adequate understanding of what is meant by saying that God is "wise" or "good" or "intelligent" or "living".[41]

To predicate a positive quality of God always requires humility that acknowledges that this quality is both like and unlike how it has been known by us—the dynamic of analogy.

Drawing on the currents of historical consciousness and the principle of embodiment, starting from the base of experience common to all liberation theologies, a feminist theology argues that Aquinas's description of God as good is flawed because he began his consideration with abstract notions of the good. The "perfection-language" Aquinas used to describe God emerges (as it must) from a human mind that can do no other than employ its best descriptions of goodness as the person conceives of it, or experiences it, and that then pushes this language of goodness to its ultimate possibility as a description of God. Since the time of Augustine, Christian perfection-language used to speak of God's goodness was based primarily on Greek philosophical conceptions of the pinnacle of human perfection—the free male. Aquinas's conception of God as good prizes qualities traditionally associated with the male who was the paradigm of Aquinas's anthropology. For example, God who is goodness is characterized by Aquinas as impassible (not affected by external forces) and immutable (unchanging) and similar qualities of being emphasizing autonomy, otherness, self-sufficiency, etc. Johnson comments on these characteristics:

> In the patriarchal system the nonrelational human male exercising unilateral power sits at the pinnacle of perfection. Relationality and the inevitable vulnerability that accompanies it are correspondingly devalued as imperfections. Being free from others and being incapable of suffering in one's own person because of them become the goal. This patriarchal model has given the concept of impassibility its orientation and content in the human mind. . . . Feminist theology judges that the attribute of impassibility, even when posed as the ethical ideal of freedom, is found wanting when compared with the truth discerned in the lived experience characteristic of women. Self-containment and the absence of relationship are not necessarily the highest perfections but signify lack. Furthermore, the attribute of omnipotence, modeled on the power of an absolute monarch, reflects patriarchal preference for domination and control.[42]

Johnson criticizes classical Christian conceptions and language about God that neglect the language of immanence as an equally important way to speak of and understand God as fundamentally good, and she also criticizes the Christian presumption of God's neutrality in situations of conflict and God's nonrelationality to the created world.[43] These conceptions of God placed such a strong emphasis on transcendence and autonomy as ultimate characteristics of God's divinity and goodness that they neglected the correlative theological tradition of God's immanence, partiality to the poor and dispossessed, and active relatedness to creation. Feminist theological discourse of God as good reclaims this suppressed, enduring tradition of God as a valuable ethical resource for women today. James Keenan and Thomas Kopfensteiner note that, in fact, this is not just a feminist methodological turn:

> As a basic *telos* . . . autonomy is an inadequate expression for the end of the human subject. . . . A profound interest in the person whose subjectivity is constituted by solidarity with others (neighbor, God, and nature) is both the anthropological given and the moral task.[44]

David Tracy observes that perfection-language must be available to amendment. He pays particular attention to the need for language of relationality as the basis for perfection-language for God, a suggestion with which many feminist theologians would concur: "A relational model of human perfection is clearly a more adequate one for understanding divine perfection than either an ancient individualist or modern autonomous one."[45]

In spite of Aquinas's description of the person as embodied spirit, embodiment is not the starting point for his predication of God's goodness. This is understandable, since Aquinas described God as pure spirit, making embodiment a characteristic of the creature, not of the creator. Feminist theology argues that the phenomena of embodiment provide a valid and important perspective from which to develop a relatively more adequate conception of God as good. The Christian community has implicitly understood that to describe God *is* to describe the good—it is impossible that anything predicated of God is *not* good. It is not only when speaking of God as merciful and wise that the Christian community has known that God's goodness is being referenced. *All* language of God is language of the good, and therefore the language and images used to describe God are extremely important for providing a "horizon of goodness" that allows the entire community to "gaze upon" this God who is known through the veil of words (as Paul describes: "Now we are seeing a dim reflection in a mirror . . ." 1 Cor. 13:12), and to find in these images a deep truth that calls the particularity of one's own way of being human forward toward the absolute goodness that God is. The traditional language of God has not, however, provided this resonance based in experience for women. The traditional language of God as good has also worked against men who could not look toward God and discern dimensions and aspects of goodness that were a corrective to the androcentric conceptions of good that society valued.

A feminist reinterpretation of God as good rejects traditional characteristics such as immutability and impassibility to the extent that they propose God as One who is unavailable to human suffering because of an emphasis of *a-patheia* (or absence of pathos or suffering) and because capacity to change was deemed an imperfection. A feminist understanding of God as good argues to reclaim qualities of the good such as empathy, solidarity, long-suffering, faithful friendship, compassion, availability, active and fierce protectiveness on behalf of family and friends, and similar, relation-based attributes. Catherine LaCugna employs this methodology in her examination of the Christian doctrine of the Trinity, and it is equally valuable in developing an understanding of God as good that takes account of the life experiences of women:[46]

> Because of the particular direction the history of dogma took, many people now understand the doctrine of the Trinity to be the esoteric exposition of God's 'inner' life, that is, the *self-relatedness* of Father, Son, and Spirit (sometimes called the 'immanent' Trinity). But if this doctrine can speak only of a Trinity locked up in itself and unrelated to us, then no wonder so many find it intrinsically uninteresting. . . . There is an entirely different way of approaching the doctrine of the Trinity. . . . It requires that we root all speculation about the triune nature of God in the economy of salvation (*oikonomia*), in the self-communication of God in the person of Christ and the activity of the Holy Spirit . . . in contradistinction to *theologia*, the mystery of God as such.[47]

LaCugna observes that Aquinas's work (particularly the *Summa Theologica*) has been criticized by contemporary theologians (Karl Rahner, Yves Congar, Marie-Dominic Chenu, and others) for creating a seeming split between *theologia* and *oikonomia*, observable even in the placement of topics in the *Summa*. Aquinas departed from the theological method that preceded him by using Aristotle's scientific, rational approach to consider God in God's self, placing this at the beginning of the *Summa*. As LaCugna observes:

> Thomas' *theologia* assumes the *oikonomia*. But given Thomas' starting point 'in' God, the economy of redemption is not the primary or obvious basis for *theologia*. . . . In the *Summa*, Thomas first treats the Trinity in itself, not in its economic manifestation. This is "God's standpoint," not that of the creature. From the standpoint of revelation, or of human experience and knowledge, the order would be reversed: *Oikonomia* would precede *theologia*. . . . God "for us" would precede God "in Godself".[48]

LaCugna addresses the methodology of Aquinas and the resulting relationship of theological perspectives: "[T]he structure of the *Summa* makes it plain that Trinity and Incarnation, *theologia* and *oikonomia*, belong together as the two central mysteries of Christian faith, explicated according to the scheme of *exitus-reditus*."[49] She acknowledges that Aquinas's method indicates that he conceives of theology as the "science of 'God in Himself'," rather than envisioning theology as understanding about God.[50] What I propose here is certainly not a rejection of the possibilities of reason in theological method; rather, it is a call for a mutually critical relationship among the traditional sources of theology—tradition, reason, scripture, and experience—in developing and amending our understanding of God as good. Christian theology has placed such emphasis on reason (philosophy) that it needs the corrective of the other three sources for developing a more adequate theology. Feminist methodology does not reject the role of philosophy and reason in developing conceptions of God's goodness, but it insists that in the face of the near absence of the other three resources, it is necessary to give greater emphasis to the missing resources to develop a more adequate conception of God as good, particularly the resource of the experience of women.

Just as LaCugna contends that Aquinas would have argued vigorously against the marginalization of the doctrine of the Trinity, due particularly to the neo-scholastic tendency to sharply demarcate the topics and treatments found in the *Summa*, considering God as the good has in many respects become an equally marginal issue for ethicists, since God's goodness has been depicted largely in highly abstract conceptual terms that have little apparent relevance for the human community, particularly in regard to social ethics. This has been especially true for women who have attempted to understand God's goodness as a moral paradigm, and who have found in the traditional conceptions of the good little that bears resemblance to women's lives and dimensions of existence that women value.

Feminist theological method and theological ethics must reclaim the *oikonomia* as the starting point for theological method, including foundational theology. This does *not* mean rejecting the task of *theologia* in itself, but it does mean insisting that the only true ground to stand on and from which to begin any theological work is the ground of history and experience. Revelation occurs within history and is mediated through human apprehension and experience. Just as there is no uninterpreted experience, there is no perfectly speculative *theologia*; it takes place through the intellectually and historically shaped person.

A conception of God as good that does not draw in a primary way on the biblical images of God is difficult to square with the Judeo-Christian tradition. In Genesis, for example, God is depicted as one who is passionately related to creation. But a distinct relationship is described between humanity and God; Genesis emphasizes that humanity is created in the image and likeness of God—there is a relationship of resemblance between God and humanity.

Both LaCugna and Johnson reclaim the ancient Christian conviction that the community looks to the manifestation of God in Jesus to provide its most basic points of reference for its understanding of God, and of God as good. LaCugna writes:

> The starting point "in God" no longer recommends itself to us for both philosophical and theological reasons. After Kant, Feuerbach, and the philosophical revolution of the Enlightenment, the idea of an "in itself" is viewed as a philosophical impossibility, especially if God is the subject. . . . For Christians, the source for thinking about both divine and created relationality must remain the revelation of God in Christ and the Spirit.[51]

Feminist theological method finds in the biblically presented Jesus (the Scripture itself being engaged through a process of critical retrieval) a manifestation of God that grounds the most ancient Christian faith claims (Jesus Christ, God's Son, Savior), and that simultaneously grounds the contention that Christian theology and Christian ethics must begin to speak about God's goodness not from philosophical categories, but from the examination of the life, behavior, and teaching of this *person* (as distinct from the later christological formulations). The Jesus of the synoptic gospels presents an image of a deeply engaged person who wills the wholeness of everyone and *each* one, and who has a particular care for the marginal ones who were rejected by mainstream society. He uses parables to teach because they make the truth available to his hearers; he *meets* them in their misery, sinfulness, and suffering and brings *shalom* to them. He eats and parties regularly with people; he has particularly close friends including women; he is touched with sadness to the point of tears; he is angered to the point of harsh denouncements of his adversaries and physical violence in the temple. If, as the Christian tradition maintains, Jesus is an unmatchable revelation of God, then the community must take seriously the life of the historical person Jesus as a manifestation of what it means that God is good. The loss of the synoptic Jesus as a reference for understanding God as good has left us with patriarchal christological formulations that propose a cosmic, imperial, authoritative, separated reality to understand God as good. Many feminist theologians maintain that the biblical Jesus offers a powerful resource for understanding how God is—an image of God whose goodness is embodied in Jesus' passionate engagement for the wholeness of all creation and active opposition to all that defaces the dignity of the human person and creation.[52] As liberation theologians have demonstrated, it is in the biblical Jesus that the oppressed, and in this case women, find an ally who condemns the cause of their suffering and who offers hope and liberation from their oppression. The biblical account of the first Pentecost similarly offers an image of a Spirit of boldness and courage for proclamation of the truth of the one who was crucified and raised. For women, this biblical wellspring contradicts images that conceive of God's goodness as solitary "being-in-oneself" rather than goodness being fundamentally a matter of relationality. At the same time, feminist theology rejects the position that it is Jesus' maleness that constitutes a significant aspect of his "perfection," which is therefore predicated of God.

The Human Good

I will now seek to develop a minimally descriptive understanding of the human good from the confluence of Aquinas's conceptions of the human good and the feminist methodology and principles that have been outlined. Such a profile of the human good is not only descriptive, but it is also an ethical principle for an ethical judgment concerning the practical life circumstances of women and a guide to choices that are made in response to these life realities.

Feminist theology brings a hermeneutics of suspicion to the ways the human good has been described in the past, in the same way that it critiques anthropological conceptions operative in the past. In both cases, Ann O'Hara Graff reminds us:

> What was apparently unseen prior to these insights was that the abstract universal claim to describe "man" or human nature was not at all abstract. The descriptions of the human that functioned in earlier theologies were usually grounded in the particular experiences of those people who had access to the academy and were able to become published theologians.[53]

Traditional Christian conceptions of the human good, including those of Aquinas, described it deductively, from an ontological perspective on human nature that functioned as the basis of moral claims and was itself based on the "normative human": a free, educated male. As with feminist responses to traditional anthropological claims, feminist scholars judge this to be an inadequate description of the human good for several reasons. The classical conception of human nature used as the foundation for considering the human good was virtually static, not allowing for the possibility that human nature in itself is a dynamic, developing reality, shaped by contexts, environments, and circumstances. Such construals of human nature privileged the intellectual and rational capacities of the person. It acknowledged only minimally that embodiment was not just a necessary evil, but a privileged and unique aspect of the human person linked to rationality rather than opposed to it. Aquinas's anthropology certainly endowed the fact and feature of human embodiment with much greater significance than had been customary before him. However, feminists argue for the necessity of an even stronger, more positive assessment of embodiment as an anthropological feature and primary phenomenon of human nature and therefore as a principle of the human good. The experience of women regarding embodiment, both as an anthropological issue and as a moral issue in the development of a description of the human good, has been absent from Christian theology. Its inclusion in a feminist method demands a rethinking not only of the question of the human person (anthropology) but of goodness for the human person (morality) and insists that women's previously neglected voices/experiences must be given particular prominence in shaping these descriptions.

Starting in a sense from the opposite end, Valerie Saiving observed that traditional descriptions of sin have been constructed from responses to life circumstances more generally associated with male experience (which she characterized particularly as alienation and anxiety producing prideful self-assertion and aggression).[54] Saiving notes that the remedies for sin so conceived have traditionally been behaviors of self-giving, seeking the good of the other without self-interest, choosing self-mortification and self-abnegation to restrain unbridled pride, aggression, and self-interest. The good envisioned for the human person, premised on an abstract concept of both human good and sin, referencing primarily male experience, reinforced precisely the negative and destructive patterns of socialization typical for women. Questions persist about whether environmental and social influences or innate gender tendencies contribute to patterns of a decentered self and a profound focus on the welfare of others for many women to the extent of losing a sense of themselves as distinct individuals. To recommend to women that the good they should pursue will occur through *more* self-abnegation holds out to them a religiously endorsed model of goodness that in fact confirms for many women patterns of destructive relationships to themselves, others, and God. To avoid this may require modifying our understanding of the human good: while there are ways in which it is a similar reality for both women and men, its pursuit may well require different moral strategies and remedies for women than for men.

It will be easier to speak descriptively about the human good if we recall the proposition of chapter 1 regarding anthropology: anthropological descriptions are minimal in their universal claims, open to amendment, and must be concretized in each unique setting. For example, while one of the human functioning capabilities proposed by Nussbaum is "Being able to live one's *own* life and nobody else's," the *way* this is understood and occurs in Ethiopia may well be different from how it occurs in London or in Beijing. But in each case, the good that is sought is having the capacity to live one's own *distinct* life that reflects one's own agency and choice. This capability identifies a principle that is descriptive of a basic aspect of the human good and that may be employed as a principle of critique and assessment in various settings. The use of the amended set of human functioning capabilities as anthropological markers or constants enables us to speak about the human good in a universal manner without being trapped in a set of static, abstract concepts of goodness.

The natural law tradition of Aquinas is in principle a resource for feminists attempting to describe the human good. The natural law tradition *requires* the use of the best available resources to understand the truth of a thing.[55] If we understand what this truth is, we come to a clearer understanding of the constitution of *this* thing's goodness, because, as Aquinas knew, greater relationship or coherence with the truth appropriate to its nature *is* the good of something. Just as Aquinas employed Aristotle's thought in an innovative and daring way to aid in the articulation of the human good and the basic dynamic of natural law, so we must now engage the best resources available to develop the most adequate way of understanding the human good. These resources include the critical study of the Scriptures and the retrieved dimensions of the work of Aquinas (and other classical writers), the effective history of the Christian tradition regarding the human good (submitted to a searching scrutiny to identify embedded conceptions of the human that implicitly or explicitly disadvantage women), the insights of the social sciences, and, most significantly, an analysis of the experience of women. Together these resources offer a more adequate grounds for appeal to the natural law tradition.

Aquinas describes the ultimate human good primarily as the complete union of the person with God. This is the perfection consistent with and appropriate to the nature of a person. While it is a totally unearned gift and is not among earthly possibilities for the person to achieve by her own actions, human decisions and choices aid the person in her growth in acquired virtue and goodness in her natural, earthly existence.

In describing the human good, Aquinas considers it as "happiness":

> In the first sense, then, man's last end is the uncreated good, namely, God, Who alone by His infinite goodness can perfectly satisfy man's will. But in the second way, man's last end is something created, existing in him, and this is nothing else than the attainment or enjoyment of the last end. Now the last end is called happiness. . . . Happiness is called man's supreme good, because it is the attainment or enjoyment of the supreme good.[56]

Aquinas addresses questions of human good/happiness logically and philosophically, considering goodness and happiness as ultimate states because they form the true horizon for all other understandings of goodness and happiness. At the same time, Aquinas distinguishes between perfect and imperfect happiness. Perfect goodness and happiness for the person are God in God's self and the person's participation in that goodness. While imperfect happiness or goodness is not to be shunned because it is not perfection, Aquinas viewed all things in relation to the final end of a person and he was not distracted by the significance of imperfect goods and imperfect happiness benefiting what he describes as the "animal" dimension of the person. This animal dimension was of secondary significance and value for Aquinas. It is to be dealt with as necessary, but never indulged for its own sake. The happiness of the "animal body," for example, is a necessary aspect of earthly life, but one that should be guided by the pursuit of ultimate happiness and good:

> For imperfect happiness, such as can be had in this life, external goods are necessary, not as belonging to the essence of happiness, but by serving as instruments to happiness, which consists in an operation of virtue. For man needs in this life the necessaries of the body, both for the operation of contemplative virtue, and for the operation of active virtue, for which latter he needs also many other things by

means of which to perform its operations. . . . Such goods as these are nowise necessary for perfect Happiness, which consists in seeing God. The reason for this is that all suchlike external goods are requisite either for the support of the animal body; or for certain operations which belong to human life, which we perform by means of the animal body: whereas that perfect Happiness which consists in seeing God, will be either in the soul separated from the body, or in the soul united from the body then no longer animal but spiritual. Consequently, these external goods are nowise necessary for that Happiness, since they are ordained to the animal life. And since, in this life, the felicity of contemplation, as being more God-like, approaches that perfect Happiness, therefore it stands in less need of these goods as stated in *Eth.* x.8.[57]

While the practical, embodied dimensions of the person are given higher value by Aquinas (as compared to his immediate predecessors— for example, Alexander of Hales, and Bonaventure), the practical needs of the embodied person still have lesser significance in themselves in Aquinas's thought than what feminists accord them. Christian feminists argue that the human good is an *embodied* good, even while the person is constituted for an ultimate fulfillment that earthly existence cannot provide. From a feminist perspective, the human good includes substantially and directly (not just incidentally) the range of practical, personal, emotional, psychological, social, and embodied human needs, not in opposition to understanding the ultimate human good as union with God, but out of deep respect for the created reality that the person is. Christian feminists do not in principle disagree with Aquinas's position that the ultimate human good is a transcendent reality beyond the agency of the person herself to achieve. But feminist critique picks up Aquinas's acknowledgment of the embodied reality of the person, and brings it into much greater prominence and significance in light of the social scientific learning of the last 300 years, as well as the narrative learning that attentiveness to the stories of women reveals about embodied goodness, and embodied destruction.

The retrieved understanding of the human good, then, draws on the anthropological schema developed in chapter 1. It is highly embodied and identifies the human (and consequently the human good) in *dynamic* terms (i.e., *being capable of* . . .) rather than describing the human good in relation to static, definitive, abstract categories. It is a human good that the person enjoys, the human reality of being capable of effective choice. But is it possible determine whether the human good is actually being promoted and to what degree it is being approximated in a situation (or for an individual person or a particular constituency) when the description is dynamic rather than definitive? The practical human good as outlined here would be gauged or judged as present or absent according to the degree to which a person possesses (or does not possess) a capability for fundamental human functions. A person's or group's good may be assessed in light of the degree of capability for functioning that is held, by whom it is held, and in regard to what capabilities—also noting what capabilities are stunted, absent, and/or restricted and for whom. This model of the human good does not lose sight of the vision of the human person proposed in the Scriptures nor in the best of the retrieved Christian tradition such as Aquinas. The model brings together the amended set of human functioning capabilities and Aquinas's description of the human good regarding the person as an embodied spirit, created with a capacity for union with God throughout eternity. The feminist description of the human good that emerges draws together a dynamic set of anthropological markers that give rise to ethical and moral imperatives that are invoked specifically in regard to women and the human good as they know it in embedded, historical situations. Christian feminist method draws on the Scriptural images of the human person in a condition of fundamental goodness as found in Genesis and throughout the Bible—images of the human person constituted for existence marked by intimacy/relationality (with God, with oneself, and with others), rich and embodied flourishing, and *shalom* (understood as comprehensive well-being), justice, peace, etc.

Cahill reminds us that Aquinas believed that morality is "reasonable": he was aware that the labor of human intellect and reason could arrive at greater knowledge of truth.[58] This, of course, does not reject Aquinas's belief (and that of the Christian community through the centuries) in revelation as a means of coming to know the truth; it does, however, offer an endorsement from Aquinas's own methodology regarding the use of the capacities of intellect and reason (and the disciplines associated with them) to come to greater clarity regarding the truth of the human person and the human good. Aquinas believed that an apprehension of "natural justice" could be discerned through observation and reflection on the human and human experience. Here feminists find a methodological ally in Aquinas. While Aquinas himself would not have sought the experience of women as a necessary vehicle for revealing truth about the good (given his cultural and intellectual environment), his methodology provides a precedent for such an appeal by feminists. Therefore, an appeal to the amended set of human functioning capabilities is in principle grounded in Aquinas's own methodology for discerning the moral good. A more adequate, embodied conception of the human good provides a more adequate ethical foundation on which to base claims regarding abuse of the human rights of all people, and particularly of women.

The proposed amended anthropology means that the benefits, obligations, and responsibilities Aquinas associated "naturally" with the male because of what he judged to be the male's greater capacity for rational discourse and intellectual pursuits, suiting him more aptly for public discourse and decision making, belong to women as well. But more than women simply inheriting the classical understanding of the human good, feminists insist that the way in which the human good is understood must be reshaped by particular attention to the experiences of women. This amended conception of the good provides a changed set of markers for judging whether the good of any person in the community is being pursued, not only women.

The work of Edward Schillebeeckx is useful here. Using a critical, liberationist methodology, Schillebeeckx insisted that the situation of most people in the world is so diminished and marked by suffering, that rather than developing deductively a set of principles of the human good, it is far more appropriate to attend to the actual situations of suffering that stand as a negation or denial of a good that is required for the human good to exist.[59] Schillebeeckx believes that suffering functions as a type of "negative marker" about a good that *should* be present. As an aspect of feminist methodology, *particular* attention is given to the suffering of women and girl children to point to a human good that is lacking for them. For example, the functioning capability "Being able to have good health, including reproductive health, to be adequately nourished, and to have adequate shelter," describes a human good applicable to both women and men. However, having good health, including in one's reproductive capacity, has a different meaning and requirement for women for whom sexual intercourse holds the very real possibility of pregnancy. Multiple pregnancies, too close together, are a serious threat to the physical health and lives of many women. Adequate nourishment means something different for pregnant and nursing women than for a man. Adequate nutrition as a functioning capability from a female perspective calls attention to the fact that in impoverished settings, it is not unusual for the male children to receive a greater share of a family's food, with the result that death from malnutrition is higher for girls than for boys.[60] This same capability is a worthy measure of an aspect of practical human good that applies equally to women and men; however, this functioning capability as a moral measure of human good demands attention to the particularities of situations as they are experienced by women.

As Nussbaum reminds us, it is insupportable to substitute an abundance of one of the functioning capabilities with the presumption or expectation that this compensates for the lack or absence of another. Lack of choice regarding sexual options or poor nutrition is not redressed by providing good housing. Each of these is a distinct functioning capability that must be met on its own terms.

Aquinas noted that people need to live in community as part of their practical human good not only to receive from the community things they cannot achieve for themselves, but because it is as a member of a community that a person has the opportunity to exercise choice that fosters acquired virtue and thereby to grow in affinity with the good. It seems reasonable to imagine that women have the chance to live out a different type of historical goodness when they do not live in terror, when they are able to respond to the contingencies of life out of their own best insights and free choices and initiative, when they participate in decisions that concern their fate, etc.

The Common Good

A feminist retrieval of the principle of the common good privileges the experience of women within the community as a moral measure. Aquinas does not describe in his writings how the practical common good of the community should be pursued; however, it seems reasonable to imagine, given his anthropological convictions regarding women (and the cultural setting in which he lived), that he likely would have presumed a different participation by women in the practical common good than was considered proper to or normative for men. Significant differences between Aquinas's horizon for the lives of women and the horizon envisioned by contemporary feminists would almost certainly exist in regard to women's education and their active participation and choice in matters that involve their lives and well-being.

Aquinas's anthropology deemed a situation in which women are subordinate to men a benefit to women (whom, he judged, profit from the protection and guidance of the male) as well as a benefit to the male, who enjoys the practical companionship and comradeship of his wife in the project of their shared life. Feminists reject this aspect of Aquinas's anthropology and also reject the presumption of subordinate positions for women as normative and as being consistent with "God's plan," manifesting appropriate justice for women. Moreover, as I have noted, Aquinas believed that it is sometimes appropriate (in extreme situations) to take from the excess of the community or of another what someone lacks as a necessity for sustaining life—though he does not indicate *who* would be in a position to do the taking. This principle, I believe, is valuable for feminists today because it locates in Aquinas's thought the principle that people have the right to certain necessities of life and that the community is responsible for providing these even at the cost of the bounty of the more advantaged.

A retrieved principle of the common good, privileging the experience of women's suffering as an evaluative and interpretive lens, requires that the community pay *particular* attention to the situations of women at each life stage, using the proposed anthropology (particularly the human functioning capabilities) as a gauge to determine the degree to which the full human flourishing of women is occurring or is absent. The premise of this retrieved principle of the common good is that the genuine common good of the community is *only* pursued to the extent that those who are most at risk within the community receive particular attention and are attended to with moral and practical seriousness in an effort to understand and change the circumstances that contribute to this group's lack of participation in the benefits of the common good. Since pursuit of the practical common good is based on the dynamic relationship between justice as it concerns the individual person and justice as it concerns the community (to be discussed in the next section), considering the common good from a *feminist* perspective requires an insistence that the situation of women (particularly situations of suffering) must be a primary concern and moral measure for the community. This feminist retrieval of the common good further insists that precisely *as* an issue of the common good, the systems, structures, and traditions that support the order of community living that are destructive of women must be changed. This is not a "woman's issue"; rather, it is an issue of justice and the common good for the entire community.

This conviction, that the situation of women must be actively sought in any situation where justice is a value in shaping the practical life of a community's members, recalls the principle of the "option for the poor,"[61] a critical principle of liberation theology and of contemporary Roman Catholic social teaching.[62] Discussions about the implications and demands of this principle have ensued since it was introduced by Latin American liberation theologians, including questions about whether this principle denies the universal call to love *all* people by singling out one class of people for particular privileging.[63] Stephen Pope argues for the appropriateness of carefully delineated forms of a preferential option for the poor. He suggests that a hermeneutical privileging of the experience and perspective of the poor is not an absolute claim, vitiating all other claims to knowledge and perspective (religious, ethical, social, political, etc.):

> Expressed in the "part-whole" language employed earlier, the preferential option works for an extension rather than restriction of the interrelationships of parts to one another and of parts to the whole. It is oriented to the proper and full participation of all parts within the whole rather than to the substitution of one system of dominance for another. . . . Unjustifiable partiality furthers the dominance of one part over others and, indeed, over the whole; justifiable partiality, on the contrary, strives to create opportunities for deprived and oppressed parts so that all parts will be able someday to participate fully in the whole.[64]

Pope describes the privileging of the poor that he suggests is warranted as appropriate cognitive inclusiveness:

> Rather than assisting the poor in a paternalistic manner, nonpoor Christians are called first to listen to, learn from, and be converted by the poor. Conscientization facilitates self-awareness and self-determination, first of all for the poor themselves but also for all other Christians. Solidarity facilitates a more comprehensive understanding by attending to, or rather taking up, views from the underside of history, which constitutes the majority of the human race.[65]

The hermeneutical privileging of the poor also demands moral inclusiveness, "insisting on the full participation of all people within the political, social and economic life of local communities."[66] Finally, Pope contends that the hermeneutical privileging of the poor must occur through religious inclusiveness: "The preferential option advances religious inclusiveness by its affirmation of both God's preferential care and universal love. . . . [O]nly by loving 'nonpersons' can Christians of any social state begin to understand the true universality and depth of God's love."[67]

The feminist theological ethic proposed here is consistent with Pope's insights regarding the preferential option for the poor along with the claim established at the outset, that women constitute the poorest of the poor in virtually every cultural setting. Aquinas acknowledges in several places that it is incumbent on a ruler to make certain that members of the society have the material goods they require in order to grow in acquired virtue and lead a good life.[68] When this is placed together with Aquinas's conviction that under certain circumstances of great need, the surplus of some may be recruited by the government and distributed to those who lack the necessities, the principle of the common good, retrieved through this feminist hermeneutics, challenges those with responsibility for the policies and decisions of the society with particular moral imperatives, among which are the need to exercise unusual vigor to determine the situation of women and women-dependent children most at risk. This requires focused investigation into the situation of girl children and women, who are consistently the groups at greatest disadvantage and risk in virtually all societies.

The retrieved principle demands more than statistical data to identify the situation of women. It requires narrative documentation to pursue and gather information about the lives of women in a society using a multidisciplinary approach—demographic information (the number of girls born and their survival rate versus the number of boys and their survival rate);[69] the general health history of women; age at the time of marriage; number of pregnancies; maternal mortality; women's participation in decisions affecting them; their educational opportunities, literacy rates, ability to own property, obtain credit, and run a business, etc. While even the best strategies will have limitations and gaps, the retrieved principle of the common good commits those who have the responsibility to govern to a deliberate, ongoing, creative, and aggressive pursuit of the situation of women in society and to action that promotes their well-being.

THE INDIVIDUAL GOOD AND THE RETRIEVED PRINCIPLE OF THE COMMON GOOD

Is there a resource in Aquinas in which feminists may find particular promise regarding the relationship between the individual and the common good, a resource that is able to provide a methodological principle that promotes the well-being of women? A principle that, in the face of the dialectic between the individual and the common good, does not repeat the model of the past that has sought the good of a select group at the expense of women in particular? I argue that Aquinas's description of the moral and intellectual virtue of prudence offers such a resource.

According to Aquinas, prudence resides in the reason, and its purpose is to guide the will to right action. "The worth of prudence consists not in thought merely, but in its *application to action*, which is the end of the practical reason."[70] Most fundamentally and repeatedly, Aquinas describes prudence as "right reason applied to action." Prudence is "wisdom about human affairs."[71] Aquinas explains that right reason, when applied to production, results in dependable principles that might be considered "art": one learns or is able to learn what it means to produce something according to the specific standards that guide that art. With regard to speculative reason brought to bear on the myriad situations and circumstances in which a person may exist, however, no such precise "art" exists in which predetermined practices guide a person in *this* particular situation. Here "speculative prudence" assists the person in coming to know the most appropriate choice in a concrete instance in light of the ultimate end of the person.

Aquinas repeatedly emphasizes that to prudence belongs

> not only the considerations of the reason, *but also the application to action*, which is the end of practical reason. But no man can conveniently apply one thing to another, unless he knows both the thing to be applied, and the thing to which it has to be applied. Now actions are in singular matters, and so it is necessary for the prudent man to know both the universal principles of reason and the singulars about which actions are concerned.[72]

Aquinas confidently instructs the person to seek justice in a particular setting guided by the virtue of prudence, which helps to implement the demands of justice with an awareness of the particular realities of the situation. Since "the infinite number of singulars cannot be comprehended by human reason . . . our counsels are uncertain. Nevertheless experience reduces the infinity of singulars to a certain finite number which occurs as a general rule, and the knowledge of these suffices for human prudence."[73] Experience helps shape general counsels to guide a person's actions or responses in particular situations. Prudence assists the person in moving from the general principle to the particular action that *this* situation requires in order to seek the individual and common good.

Importantly, Aquinas himself invokes the guidance of experience in shaping the wise counsels that prudence must consider in a particular situation. This is again a conviction within Aquinas with which feminists agree, but for them the conviction is focused on women's experience in order to remedy the previous neglect of the experience of women who, in fact, bear an unjust weight of suffering in the community. General principles that are shaped without being informed by women's experience are deficient, and cannot authentically orient the community or those who are making decisions and choices to the true common good of the community. Since the end of moral virtues is the human good,[74] prudence guides the application of all virtues to the choices and actions that will promote this human good.

Aquinas identifies three acts which constitute right reason and are required for the act of prudence. These three are the taking of counsel (an act of discovery and inquiry), the act of judgment wherein one assesses what one has discovered, and the act of command that occurs as the person puts into action the counsel and judgment. Prudence, which benefits from and requires all three acts, functions in the third step, the movement into choice and action.[75] The "taking of counsel" might easily be seen to involve the investigation into the experience of women in the society.

Aquinas specifically addresses the virtue of prudence in regard to the relationship between the individual good and the common good:

> According to the Philosopher (*Ethic.* vi. 8) some have held that prudence does not extend to the common good, but only to the good of the individual, and this because they thought that man is not bound to seek other than his own good. But this opinion is opposed to charity, which seeketh not her own. . . . Moreover, it is contrary to right reason, which judges the common good to be better than the good of the individual. Accordingly, since it belongs to prudence to counsel, judge, and command concerning the means of obtaining a due end, it is evident that prudence regards not only the private good of the individual, but also the common good of the multitude.[76]

At this juncture Aquinas offers an intriguing insight into prudence: "Just as every moral virtue that is directed to the common good is called *legal* justice, so the prudence that is directed to the common good is called *political* prudence. . . ."[77] Prudence can in no way be construed as a cover for timidity or for maintaining the status quo. Prudence, guided by right reason (counsel and judgment) commands the will to courageously choose those actions that are for the human good. But prudence also guides the pursuit of the common good as political prudence: those who govern are expected to do so in a way that genuinely and actively pursues the common good. If, as has been suggested, the common good is pursued only when the situation of those most at risk in a society is sought as an informing, critical and moral element in the pursuit of justice, and if in any setting, the situation of women is most likely to be that of the most oppressed and suffering of the society, then political prudence demands action to redress the situations that cause the suffering for women.

While Aquinas's emphasis on the common good over the individual good has raised concern among some that the individual good will be lost, he reminds us that

> he that seeks the good of the many, seeks in consequence his own good for two reasons. First, because the individual good is impossible without the common good of the family, state or kingdom. . . . Secondly, because, since man is part of the home and state, he must needs consider what is good for him by being prudent about the good of the many. For the good disposition of parts depends on their relation to the whole.[78]

Aquinas delineates the ways prudence guides the choice of action:

> The individual good, the good of the family, and the good of the city and kingdom are different ends. Wherefore there must needs be different species of prudence corresponding to these different ends, so that one is prudence simply so called, *which is directed to one's own good*; another, domestic prudence, *which is directed to the common good of the home*; and a third, political prudence, *which is directed to the common good of the state or kingdom*.[79]

In Western liberal capitalistic cultures, individual rights and the individual's good have become privileged to an extreme degree. In this setting, discussion of the common good can sound either quaint or dangerous, a hemming in of unrestrained individualism. However, it has become clear that the privileges of some (which are now considered by them to be their right) have very often been achieved by ignoring the needs and rights of others in the community. To this degree, Aquinas's emphasis on the *common* good serves as a needed corrective to the reigning Western preference. But Aquinas further specifies political prudence as *legislative* prudence (belonging to rulers), "while the other [form of prudence] retains the common name *political*, and is about individual actions. Now it belongs also to subjects to perform these individual actions. Therefore, prudence is not only in rulers but also in subjects."[80] Finally, Aquinas advises that domestic prudence is directed to the common good of the home.[81]

Aquinas's approach to the relationship between the individual and the common good suggests a dynamic interplay between the human good, the individual good, and the common good. His discussion of the virtue of prudence supports his insistence that speculative reason is engaged in constant moral discernment, not the application of once-and-for-all established procedures. The function of prudence is not timid, or a fierce protection of the status quo, but thoughtful assessment of the situation (experience) and the ways that the end of the good understood essentially may be pursued in a particular situation, gauging and balancing the claims of the individual and the common good that are at hand. When Aquinas's description of prudence is joined with historical consciousness and the necessity of attending to the claims of the poor (through attention to the preferential option for the poor, as described above), prudence orders the actions and choices of both individuals and the community to redress in practical terms the situation of those whose good has been denied or thwarted. Prudence considers whether the benefit of some has been achieved by means of injustice toward others, and insists that the claims of the advantaged must be balanced against the needs of those who suffer. Here prudence challenges a privileging of unbridled individualism and autonomy so the just claims of the less advantaged may be met. Since women historically and in current fact constitute the most needy in virtually any cultural and national setting, prudence insists that any individual or group who subscribe to the common good as it has been retrieved choose actions to address the situations of exclusion and injustice of the women in the society.

Prudence cannot be satisfied with theoretical statements about equality of people, but functions as a demand for *action* that pursues the individual and the common good. In Aquinas's consideration of prudence there is a practicality and an endorsement of embodiment—

prudence assists in the choice of actions that enable the embodied person(s), and by extension, the community as an embodied reality, to labor for a good that is embodied (practical and contextual) even while these are choices that Aquinas maintains also assist in orienting the person and the community to their ultimate good. The practical human good has been described in the amended set of human functioning capabilities; prudence requires choices and actions that foster these capabilities with particular attention to the ways in which these capabilities are present or absent for women as long as it is true that women are those for whom the capabilities are most denied. The biblically based option for the poor orients the focus of the community (Whose questions are heard? Whose suffering counts? Whose situation has first claim on the resources of the community?) and claims the ancient covenant tradition as a still-operative moral force within the community, guided now by the awareness of the suffering of women as a systemic, cross-cultural reality.

The convictions in Aquinas regarding the function of the virtue of prudence in relation to the common and individual good may be contextualized now in settings that embody political processes in contexts that are very different from that of Aquinas. The issue is not the precise political system or form that is engaged, but the degree to which any political and economic reality fosters full human flourishing and particularly the full human flourishing of women, using the amended human functioning capabilities as a gauge to assess this.

JUSTICE AND THE COMMON GOOD

Justice is not a separate reality from the common good, but is pursued in the interplay between the individual good and the common good.[82] For feminists, justice is not understood as moral neutrality in decision making, reminiscent of John Rawls's veil of ignorance.[83] Justice for feminists (and for all whose ethical principles are based on a liberationist tradition) is pursued with particular attention for the constituency that has suffered and been discounted in the history of the community; that is, justice is partisan insofar as it is a rectifying of an inequity suffered by a particular group. It is a false dichotomy to pit justice for women against the common good, a dichotomy Aquinas would not have recognized as representing the relationship between the individual and the common good. In essence, such a dichotomy suggests that the community cannot "afford" justice because too much would have to change in order to alter the historical situation to enable those formerly oppressed to have redress. In such a conception, the pursuit of the circumstances that foster the full human flourishing of the oppressed constituency is cast as the enemy of those who traditionally have enjoyed the full benefits of the community. Justice for women in this construal (or for any group that has been excluded and oppressed) might indeed appear as a threat to the advantage of some men. Of course, this presumes that what *has* existed has *been* the common good, when in fact it has really been a situation that benefited certain members (the men of the community) at the expense of women. This is not the common good, nor has it been authentically pursued.

If justice is understood, as Aquinas suggests, as the *habit* of giving each person (or constituency) what is properly theirs, guided by prudence (informed by experience and practical reason), then a feminist construal of the relationship between justice and the common good begins with the insistence that the experience of women must be sought as a matter of priority to uncover women's descriptions of their lives. Justice is understood in and through description, through narrative, not just through statistical data. Feminists insist that to truly pursue justice commits us to hearing the testimonies of women. This has been absent in moral and ethical theories that have used a deductive conception of justice not premised on a narrative base of *testimony* through which the accounts of those who suffer *because of* the status quo provide a witness to its destructive dimensions.[84] Feminists reject an abstraction of justice from the concrete, historical realities of women's lives—a deductive conception of justice and the common good that is utterly unable to respond to the specific realities of a situation.

Rebecca Chopp highlights the traditional split between theory/theology and faith/witness/testimony and proposes a different way of understanding the relationship between these two sets of theological and ethical components. Her reframing reflects the feminist contention that the experience of women is traditionally absent as the base from which to encounter and understand the current situation and offer an ideological critique of the status quo. Moreover, the traditional relationship between theory and experience perpetuates the destructive dichotomy of spirit/matter, reason/experience, male/female. She insists on the need for reconceiving the relationship between these components so that the "poetics of testimony" is part of the theory of emancipatory praxis itself:[85]

> Testimony is, in other words, a discursive practice, as opposed to a pure theory. . . . This poetics of testimony challenges how the real is both represented and created in culture by summoning us to question the role of modern theory as the court of the real.[86]

A feminist understanding of the relationship between justice and the common good requires the "poetics of testimony" to disclose and inform the community about a *lack* of justice within itself. This is an apt way to describe a feminist construal of the relationship between justice and the common good, because it refuses to separate and isolate the "tales" of suffering and oppression from the moral claim the experience makes on the community and the community's response to the suffering. As Chopp observes:

> Testimony invokes a moral claim; it is from someone to someone about something. A decision is called for, a change in reality is required. This responsibility is . . . a social reality. The moral responsibility is to change the rules, not simply this particular verdict. . . . The poetics of testimony place all theory, even contemporary theories of culture, on trial for their moral responsibility to engage this "reverence for life." . . . Testimonies, I am suggesting, summon even theory to serve those who suffer and hope, those whose voices testify to survival, those who imagine transformation. Theory is neither objective judge nor subjective experience; rather, it is now summoned to help, to aid, and to serve.[87]

In order to practice or foster the virtue of justice, the community must *always* be in the process of hearing the testimonies that describe a reality usually ignored or only included as anecdotes rather than demanding response and redress that reshapes the community's "social imaginary"—the way in which the "normal" is imagined and the multiple relationships that contribute to the practical common good are embodied. "Indeed," Chopp writes, "we might even say that these contemporary testimonies of extremity allow us to imagine different ways in which the ordering of the particular and the universal or the specific and general might occur."[88]

The good of women as a group (in a sense, a type of individual good to be understood in relation to the common good) is not in opposition to the common good. Rather, feminist ethics insists that these two goods are in an integral and dialectical relationship. The authentic common good cannot occur, and is not even being approached, to the extent that the benefit of some is purchased at the expense of women. Similarly, the good of women cannot be achieved over against the *common* good. As Aquinas explained, the good of the individual (or in this case, of women) *requires* the good of the whole to which it exists in necessary relationship. At the same time, feminists might find in Aquinas support for their claim that circumstances of society that have shaped and endorsed the unjust treatment of women, and that depend upon such treatment for their maintenance, must be changed, even if this change results in relative discomfort for those who benefit from what has existed. Aquinas's conception of the common good holds that at times it is necessary for a person to relinquish (or to have taken from them) some private good, for the sake of the common good. The challenge of actually embodying this feminist conception of justice and the common good will require different practices in different settings. From sub-Saharan Africa, to Brazil, to North America, to China, different historical responses are required in different contexts to pursue justice and the common good in a way that offers redress to the historical reality of the suffering of women.

CONCLUSION

In this chapter, I employed a hermeneutical method to recommend that the common good be seen as a moral norm that is valuable in shaping the ethical horizon or imagination today. Even more specifically, I have tried to demonstrate that through the use of a critical feminist hermeneutics, the principle of the common good functions as a valuable resource for the pursuit of justice on behalf of women.

The heart of this chapter lies in the critique of Aquinas's anthropology and in the amended anthropology that has been proposed. This anthropology is the foundation for understanding the common good because Aquinas's work is an exploration of the ideal relationship between the individual person and the community. The common good, therefore, is sustainable as an ethical principle to the extent that it is based on a valid conception of the normatively human and of what, in principle, human flourishing requires.

In the next chapter, I will consider the issue of health care for women in the United States, thus moving from the conceptual to the practical. The guiding question is simple: How would an analysis of the health care crisis in the United States be affected by the use of the retrieved principle of the common good?

CHAPTER 4

The Retrieved Principle of the Common Good and Health Care in the United States

Now that we have retrieved Aquinas's principle of the common good through the proposed feminist hermeneutics, we should inquire about its significance for the community. What is this retrieved principle capable of? What does it offer the human community? On the one hand, the distinction between fundamental ethics and applied ethics ought to be left intact; certainly the two moments in ethics are distinct and should not be blurred into one another, nor should one be reduced to the other. On the other hand, from several quarters we find an expectation if not a demand that theoretical considerations be extended into a logical or reasonable terminus in concrete or applied realms. Hans-Georg Gadamer insists that "understanding always involves something like the application of the text to be understood to the present situation of the interpreter."[1] Taking legal hermeneutics as his model, he says that theological interpretation is like the act of a judge interpreting a law. After the history and meaning of the law is studied, the interpretation of the judge has to do with its applicability. But application here, Gadamer says, "does not mean understanding a given universal in itself and then afterward applying it to a concrete case. It is the very understanding of the universal—the text—itself."[2] Understanding the meaning and truth of the past is constituted precisely by understanding its significance and relevance for life in the present-day situation.[3]

What Gadamer discusses as application has resonance in the methodology of liberation theologians who employ a "hermeneutic circle" that requires not only the moment of analysis but implementation of a new practice informed by the analysis—which then itself is the focus of further assessment.[4] Liberation theologian Míguez Bonino maintains that the moment of strategy for social change completes the process of ethical reflection by bringing together relevant sources to offer a synthetic moral judgment about what should be done differently to promote the greater flourishing of a previously neglected constituency.[5] In this, Bonino echoes Martha Nussbaum's method for determining the criteria that should both inform the community about the existence of suffering and injustice in their midst and guide the choices of strategic action. The basic ethical criterion or principle of justice for Bonino is the "maximizing of universal human possibilities and the minimizing of human costs."[6] He uses the term 'universal human possibilities' to refer to distinctively human goods, "such as freedom; better human conditions, such as employment and housing; and space for human community, guaranteed by respecting human rights. Under 'human costs' he would include the loss of human goods, material conditions, and human rights."[7] As a constitutive element in the methodology of liberationist ethics, the movement to strategic planning and action to address a situation of suffering is informed by foundational convictions regarding the human good, and by careful assessment and analysis of a particular situation of suffering.

This chapter is not a strict application of the retrieved principle of the common good. Rather, it offers a specific situation of anxiety, distress, and in real ways, suffering, specifically, that of health care in the United States. I recognize that the proposal to address this particular social reality could be met with criticism: it could be argued that it represents such a uniquely first-world situation that it invalidates the attempt to argue for the significance of the retrieved principle of the common good as a principle that might or should be used in developing analyses of situations of suffering and strategic responses in any society. However, if it can be shown that the retrieved principle of the common good, applied in this situation, produces different questions, different perspectives, different demands on the community to which a response is required, there is no logical reason to conclude that it would not produce the same results in other settings. That, in fact, is the explicit goal of this entire work—to demonstrate that a feminist liberationist perspective on the principle of the common good causes different situations to be seen as more troubling than they are usually considered, and that the questions raised by this interpretation of the common good and the process of investigation that is necessary are different from what would occur in traditional Christian social ethics. This perspective causes different priorities to be exercised in the development of strategic responses; it places different demands on the community and in doing so demands that the community—to the extent that the community chooses to be faithful to its own beliefs—alter its dedication of resources to respond to these situations.

This chapter emphatically does not offer a complete analysis of the health care system in the United States, but it offers a way of considering this particular situation and any social reality that deeply affects in a negative way the lives of many members of the community. This same analysis could be used to consider welfare reform, education, debt relief, female genital mutilation, and other social realities whose contours are often hidden from view. The retrieved principle of the common good recalibrates the measure of the good of the society and the balance for moral and practical attention by the community. The experience of those who suffer because they are deprived of some of the vitally necessary goods of the community is a primary criterion of social moral evaluation.

Health care is the focus here because it strikes at the heart of being human—being alive, being healthy enough to participate in and enjoy life, being treated with dignity when one is vulnerable because of illness, being able to have the health of one's children adequately protected. While many other social issues might have been examined, adequate health is a prerequisite for most of them. The use of the retrieved principle of the common good orients attention to the experience of suffering and lack—here, not the suffering of a particular illness generally, but the suffering that occurs when members of a group (and here, many members of large groups of people) experience the anguish of worrying about whether they or their dependents will be able to receive health care when they need it. This is also a type of anguish that goes beyond worry about possible lack of health care to the anguish of experiencing oneself or one's dependents as bearing the consequences of the injustice of inadequate health care and being unable personally to change the situation, particularly when suffering from a disease that could have been prevented with better health care or earlier treatment.

THE CHANGED REALITY OF HEALTH CARE IN THE UNITED STATES

There is probably general agreement that health care in the United States is in a state of crisis. In the past, health insurance was generally a presumed and expected benefit that came with employment. While those who were hospitalized often spent longer in the hospital than patients do today, the technologically based medical treatments that were available were less numerous and less normative. X-rays were for the most part the extent of noninvasive diagnostic tools available. Those who did not have health care coverage generally were those who did not work. Charity wards in hospitals were available for those who did not have some form of health insurance.

While a universal right to health care is not a legally defined and protected right in the United States, throughout U.S. history the government has gradually provided health care coverage for specific groups of people who were judged to be particularly vulnerable, for those serving in the military, and for veterans.[8] In 1965, legislation was passed enabling the government to provide health insurance for two specific groups of people—those over sixty-five and the poor—through Medicare and Medicaid. The existence of Medicare and Medicaid leaves many with the impression that a limited but adequate form of universal coverage already exists in the U.S.

Today, however, health care insurance can no longer be presumed or expected to be a paid benefit accompanying employment. When it does accompany employment, it provides only a limited contractual right to some health care. An increasing number of employers from the 1950s onward began to offer health insurance to employees because of the preferential tax treatment that accrued to employers who offered employee health benefits. This increased the number of for-profit insurers, and competition for low-risk groups intensified. The competition for these groups has led to more and more exclusions based on preexisting conditions, which has also come to involve the exclusion of those who are judged likely to develop certain medical conditions. As an alternative to paying escalating premiums for health insurance for employees from an outside provider, many firms have chosen to self-insure, saving them the cost of insurance company commissions, overhead, and profits. The Employee Retirement Income Security Act (ERISA) of 1974, which governs employer health benefits, also exempts employer health plans from state insurance regulations and taxes, and provides another financial incentive to self-insure. This means employers are protected from lawsuits by employees for damages when covered benefits are denied. "ERISA also permits employers to cut benefits for specific conditions, even after an employee has become ill."[9]

The situation, however, is very difficult for those who have had health insurance through their employer during their working years (which often includes some form of prescription coverage), and who lose their health insurance upon retirement. Then most Americans turn to Medicare as their primary form of health care coverage, and precisely when their health care needs often increase, their benefits sink dramatically. Medicare is a single-payer, national health insurance program originally intended to cover only persons over the age of sixty-five. It is sometimes mistakenly thought of as a program that guarantees a right to comprehensive health care for those covered, when in fact the program guarantees only a limited coverage for hospital services. This is covered through the Medicare Hospital Trust Fund, Part A. Enrollment in Part A is mandatory for virtually all those sixty-five and older. It requires no premiums and it establishes an entitlement to most *hospital* services, hospice care, and a very limited post-acute nursing home and home health benefit. To have coverage for physicians' services and other outpatient services, those using Medicare need to purchase Medicare Supplementary Medical Insurance, Part B, for an annual premium. This premium is subsidized from general revenues, regardless of a person's income. The overwhelming source of Medicare revenue comes from payroll and income taxes on workers under sixty-five.[10]

For persons who are below the poverty level, Medicaid pays the Part B premium, the deductible, and any copayments incurred. However, only one-third of the poor elderly are eligible for this Medicaid coverage. For the near-poor elderly who can't afford the Part B premium and who are ineligible for Medicaid, their entitlement to health care is limited to hospital coverage. Medicare provides very limited coverage of prescription drugs, and it does not cover many preventive and early diagnostic services or long-term care. The hospital coverage is subject to an annual deductible fee, and there is substantial cost-sharing for long hospital stays, no cap on out-of-pocket liability, and no coverage for persons needing very long hospital care. Deficiencies in coverage for expensive items such as prescription drugs and extensive cost-sharing impoverish one-third of the near-poor elderly each year, leading a high percentage of persons over sixty-five to purchase supplementary coverage through private "Medi-Gap" policies.[11] While these policies pay all of Medicare's *cost-sharing* requirements, they do not pay for benefits that Medicare does not cover, specifically prescription drugs and long-term care.

While Medicaid is sometimes considered to be a safety net that provides adequate health coverage for the poor, very strict categorical eligibility and unrealistically low-income requirements greatly reduce the number of poor persons actually eligible for Medicaid. The realities of Medicare and Medicaid point to programs that, while well-intentioned in their genesis and purporting to offer health coverage to several needy groups (the elderly and the poor), in fact offer such limited coverage that those who do use it still often find themselves (or their families) impoverished in order to cover medical bills not included in Medicare's benefits.

The limitations of a person's health coverage often are not understood or appreciated until the person or one of their presumably covered dependents becomes ill. Most Americans report a high level of satisfaction with their current health insurance coverage; it is when a catastrophic illness or accident occurs requiring a wide range of medical, rehabilitative, and support services that they discover how few services their policies really cover. According to Janet O'Keefe: "They also find that hospital and physician charges which the insurer determines are above 'usual, customary, and reasonable' charges, are neither paid by the insurer nor applied to the out-of-pocket limits. Thus, actual out-of-pocket expenses are often far higher than stated limits."[12]

U.S. ATTITUDES TOWARD TREATMENT AND DEATH

In the United States, death is a reality often viewed from two seemingly conflicting but oddly related perspectives. On the one hand, death is seen as a reality to be fended off at any expense, through any treatment, because it is now possible to do so for extraordinarily long periods of time, requiring dollar outlays for treatments that in the past simply did not occur. Treatments are used at much later stages of disease progression and at later points in chronological life to prevent death for a limited amount of time and frequently with doubtful expectations for quality of life, raising questions concerning discretionary judgments in treatment options. Patients themselves or their families may demand technological or medical treatments even though such treatments no longer offer any possibility of improvement in the patient's condition. The other perspective on death in the United States arises from a fear of being overtreated and a demand to face death on one's own terms, rather than on the terms allowed one by an overly aggressive treatment regimen. From this have come the increasing use of do-not-resuscitate orders, advance directives, and living wills, as well as arguments concerning a person's right to die on their own terms (e.g., euthanasia and physician-assisted suicide). The technological and medical possibilities for extending life have become, for some, so unwanted and the fear of becoming trapped in a treatment regimen is so great that support grows for proactive ending of life before the expense and futility of treatment bankrupt everyone concerned. At the same time, growing fears about a culture of "euthanization" provoke questions concerning the need to carry "do not euthanize" cards for fear of not receiving aggressive medical care in an emergency. As Daniel Callahan observes:

> The most striking result of the success of medical technology is the very strong trend toward the combination of longer lives and worsening health. Despite efforts to reduce the burden of sickness, sickness has increased as life has lengthened, and both the duration of illness and the number of disabilities have increased as well.[13]

At times, members of the medical community insist on or recommend treatment options that offer no realistic curative possibility. This may occur because of a physician's sense of a personal failure in the face of the "enemy," death. It may occur because the caregiver him- or herself is convinced that they are obliged morally to use every aggressive treatment option to protect the life of the patient. On occasion the sheer momentum of treatment propels caregivers into initiating treatments that can be legally difficult to discontinue at a later point. And sometimes treatment protocols are initiated because doctors are concerned that they could, at a later point, be sued for malpractice if there is not evidence of aggressive treatment. Whatever the reason in a specific situation, the reality is that in the United States great paradoxes exist in medical care: Some people do not receive important preventive treatment because it is not covered by their insurance or by government-sponsored programs, while others receive treatments of doubtful value that are covered in some form (through an insurance program or through Medicaid) or at great personal and/or social cost. Often the reality of the common good in health care is lost, if it ever was a factor.

Aggressive and expensive treatment options are not only realities affecting the patient and/or their family, but the availability of health care services for others. The problem facing the entire health care system in the United States is one of determining what justice means for all members of the community in the area of health care. "In the last analysis," Albert Jonsen writes, "the principle of equitable access is noble. It is probably the best statement of the principle of justice in health care that our present wisdom can generate. But the ability to carry the principle into practice eludes us, given our current health-care budget system."[14]

HEALTH CARE AS AN ELEMENT OF THE COMMON GOOD

Should health care be understood as a fundamental human right, an element or aspect of the "common good" to which all people in a society are entitled? In the United States, health care has not been identified as a right to which a person is entitled by virtue of being a citizen, a legally defined right for which people can sue if it is denied them. But whether the right is legally defined as an entitlement of the citizens, the question remains as to whether this social reality in fact should be understood *morally* as a basic human right, irrespective of whether a country chooses to grant it the status of a legal right. According to Charles Dougherty:

> One of the most important issues at stake in the contemporary health care debate is the claim that the intrinsic value of persons requires a right to a basic level of health care. The argument is simple but powerful. Respect for the incalculably great value of each person creates a duty not only to refrain from destroying health—a negative right— but also a duty to take reasonable steps to preserve and restore health by ensuring access to basic health care. Failing to act on this duty, by allowing lives to be shortened or diminished in quality because of lack of access to basic health care, expresses callous disregard for the dignity of human life. Thus, the intrinsic value of the person supports the claim of a positive legal right of access to some level of health care.[15]

The World Health Organization in 1958, and before that the United Nations in the Universal Declaration of Human Rights in 1948,[16] identified good health as a fundamental human right: "The enjoyment of the highest attainable standard of health is one of the fundamental rights of every human being without distinction of race, religion, political belief, economic or social condition."[17] This "highest attainable standard of health" was described as "a state of complete physical, mental and social well-being and not merely the absence of disease or infirmity."[18]

While there is no mention of health care in the United States Declaration of Independence or in the Constitution, historically the government has taken increasing responsibility for providing certain services for the citizens, such as clean water, or in insisting on quarantine during outbreaks of contagious diseases, and requiring the immunization of children.[19] These actions were taken because without them the physical health of the populace would have been jeopardized and weakened, and the circumstances necessary for good and secure living would have been impossible to maintain. The President's Commission on the Study of Ethical Problems in Medicine and Biomedical and Behavioral Research, established under President Jimmy Carter, reported in 1983 as its first and principal recommendation, that society has an obligation to assure equitable access to health care for all its citizens.[20]

I would argue that access to a decent minimum of health care is a basic human right that should be given legal status and has already been recognized as such by many countries. It is inadequate to reject such a suggestion by arguing that health and health care are not mentioned in the U.S. Bill of Rights drafted in the late 1700s:

> Human rights are universal because they are understood to derive from the inherent dignity of the human person. Because all human beings have the same nature and dignity by virtue of their humanity, they have the same rights. Nevertheless, the delineation and interpretation of those rights reflect a particular political conception of what it means to be a human being. . . . [I]n the late eighteenth century rights were interpreted as fences or protection for the individual from the unfettered authoritarian governments that were considered the greatest threat to human welfare. In late twentieth century democratic governments do not pose the same problems and there are many new kinds of threats to the right to life and well being. Moreover, varying resource levels historically and contemporarily amongst societies at different levels of development translate into different capabilities for promoting human and societal development; the commitment to providing basic and adequate health care or other types of positive entitlements is far more appropriate and possible for a late twentieth century advanced industrial economy than for an eighteenth century agrarian economy.[21]

Several of Martha Nussbaum's proposed human functioning capabilities point to the significance of having access to health care: among these are the ability to live to the end of a human life of normal length, being able to have good health, being able to avoid unnecessary and nonbeneficial pain, and having choices in matters of reproduction.[22] As Carl Cochran notes:

> [H]ealthcare is part of the proper functioning of a community life. People who are free from disease and whose injuries are repaired are better able to pursue their own goods, to contribute to the common good, and to share communal interactions with fellow citizens. Because modern medicine can do much to repair injury and cure illness, it is an essential aspect of the common good of modern societies.[23]

From a theological perspective, access to a decent minimum of health care is a fundamental human right because an individual is created in God's image and has a claim on the conditions that will allow her to live in human dignity and well-being as befits a creature of inestimable value. A healthy person is more able to participate in society, contribute to it, and turn her attention to God in praise and thanksgiving. But good health is not something simply to be devoutly desired and hoped for. Leaving good health to good luck is inadequate. In each social and cultural setting, means exist for protecting good health and receiving treatment when one becomes ill. Good health, then, is directly linked to appropriate and adequate health *care.*

SOCIAL VALUES IN THE UNITED STATES

The dominant social values in the United States are autonomy, individualism, and unrestrained personal freedom. This is evident in the ferocity of the arguments that erupt when limits on personal choice are broached: for example, proposals for restrictions on gun ownership, the abortion debate, and arguments supporting euthanasia and physician-assisted suicide. The only limit usually placed on the scope of individual choice is that one's personal freedom and choices should not interfere with the personal freedom and choices of someone else. As Daniel Callahan writes:

> For lack of a more graceful term, I will call those values a "minimalistic ethic." That ethic can be stated in a simple proposition: One may morally act in any way one chooses so far as one does not do harm to others. . . . It seems to be saying that the sole test of the morality of an action, or of a whole way of life, is whether it avoids harm to oth-

ers. If that minimal standard can be met, then there is no further basis for judging personal or communal moral goods and goals, for praising or blaming others, or for educating others about higher moral obligations to self or community.[24]

Such privileging of autonomy and individual choice is at the heart of much of the resistance to implementing meaningful health care reform, particularly through universal coverage. Many in the U.S. hold the simple and unquestioned belief that they are entitled to any form of treatment they desire, regardless of the impact of that choice on the pool of dollars available for health care generally:

> We are faced with a paradoxical situation in which the power to make individual treatment decisions exists in the absence of any guaranteed access to medical care for all citizens. The result is an almost unrestricted right for those within the system, but no guarantee of initial access to anyone except the well insured or those with specific entitlement programs. The right of specific patients to choose is provided with total disregard for the general right of access for all.[25]

Initially the concept of autonomy emerged in bioethics as a protest against unrestrained research (such as the Tuskegee experiments) and paternalistic physicians who made decisions for patients or conducted research on them without their consultation or knowledge, sometimes couched as protection of patients from difficult realities or matters they supposedly could not understand. Thomas Murray contends:

> It [autonomy as a predominant value in bioethics] found deep ideological resonances within American popular, legal and political culture: our celebration of the individual, our anger at infringements by others, our constitutionalized protections of personal liberty, and our faith in markets as fair and efficient methods for distributing social goods from bathtubs to—babies? Autonomy was an exceptionally apt tool with which to confront the problems bioethics faced at its birth. But it is not the all-purpose solution that some of its enthusiasts claim.[26]

If the chance to enjoy good health, and therefore access to meaningful health care, relatively speaking,[27] is a fundamental human right, it is not an absolute individual right (one which trumps all other rights), just as, in the Roman Catholic moral tradition, life is a very high value, but not an absolute value. As a member of a community, a person does not have the right to such a full claim on all the medical care that they *desire* to the degree that it imperils or diminishes the common good of others. At the same time a basic degree of health is necessary if people are to have the possibility of living out their lives with a measure of fullness, vigor, and dignity, making full use of the choices that are part of their life, contributing appropriately to the community. Those who are sick (chronically ill, victims of accidents, or those terminally ill) have fewer choices than healthy people. Their life energy is far less available for ordinary choices (or for creative and noble ones). If a basic standard of health is the fundamental right of citizens, then all of the people must be enabled to enjoy this right.

Giving health and access to health care the status of a universal human right and a component of the common good of the society means, by extension, that the means of *securing* this good are also part of the common good.[28] For a society to pursue the common good of only a limited segment of its members or to ignore patterns of poor health/lack of health care for whole groups of people is morally unjustifiable and ultimately self-defeating.

An adequate base or "decent minimum" of health care in the United States would guarantee something more inclusive for the entire populace than exists now but less indulgent than the individualistically oriented health care choices that frequently occur now. Mary Ann Baily addresses the goals of establishing a basic or decent minimum of health care as a progressive reality:

> [T]he "decent minimum" should not be seen as a list of conditions and treatments to be developed once and for all and imposed on the health care system. Only when the adequate level is seen as an entire standard of care can appropriate trade-offs be made among health benefits and between health benefits and other kinds of benefits. Given this, defining adequacy requires detailed information on both medical technology and preferences, with the definition open to constant revision, since medical technology, resource availability, and preferences vary over time. What is needed, in other words, is an ongoing *process* capable of defining a *standard of care* that *evolves over time* to incorporate changes in technology, preferences and resource availability.[29]

The retrieved principle of the common good offers a principle of personal and corporate moral *formation*[30] to the community, supplying a corrective to the contemporary emphasis on individualism and auton-omy. This is expressed by Ron Hamel:

> [F]rom the point of view of the common good, the good of each is bound up with the good of the whole community. The common good seeks both the good of all and the good of each, in contrast to the tendency in American society for each to pursue his or her own good without much consideration for its impact on others and on the whole. . . . Abstract as it may be, the notion of the common good, as part of a world view, can be a significant *formative and transforma-tive* influence. It keeps before our eyes essential dimensions of who we are as individuals and communities, dimensions that are easily ne-glected in a society that prizes the individual. It also beckons us to be ever engaged in creating environments in which human beings can flourish.[31]

The contemporary culture generally bestows the label "valuable" on things that are utilitarian or gratifying. The retrieved principle of the common good does not offer that; instead, it orients the community to a commitment to ongoing social-moral discernment, praxis, and evalu-ation, using the experiences of those who are most excluded from the benefits of the community as the evaluative measure of the degree to which the common good is authentically being sought. Correlative to this, contemporary Western society primarily values things that have distinct, quickly achieved end points. In a culture with an increasingly short attention span, things that require sustained awareness, ongoing reflection, assessment, and evaluation, incremental growth toward a goal, subtle distinctions, patient and slow progress, conundrums and difficult conflicts are dismissed as unwanted and unvalued because they are "unuseful": they do not quickly yield a clearly defined result. In light of that, the common good stands as a countercultural discipline: "[T]he common good refers to the overarching goal of social action, the good common life of society itself. In this sense, the common good is never attained. Imperfections are always present; progress is always possible (although never guaranteed)."[32] As a formative agent, the common good shapes the social and moral imagination of the commu-nity to a commitment to the long haul: it fosters an approach to social problems that is less easily seduced by quick fixes that benefit only a limited segment of the community, and holds the patience and courage of the community to a longer and broader vision of what constitutes the "good," requiring sustained behaviors of generosity, even sacrifice.

U.S. HEALTH CARE TODAY

Often health care is thought of as an unlimited resource in the United States. Surely there are enough doctors, nurses, and hospitals. However, adequate health care in the United States is a limited resource primarily because of choices in spending. Health care spending rises annually in the U.S. at double-digit rates, consuming an increasing percentage of the nation's total economic output.[33]

To place this in perspective, health care spending in Canada, Britain, Germany, Sweden, France, and Japan in the 1990s ranged between 6 and 9 percent, while providing universal health insurance for their populations.[34] The limits of the current system of health care in the United States are becoming frighteningly apparent, and the need for significant reform that provides adequate coverage to every person also appears increasingly evident. And yet while this appears obvious at one level, it is far from obvious in terms of public policy or public sentiment. Health care is viewed by many, claims Charles Dougherty, as one more among the array of services that are properly controlled by market forces:

> From virtually every corner of the reform debate there is insistence on preservation of traditional prerogatives and personal freedoms. Physicians want to retain or restore autonomy of practice. Hospitals want market choices but protection from market discipline. Suppliers of medical devices and pharmaceuticals want the widest range of proprietary control in the development and marketing of products and drugs. Insurers want release from cost shifting and mandated benefits and freedom to exclude high-risk individuals. Patients and consumers of health insurance want the greatest range of coverage at the lowest cost and access to the highest quality of medical care—without gatekeepers, waiting lists, or rationing of care. American taxpayers do not want to sacrifice the freedom represented by their disposable incomes, and many are reluctant to abandon unhealthy habits. In short, the politics of American health care is dominated by an individualism that asserts self or group interest over the common good—or simply identifies the one with the other.[35]

Market forces based on an exercise of personal freedom have produced the current situation in which approximately 41 million Americans are without health insurance,[36] and as many as 70 million people may be substantially underinsured.[37] Those who have health insurance often are very vulnerable in regard to adequate coverage by their health care provider: Tests recommended by one's physician may be disallowed by the health care provider. Prescription coverage (if available) may be only for drugs listed on the provider's formulary of approved drugs or generic alternatives when the prescribing physician believes greater benefit would be obtained by using a specified drug that is prohibitively expensive for the patient. A person may reach coverage limits for themselves or a dependent because of the need for long-term care, rehabilitation, or a catastrophic illness that exceeds one's coverage and yet leaves need uncovered. Many face a loss of health care coverage through job change; many fear disallowance of preexisting conditions in themselves or their dependents, particularly if their employer changes health care providers; and millions face inadequate coverage for psychiatric and mental health needs. Private health care coverage ends for many at retirement, often leaving the person (and often a dependent spouse) searching for affordable health care coverage to supplement Medicare, particularly for expenses such as prescriptions, precisely when income has been reduced and health needs increase. Janet O'Keefe writes:

> The lack of security in the private insurance market has recently become even more acute for retired workers under the age of 65, some of whom retire due to poor health. As of 1993, the Federal Accounting Standards Board requires companies to include the cost of retiree health benefits as liabilities on their balance sheets. As a result, many employers are cutting back or entirely eliminating retiree health benefits. Recent Congressional hearings highlighted the problems faced by retired persons with serious health conditions who are unable to purchase private insurance because they are considered "medically uninsurable," and who will not be eligible for Medicare for many years. Even for those retirees who may not be excluded for health reasons, the cost of health insurance is often prohibitive, amounting sometimes to one half of their annual pension. Some retirees have had to re-enter the labor force, solely to obtain health insurance.[38]

The number of uninsured continues to rise, even as national unemployment rates have dropped to generational lows. Who are the people without health insurance? They are mostly adults, and not poor (80 percent of the uninsured have family incomes above the poverty level; half of them are from families with incomes twice the poverty level).[39] They are disproportionately nonwhite and increasingly they are employed. Twenty-two million workers (17 percent of the workforce) are without health insurance. Fifty percent of people without health insurance are from families with a full-time worker, and another 25 percent are from families with a part-time or part-year worker.[40] Lack of health insurance, and therefore lack of access to health care, is no longer limited to the unemployed.

Employment-based health insurance was a wonderful reality while it existed as the virtual norm, but it can no longer be depended on as such. This has happened mainly for two reasons: The greatest number of new jobs created since 1985 have been in small businesses, non-unionized industries, and in the service sector (generally low-paying jobs with few benefits). Second, health care costs have risen—and are rising—exponentially, making it almost impossible for many workers who do not receive health care as part of a benefit package from an employer to afford it out of their own pocket.[41]

Attention to the numerical dimensions of health insurance today makes it abundantly clear that the old order has passed away—the security of having one's health needs and those of one's family covered unlimitedly by health insurance that was part of a compensation package is not the norm for many people in the United States. Health care is uncertain or absent for many, and good health is at risk for increasing numbers of people.

WOMEN AND HEALTH CARE IN THE UNITED STATES

In the United States, social issues often do not receive attention and concern until they impact the wealthy and the middle-class, or until an advocacy group finds a way to demand attention for a situation it considers unjust. The application of the retrieved principle of the common good to this issue leads to an approach that differs from the standard one in two areas—the "provoking" situation, and the process that would be followed because of it. As a matter of process, the retrieved principle of the common good searches out and focuses on situations of those who suffer as a distinct constituency, rather than focusing on individuals who feel their situation is unfair. Obviously each constituency is composed of individuals with individual situations that, when brought together, point to a group being excluded from the benefits of the common good. However, the retrieved principle of the common good, based as it is on a liberationist orientation, has a different point of reference than a liberal interpretation of the common good. To the extent that the principle of the common good has been invoked in liberal society, it has frequently focused on individual rights. The retrieved principle of the common good focuses much more on groups within the community who are excluded from participation in the benefits of the community in some way, rather than focusing on the ways in which the rights of individual persons may have been violated. The proposed retrieval of the principle of the common good would be triggered by the judgment that this *group* is suffering, rather than that this *person* is demanding redress. Second, the retrieved principle of the common good, functioning in a liberationist methodological framework, requires that the process of responding to the suffering of the constituency that has been identified (including the development of new social policy) must continually refer to the experience of the group that has most suffered as the measure of the adequacy of the reforms. This includes developing assessment protocols that seek out and use the narrative accounts of this constituency as significant data for evaluation of the new policies.

The retrieval of the common good developed here is based on the contention that women are a constituency within the community (any community) who usually bear the brunt of unjust treatment and disenfranchisement from aspects of the common good of a society. The particular orientation of the retrieval developed here, then, requires that the women's experience of suffering—particularly the experience of poor women and women of ethnic and racial minorities—must be sought as a gauge for the adequacy of social relationships in a society. The "provoking reality" would most likely be visible only to those who chose to examine a social reality of the community from a liberationist perspective and, further, to those who are persuaded that it is in examining the situation of women in a community that the experiences and circumstances of those most disenfranchised are exposed.

Thus far in this chapter, I have proposed that access to a decent minimum of health care be viewed as a dimension of the common good and a fundamental human right. Without this, it would not be possible to pursue the next point: Ample evidence suggests that many women have distinct problems in achieving adequate health care coverage and adequate health care treatment in the United States, and therefore women have distinct obstacles in maintaining good health and suffer distinct hardships and often physical consequences because of this lack.[42] This evidence includes the data that women use more health care services than men, and pay more for them as a proportion of their income; have less access to health insurance through their own employers than men do;[43] are more likely than men to have some insurance, but are twice as likely to be underinsured;[44] have generally lower incomes than men and constitute a majority of part-time and service workers whose employers provide either no health insurance or only catastrophic-care coverage (not preventive care, such as yearly mammograms).[45] Employment in the service, retail trade, and wholesale trade sectors is growing rapidly in the current economy. However, while many new workers generally, and particularly many women, have found employment there, many employers in these sectors (particularly small businesses) do not offer health insurance, or if it is offered, it is frequently one of the first benefits to be cut due to rising health insurance premiums that small employers cannot afford to pay. This has had the effect of increasing the number of uninsured people, and particularly the number of uninsured women (who make up the majority of workers in lower-paying and service jobs). If the male wage-earner in a household finds employment in this sector, frequently he does not receive health insurance, and obviously his dependents do not. They become part of the growing number (noted earlier) of the employed who are without health insurance. Many women who obtain insurance through a spouse are vulnerable to the loss of their coverage (and the coverage of their children) if the marriage dissolves or if employers decrease or eliminate dependent coverage.[46] Fourteen million women of childbearing age remain without any coverage, and five million have insurance that excludes coverage for prenatal care and delivery.[47] Twelve million working-age women do not have health insurance of any kind, and a disproportionate number of these are women of color. Medicare provides better coverage for illnesses that are more common in men than it provides for those that are more prevalent in women. This is because acute illnesses more common in elderly men (e.g., lung cancer, pneumonia, prostate disorders, myocardial infarction) require lower out-of-pocket patient expenses than chronic diseases more common in elderly women (e.g., breast cancer, depression, hypertension, arthritis).[48] Women are least likely to have health insurance during their prime childbearing years, and women under the age of thirty are the most likely to be uninsured. Both women and their children are likely to suffer if health care is difficult to obtain.[49]

Supplemental policies that supposedly help senior citizens cover gaps in their major health care coverage add to these discrepancies.

Sixty percent of persons over sixty years of age and 71 percent of those over eighty-five are women. Therefore, women who are senior citizens are more likely to be using limited income to pay for premiums for supplemental policies. Demographic trends predict an increasing proportion of elderly women in the future, as baby boomers cycle into the ranks of senior citizens.[50]

Proposals such as the rationing of health care based in part on age have been broached as an option for dealing with this expense. Most proposed implementations of this suggestion, while not explicitly directed at women, would have disproportionate negative effects on women. A greater number of women than men would be subjected to age-based rationing, because the population of older adults includes more women, who live longer than men. Moreover, older women rely more heavily than older men on publicly funded insurance to pay their health care expenses.[51]

A further issue in regard to the use of health care by women is that, as M. E. Lutz writes,

> women assume a disproportionate burden as caretakers for family members of all ages: the young, the sick and the elderly. This often disrupts employment and consequently, insurance coverage. The caregiver's role may also present nonfinancial obstacles to obtaining necessary care, especially preventive services.[52]

The retrieved principle of the common good, used here in regard to women and health care, could be used on behalf of other underserved and neglected constituencies to highlight their distinct needs and the ways they are underserved by the health care system and other social systems in the United States. Particular constituencies among women in general (e.g., constituencies broken down according to ethnic and racial background, age, education level, sexual orientation, marital status, and other distinguishing factors) make the reality of women in regard to health care quite varied. These differences in themselves require investigation to determine how different women are affected differently in regard to health care.

This moment in examining health care in the United States corresponds to Edward Schillebeeckx's sense of anger and outrage, the sense of "this should not be" that provokes the judgment that something is wrong with the given order that must be redressed. This awareness, that the experience of women in relation to health care is pervasively one of lack and suffering, means that fair and equitable participation by women in the benefits of health care in this society cannot be allowed to occur accidentally, as a by-product of general health care reform. Rather, using the retrieved principle of the common good, the experience of women functions as a primary element of exposition of the reality of health care and the common good and an evaluative measure for proposals in health care policy.

BLACK WOMEN AND BREAST CANCER

The question arising from a liberationist perspective is: "Who is suffering here because the situation is the way it is?" In regard to health care, we see that the answer exposes the situation of women in the United States who suffer because health care is organized the way it is. The liberationist question, however, is not finished when it functions at a general level to illuminate a general social reality in which some suffer from exclusion. Once a social construction or a social reality (such as health care) is identified and the first level of response is given, the same question must be brought to the narrower focus of that group that has been identified as particularly impacted negatively.

The situation of women and health care discussed thus far establishes the fact that *women* have distinct problems in regard to health care in the United States, and frequently are significantly disadvantaged in their ability to obtain health care coverage and therefore to receive the health care they need. But in order to let the dynamic of the retrieved principle of the common good function in an integral and appropriate way, we must appreciate that the experiences of women in this area (or any area for that matter) are not all the same. If we proceed as though identifying one group of women (or women as a generic reality) who are excluded is enough to expose the entire story, then, as feminist scholars have pointed out, we fail to address the oppression of women who are additionally marginal within an already marginalized constituency (e.g., women of color, older women, lesbians, ethnic and racial minorities, women in rural settings, refugee women, etc.). Among the constituency of women, therefore, the retrieved principle of the common good requires that we ask: "Among *this* group, who suffers in distinct ways from the fact that health care does not serve *women* adequately? And what tells us this?" There are many answers to these questions, and they are probably all valid or at least worth serious investigation. While the right initial question has been asked, it is necessary to let the variety of women's experiences provide further responses, not in competition with each other for the status of "most disenfranchised" or "most suffering," but for the sake of seeing both distinct problems of this constituency generally, and the overlapping realities among different segments of the population of women in relation to health care.

When we raise the liberationist question "Who suffers because the situation is the way it is?," the situation of black women and breast cancer emerges as one of suffering by a distinct constituency of women in the United States. I will investigate it briefly here as an example of the types of situations that become visible when this retrieved principle of the common good is brought to bear on a social relationship of a larger group. I will use the issue of breast cancer because of its virtual uniqueness to women,[53] and because often it is the disease women find most frightening for many reasons: for example, the socio-psycho-sexual-biological significance of the breast; treatment options and accompanying side effects (lumpectomy, mastectomy, radiation, chemotherapy); the disease progression; and often the experience of having watched another woman (friend, sister, mother, grandmother, etc.) who struggled with and possibly died from breast cancer. These experiences leave an indelible mark in the minds of women, even though in fact heart disease annually claims more victims in this country among women than does breast cancer.

Among women who experience breast cancer, then, the guiding question of the retrieved principle of the common good recurs: Who, in *this* group of women who suffer from breast cancer, are those at particular risk? Who are those who are receiving less adequate treatment, and why? Who are those who, as a group, experience different outcomes, and why? The answers expose the fact that it is women of color, particularly black women, who have the most markedly negative experience dealing with this disease. According to statistics released by the National Cancer Institute, from 1973 to 1995, mortality from breast cancer *decreased* 7.1 percent among white women of all ages in the United States while *increasing* 19.4 percent among black women.[54] This statistic provokes a pause and a number of questions: Why do black women have a higher mortality rate from breast cancer? Is it due to genetics? Is it based in differences in diagnosis and/or treatment? What clues should be pursued? How should the larger community respond? A situation in which a distinct constituency of women endures a rate of mortality from a disease that is significantly higher than the rate for another constituency is a profound indicator that these women are, most likely, not participating in the common good of adequate treatment for breast cancer. They are being denied the full range of life that they had reason to expect for themselves. It is a fundamental moral principle and a point of simple logic that while good health and the best of health care cannot prevent death, unnecessary sickness and suffering and untimely death that can be prevented should be, insofar as it is possible.

Not surprisingly, there is no definitive answer to the question of why these statistics are so different for white and black women. Emerging data point to some directions for further investigation: The overall *incidence* of breast cancer is *lower* for African American women than for white women (9.57 percent for African American women, 13.15 percent for white women).[55] However, the *death rate* for black women is much higher.[56] The five-year survival rate for white women is 85 percent, but the rate for black women is 69.8 percent. This discrepancy holds true for women under the age of fifty, where the survival rate for white women is 82.4 percent, and the rate for black women is 67.2 percent.[57] From 1976 to 1996, cancer mortality trends showed a decrease of 21.5 percent for white women under fifty, and a decrease of only 0.7 percent for black women under fifty.[58]

Reasons for these differences are not yet clear, but it appears that at least part of the reason is that black women often are diagnosed when the cancer is at a more advanced stage, reducing their chances of survival. Why are they diagnosed at later stages of the disease? Once again, this is not clear, but some reasons are being offered. In 1994 the Institute for Women's Policy Research issued a briefing paper on women of color and their access to health care. It claimed:

> Out of 11.7 million uninsured women who are between 18 and 64 years old, about 40 percent or 4.6 million are women of color. . . . African American women are twice as likely as white women to lack health insurance. . . . Related to their higher rates of uninsurance, women of color are more likely than their white counterparts to face negative health outcomes. Because of more limited access to preventive tests, a higher proportion of women of color die from heart diseases, breast cancer and cervical cancer, compared to white women.[59]

When women do not have health insurance, they are less likely to receive regular preventive care such as mammograms. Some cancer researchers report that the Tuskegee experiments are still very alive in the memory of the black community and are invoked when black participants for clinical trials of cancer treatments are sought.[60] The social and medical legacy of the Tuskegee experiments is not simply the memory of how the black men who participated in them were treated shamefully and unjustly, but the fact that those experiments have produced a barrier of skepticism and suspicion that still influences the relationship between some in the black community and medical researchers today.

If we follow the retrieved principle of the common good, using as our standard the situation of those most disenfranchised, those who suffer most egregiously in a situation, then (1) we should clearly identify the disparity in the prognosis for white and black women with breast cancer; (2) we should commit ourselves to the work involved in understanding the underlying causes of this disparity (medical and social); and (3) to the extent that the causes are humanly controllable variables, we should seek to provide opportunities for black women to have the same rate of diagnosis at the earliest possible stages of cancer, the same opportunities for treatments, and the same possibilities of survival as those of white women. If we follow this retrieved principle, we will not be morally content merely with an emphatic statement of "ought" (black women *ought* to have roughly the same prognosis in the face of breast cancer). The retrieved principle of the common good requires that we take meaningful, timely, and appropriate action to move from "ought" to a closer approximation of an embodiment of that end. This "closer approximation" recalls the point made earlier, that the success of our use of the retrieved principle of the common good cannot be judged in terms of whether it produces complete and definitive solutions to a social inequity. This retrieved principle requires the long view, a patient yet paradoxically impatient fidelity to the task of laboring to bring into existence more just relationships, and ultimately an appreciation that no social system can or will perfectly reflect in its concrete relationships the ideal of justice and equity that the transcendent horizon of God as the ultimate common good establishes.

When approached using the retrieved principle of the common good, the reality of the survival rate of black women from breast cancer demands a commitment from the community to pursue *aggressively* the underlying causes of the disparity in survival rates (which means providing the funding necessary for this) and to develop the responses that will bring about a change in those rates (this again requires an appropriation of the money necessary to implement the responses).

THE FUNCTIONING OF THE RETRIEVED
PRINCIPLE OF THE COMMON GOOD

When the retrieved principle of the common good is used as a moral guideline, it yields key moral priorities to be used in the development of social policies and practices generally, and (in the present case) in regard to health care. The key moral priorities that emerge must be creatively and faithfully used to develop policies and practices that, in turn, must constantly be evaluated against the experience of those who are most at risk or who have been most negatively affected by the injustice and inequity. They and their experiences are the moral evaluative measure of the degree of justice a society embodies. In doing this, the needs of the more advantaged are not ignored, but they do not serve as the moral measure or function with the same moral demand within the community. The more advantaged *have been* enjoying the benefits of the common good to a substantial degree. The moral measure of a society is the degree to which it makes the benefits of the common good available to those who have been excluded from the common good.

What key moral priorities would the use of the retrieved principle of the common good produce in regard to the situation of women and health care in the United States? The situation of black women and of women generally is embedded in the larger health care crisis in the United States. In order to more justly serve the health care needs of women in the United States, it is necessary to reshape and redesign health care generally. In doing this, the moral measure of the adequacy of proposed policies and practices is the well-being (or lack of it) of women generally, but particularly of women who are additionally marginal within the constituency of women.

First, the moral priorities that would result from using the retrieved principle of the common good in relation to health care would be based on fundamental principles of justice and equity. These moral priorities are based on the conviction that all citizens have a fundamental human right to adequate health care:

> [I]t is necessary to reassert the moral priority of equity. All Americans, rich, middle class, and poor alike, should be entitled to a decent level of health care. As a nation, it is our collective responsibility to provide all individuals with a level of care necessary to maintain and restore health, and to eliminate anxiety about risk of future illness. . . . Whether the demand for the reform of the health care system is

framed in terms of a "right to health care" or a "societal obligation" to guarantee access to health care is less important than recognizing a moral commitment to one overriding goal: all Americans must have access to the full range of necessary health care services.[61]

Each person has a claim on a decent, minimal level of the goods and services of the community in order to protect their health. While this may sound like a benign priority, not reflecting the radical demand of a liberationist perspective, given the situation in the United States at the current time this moral priority would require a distinctly different expression of justice and equity in the United States—an approach which, up to the current moment, has been strongly resisted. Achieving a basic minimum of health care is not, morally, something that can be left to a person's good luck, and it is also morally inadequate to leave it only or primarily to the exercise of charity or private philanthropy to help those who suffer the absence of a basic human right:

> Without such protection, individuals will be dependent upon the charitable impulses of the community and the availability of public clinics and hospitals established to provide services to the poor and uninsured. Neither private philanthropy nor local governments alone can provide the foundation for a just and adequate health care system. By its very nature charity is a voluntary act. Those who believe they ought to share their resources with others who are less fortunate determine the level of effort and commitment. Although modern hospitals developed as charitable institutions, and physicians historically offered their services free of charge in clinics, it is clear that the level of such provision has always been inadequate to meet the needs of the poor, the uninsured, and those whose insurance protection is inadequate.[62]

The retrieved principle of the common good yields the moral priority that the most underserved constituencies are the evaluative measure of the adequacy of all health care reforms. As Audrey Chapman writes:

> A human rights approach requires a pattern of distribution that confers priority on the disadvantaged and those with greatest need. Hence, improved security and comprehensive benefits for the middle class should not be financed at the expense of the poor. More equitable budgeting would provide subsidies to cover the full cost of premiums, copayments, and fees for persons below the poverty line and

offset the increased costs of participation in regional alliances to the working poor.[63]

Given the situation outlined in this chapter, this means the experiences of women in relation to health care must serve as a significant evaluative principle. Moreover, the experiences of women who presently are *most* underserved and excluded from adequate health services must hold the highest priority in evaluating the adequacy of health care services and reforms.

A final moral priority that emerges from the retrieved principle of the common good used in relation to health care is the demand for the development of different and better means of gathering information on the situations and experiences of all people, and particularly the experiences of women with respect to health care. But it is especially the stories of women who are most disadvantaged presently in regard to health care services that must be sought. "Different and better" means that in addition to sheer statistical information, the narrative testimonies of women must be sought and used as part of the evaluation of health care as a social reality. These stories function as moral data, and those who are responsible for developing health care policy must accord them a significant role in shaping that policy. As important as good statistical information is, it is inadequate by itself to expose the lived experiences that have a moral claim on the community.

Perhaps an analogy will be useful here: It is generally accepted that six million Jews died during the Holocaust (this figure does not include gypsies, homosexuals, mentally handicapped people, and others the Nazis felt were only a burden on society). This is a horrific number, so huge that one struggles to imagine "six million." However, going through the Holocaust Memorial/Museum in Washington, D.C.— where one receives at the entrance a small, passport-like document with a picture of someone who was a prisoner at one of the death camps and a brief synopsis of their story—reshapes one's sense of relatedness to the victims of the Nazis. The number, "six million," is enormous, mind-escaping. It is obviously terrible. The story of the *particular* person one follows as one proceeds through the Holocaust Memorial reorients the focus from the level of the enormous to the level of the individual whose face one sees. Including the narrative element as a moral factor in the development of more adequate health care provisions for women in general, and for women of color in particular, functions in a similar manner, bringing the moral issue back from the level of the overwhelmingly enormous to the level of the visible human person who, as a member of a particular constituency, suffers injustice.

CONCLUSION

This chapter has offered an example of the way in which a fundamental ethical principle, retrieved through a feminist hermeneutics, might be engaged on behalf of women in their pursuit of justice in a practical reality of life: health care. This is a point at which contemplation of the experiences that are part of women's lives leads us to question whether ethical theories make any difference in the practical challenges of life. Specifically, the focus has been on the way in which the principle of the common good, retrieved through a feminist hermeneutics, might address the concrete social issue of health care for women in the United States.

If the method that has been proposed here is judged to be valid in itself, and if the use of the retrieved principle of the common good in regard to women and health care in the United States is accurate (both in the practical data regarding women and health care and the use of the critical principles for evaluating the practical data), then we may rightly conclude that the experience of women must be given priority both in assessing the reality of health care and in devising policy responses to the situation. The experience of women is given this priority because of the presumption—a hermeneutics of suspicion—that the conventional ways of looking at the issue of health care do not reveal the realities of suffering being experienced by a particular constituency: women. In using this liberationist, feminist hermeneutics, we seek to explore the experience of women—and particularly the suffering of women in the realm of health, health care, and health preservation— and to use that experience to make a claim against the larger community. This claim is not for more adequate health care *only* for women. But until the inequities of women's health care in the United States are addressed and rectified, the common good is not being pursued.

Afterword

THE PRINCIPLE OF THE common good holds considerable promise for improving life both in American society and globally, particularly when it is reinterpreted through the lens of women's experience. It has become commonplace today to recognize that a significant cultural blinder in the United States is individualism, and that nation-states internationally are all too often guided by narrow national interests rather than what is best for the global community. The retrieved notion of the common good can serve as a necessary corrective, whether discussing health care policy, as this book has done, or other domestic social issues such as welfare reform, affirmative action, urban poverty, or even such global issues as third world debt, immigration policy, and war in its many forms. A retrieval of Aquinas's principle of the common good, such as has been proposed here, can help in the project of making the world at once more interdependent and more just.

Similarly, the feminist hermeneutical method proposed in this book can be applied not only to the common good, but also to other significant moral principles drawn from the Christian tradition: for example, love, forgiveness, solidarity, justice, and human rights. Reinterpreting these principles from the perspective of the good of the community, particularly of those who are excluded, deprived, or unfairly burdened within the community, requires that the community must attend to the realities of groups whose situations have traditionally not even registered as problems and that it must grant strategic priority to their just demands.

Notes

INTRODUCTION

1. "Postmodernism" is a fluid term, not easily defined. Mary Ann Tolbert writes: "With some oversimplification, postmodernism might be described as the intellectual ferment in science, architecture, art and the humanities, originating in the late 1960's and early 1970's, that radically calls into question many of the Enlightenment foundations of modern Western thought and society. Specifically under attack are the Enlightenment belief in the supremacy of human reason to transcend historical and cultural particularity in order to arrive at objective, value-neutral assessments of 'natural law' or universal 'truth.' . . . The various proponents of postmodernism argue that all human theorizing is culturally constrained and historically limited; that there can be no absolute division between objectivity and subjectivity even in science because the methodological and theoretical assumptions of the observer always shape the outcome of the observations; that methodological and theoretical assumptions, moreover, always involve the privileging of certain values or categories over others; and, perhaps most fundamentally, that language does not merely represent some reality 'out there' but itself makes up that reality as it weaves the very fabric of human interaction in historically specific, socially constructed, and thoroughly political ways." See Mary Ann Tolbert, "Social, Sociological, and Anthropological Methods," in *Searching the Scriptures: A Feminist Introduction*, ed. Elisabeth Schüssler Fiorenza (New York: Crossroad Publishing Company, 1993), 258. The works of Jacques Derrida, Michel Foucault, and Jean-Francois Lyotard are particularly significant in shaping the postmodern sensibility that emphasizes the plurality of expressions of humanity and a distrust of universal claims (particularly anthropological claims).

2. Paul Lakeland's *Postmodernity: Christian Identity in a Fragmented Age* (Minneapolis: Fortress Press, 1997) offers an excellent and insightful summary

of interpretations of postmodernity and the Christian expressions of and responses to postmodernity.

3. Elisabeth Schüssler Fiorenza's work represents this response in her suggestion of a development of a canon within the canon. According to this view, within the Scriptures traditionally deemed canonical, some are judged revelatory, meeting the criteria for canonicity because they offer a vision of humanity that does not view women in a derivative, diminished, or negative manner—a vision that is inclusive of women as bearers of the revelation of God's salvation and equal recipients of all that salvation means.

4. Both Margaret Farley and Rosemary Radford Ruether represent this response in their claims that any text or doctrine that does not promote the full dignity and flourishing of women cannot be considered revelatory by the community. See note 5.

5. Rosemary Radford Ruether, *Sexism and God-Talk: Toward a Feminist Theology* (Boston: Beacon Press, 1983), 19. Margaret Farley endorses such an approach to feminist reinterpretations of scripture in her article "Feminist Consciousness and the Interpretation of Scripture," *Feminist Interpretation of the Bible*, ed. Letty M. Russell (Philadelphia: Westminster Press, 1985), 41–54.

6. Mary Daly and Carol Christ are feminist scholars who have chosen this option in relation to the Christian tradition. For representative texts, see Mary Daly, *Beyond God the Father: Toward a Philosophy of Women's Liberation*, 2d ed. (London: Women's Press, 1986); Daly, *The Church and the Second Sex* (Boston: Beacon Press, 1986); Daly, *Gyn/Ecology: The Metaethics of Radical Feminism* (Boston: Beacon Press, 1978); Carol Christ, *Rebirth of the Goddess: Finding Meaning in Feminist Spirituality* (Cambridge, Mass.: Perseus Publishing, 1997); and Christ, *Womanspirit Rising: A Feminist Reader in Religion* (San Francisco: HarperSanFrancisco, 1992).

7. Stanley Hauerwas is an ethicist whose large body of work reflects this postmodern position. For representative selections of his thought, see Stanley Hauerwas, *A Community of Character: Toward a Constructive Christian Social Ethic* (South Bend, Ind.: University of Notre Dame Press, 1988); Hauerwas, *The Peaceable Kingdom* (South Bend, Ind.: University of Notre Dame Press, 1984); and Hauerwas, *After Christendom? How the Church Is to Behave If Freedom, Justice, and a Christian Nation Are Bad Ideas* (Nashville: Abingdon Press, 1991). George Lindbeck's thought has been very influential on many postmodern scholars. See especially his *The Nature of Doctrine: Religion and Theology in a Postliberal Age* (Louisville, Ky.: Westminster/John Knox Press, 1984).

CHAPTER 1. FEMINIST THEOLOGICAL HERMENEUTICS

1. David Tracy, "Interpretation (Hermeneutics)," in *International Encyclopedia of Communications*, ed. Erik Barnouw et al. (New York: Oxford University Press, 1989), 343.

2. "Hermeneutics" is usually understood to refer to an interpretive task focused on texts. However, events are also realities that are interpreted, and their interpretations may be varied and may change over time.

3. Roger Haight, *Dynamics of Theology* (Mahwah, N.J.: Paulist Press, 1990), 171–74. On the hermeneutics of suspicion, see note 43.

4. Ibid., 172.

5. This principle is important from a feminist perspective. An interpretation or reinterpretation of a text or tradition that is truly not coherent with the experience of the suffering of women is an interpretation that fails to carry meaning for them.

6. The understanding of the term "classic" will be discussed later in this chapter.

7. A theological method of mutually critical correlation is frequently associated with fundamental theologian David Tracy. Drawing on the work of Paul Tillich, who proposed a method of mutual correlation between the questions in the contemporary situation and the "answers" to be found in the Christian tradition, Tracy describes mutually critical correlation as "a general heuristic guide to alert theological interpreters that they must attend to three realities: first, the inevitable presence of the interpreter's own pre-understanding (situation); second, the claim to attention of the text itself; third, the conversation as some form of correlation (identity, similarity or confrontation)." See David Tracy, "Theological Interpretation of the Bible Today," in *A Short History of the Interpretation of the Bible*, ed. Robert Grant and David Tracy (Philadelphia: Fortress Press, 1984), 171. Tracy also notes: "My own formulation is that the task of contemporary Christian theology demands the critical correlation of the meaning and truth of the interpreted Christian fact (including therefore the texts, symbols, witnesses, and traditions of the past and present) and the meaning and truth of the interpreted contemporary situation." See Tracy, "Particular Questions within General Consensus," in *Consensus in Theology? A Dialogue with Hans Küng and Edward Schillebeeckx*, ed. Leonard Swidler (Philadelphia: Westminster Press, 1980), 34. Finally, Tracy refers to his evolving understanding of the project of mutually critical correlation: "I continue to believe that some form of revised correlational method (i.e., correlating an interpretation of the tradition with an interpretation of our situation) remains the best hope for theology today. I have continued to revise my form of correlation method when it seemed necessary. For example, I have in the last ten years (but not before) always added the important qualifier 'mutually critical' to the word 'correlation' in order to indicate the fuller range of possible correlations between some interpretation of the situation and some interpretation of the tradition. This signals that theological correlation is not always harmonious (much less 'liberal'), but covers the full range of logically possible relationships between situation and tradition from nonidentity (or confrontation) through analogy to identity." See Tracy, "God, Dialogue, and Solidarity: A Theolo-

gian's Refrain," in *How My Mind Has Changed*, ed. James M. Wall and David Heim (Grand Rapids, Mich.: William B. Eerdmans Publishing Company, 1991), 88–99.

8. This is not a term that Nussbaum herself uses for the elements she proposes, but it suggests a set of distinguishable elements that are distinctly human and are necessary for full human flourishing. The term "anthropological constants" is associated with Edward Schillebeeckx, who proposed a set of characteristics that he believes dependably reflect constitutive realities of the human person. These characteristics will be discussed in more detail later in this chapter.

9. In this chapter (and throughout this book) my discussion is oriented toward the interpretation, retrieval, and reconstruction of the classic texts of the community, specifically scripture, and the dogmatic positions of the faith community. While I may at times refer to "texts," I always presume that interpretation includes a much broader scope than merely textual.

10. This judgment is made by many women in the Judeo-Christian community as well as by a good number of men.

11. Sandra Schneiders, *The Revelatory Text* (San Francisco: HarperSan-Francisco, 1991), 69.

12. Sociologist Gregory Baum suggests that the origins of the Enlightenment may be understood as follows: "The two revolutions [democratic revolution and industrial revolution] embodied ideas derived from seventeenth and eighteenth-century Enlightenment thought that rejected traditional values and institutions and looked upon reason as the organ of human self-liberation. Reason here referred to demonstrable science to understand and control nature and society. . . ." Gregory Baum, "Modernity: A Sociological Perspective," in *Concilium* 179, no. 5 (December 1992): 3.

13. Sandra Schneiders, "Feminist Ideology Criticism," *Biblical Theology Bulletin* 19, no. 1 (1989): 5.

14. Ibid.

15. This is not to suggest that there were no feminist responses to scripture before the 1960s. In the 1830s Sarah Grimke, a noted antislavery lecturer and women's rights author, charged that the masculine bias of biblical interpretation was part of a deliberate plot against women. In the 1880s Elizabeth Cady Stanton was a leader in promoting alternative renderings of scripture, renderings that took seriously the experiences and situation of women.

16. Edgar V. McKnight, *Post-Modern Use of the Bible: The Emergence of Reader-Oriented Criticism* (Nashville: Abingdon Press, 1988), esp. chapters 1–3.

17. Schneiders, "Feminist Ideology Criticism," 4.

18. Sandra Schneiders, "Living Word or Deadly Letter: The Encounter between the New Testament and Contemporary Experience," *Proceedings, Catholic Theological Society of America* 47 (1992): 50.

19. Hans-Georg Gadamer, *Truth and Method* (New York: Seabury Press, 1975), 267–74.

20. Ibid., 258–67.

21. "Hence, the horizon of the present cannot be formed without the past. There is no more an isolated horizon of the present in itself than there are historical horizons which have to be acquired. *Rather, understanding is always the fusion of these horizons supposedly existing by themselves.* . . . Projecting a historical horizon, then, is only one phase in the process of understanding; it does not become solidified into a self-alienation of a past consciousness, but is overtaken by our own present horizon of understanding. In the process of understanding, a real fusing of horizons occurs—which means that as the historical horizon is projected, it is simultaneously superseded. To bring about this fusion in a regulated way is the task of what we call historically effected consciousness." Gadamer, *Truth and Method*, 306–7 (emphasis in original).

22. "No classic text comes to us either pure or autonomous. Every classic bears with it the history of its own conflictual history of reception. Indeed, every classic brings a history of effects that we can never fully explicate." David Tracy, *Plurality and Ambiguity* (San Francisco: Harper & Row Publishers, 1987), 14. At a later point in *Plurality and Ambiguity*, Tracy notes, "There is no innocent interpretation, no innocent interpreter, no innocent text" (ibid., 79).

23. Schneiders, *Proceedings*, 51.

24. Gadamer's appreciation of the text or event creating an effective history in which the reader/interpreter functions has been criticized as recommending an uncritical surrender of the reader to the distortions of that effective history. This will be addressed later, in my discussion of ideology criticism.

25. Schneiders, *The Revelatory Text*, 68.

26. Schneiders, *Proceedings*, 51.

27. Schneiders draws for her analysis of these three characteristics of language on the work of the "New Hermeneuts": Hans-Georg Gadamer, Philip Wheelwright, and Paul Ricoeur. See Schneiders, *The Revelatory Text*, xxx.

28. See Gadamer, *Truth and Method*, 456–74.

29. Schneiders, *The Revelatory Text*, 138.

30. "These recontextualizations, like diverse settings for a jewel or different environments for a plant or interpretation of a musical score by a different instrument, will exploit the surplus of meaning which the text now has in virtue of its emancipation from authorial intention." Sandra Schneiders, *Beyond Patching: Faith and Feminism in the Catholic Church* (New York: Paulist Press, 1991), 60.

31. Here Schneiders draws on Philip Wheelwright, *Metaphor and Reality* (Bloomington: Indiana University Press, 1968), 32–69.

32. Paul Ricoeur, *Interpretation Theory: Discourse and the Surplus of Meaning* (Fort Worth: Texas Christian University Press, 1976).

162 ꝏ Notes, chapter 1

33. Schneiders, "Feminist Ideology Criticism," 7, quoting Ricoeur, *Interpretation Theory*, 139.
34. The relationship between sense and reference will be discussed later.
35. Schneiders, "Feminist Ideology Criticism," 7.
36. "If we can no longer define hermeneutics in terms of the search for the psychological intentions of another person which are concealed *behind* the text, and if we do not want to reduce interpretation to the dismantling of structures, then what remains to be interpreted? I shall say: to interpret is to explicate the type of being-in-the-world unfolded *in front of* the text. . . . [F]or what must be interpreted in a text is a *proposed world* which I could inhabit and wherein I could project one of my ownmost [*sic*] possibilities. This is what I call the world of the text, the world proper to *this* unique text." Paul Ricoeur, *Hermeneutics and the Human Sciences*, ed. and trans. John B. Thompson (New York: Cambridge University Press, 1981), 141–42 (emphasis in original).
37. Ibid., 140–42.
38. Schneiders, "Feminist Ideology Criticism," 8.
39. Schneiders, *Proceedings*, 53.
40. Werner G. Jeanrond writes: "According to Gadamer, the ultimate purpose of text-understanding for the reader is the material agreement with the text; and the aim of understanding is described as the fusion of two horizons, i.e., the horizon of the text and the horizon of the reader. . . . But many problems have arisen and a number of questions remain unanswered. First of all, the question of critique. How can the reader protect him or herself against misunderstandings? Why does a text have authority and therefore can demand submission to the tradition it represents? Is the fusion of horizons a happy fusion or could it not at least sometimes be thought of also as a conflict between reader and texts? How does truth manifest itself in the interpretation of texts? . . . According to Gadamer, understanding will always be successful as long as understanding persons are willing to submit themselves to the claims of the text and to enter into the tradition which the text represents. Gadamer's insistence that this kind of hermeneutics ought to be seen as a universal aspect of philosophy has provoked sharp criticism." Werner G. Jeanrond, *Theological Hermeneutics: Development and Significance* (New York: Crossroad Publishing Company, 1991), 66–67. Jürgen Habermas has been the most notable critic of Gadamer's claim to universality in his conception of hermeneutics. "It is therefore not the concern of Habermas to reject Gadamer's concept of understanding in its totality. Rather does he wish to contradict its claim to universality and to demand that a hermeneutics which is critically enlightened in its own regard, 'which differentiates between insight and restriction of vision . . . should integrate into itself the meta-hermeneutical knowledge about the conditions of possibility of systematically distorted communication.'" Werner G. Jeanrond, *Text and Interpretation as Categories of Theological Thinking* (New York: Crossroad Publishing Company, 1988), 23, quoting Jürgen Habermas, *Hermeneutik und Ideologiekritik* (Frankfurt: M. Suhrkamp, 1971), 313f.

41. Rebecca S. Chopp, "Practical Theology and Liberation," in *Formation and Reflection: The Promise of Practical Theology*, ed. Lewis S. Mudge and James N. Poling (Philadelphia: Fortress Press, 1987), 123.

42. David Tracy has offered a succinct definition of critical theory: "Any theory that allows primacy to critical reflection is on the way to becoming critical theory. A critical theory in the full sense, however, is any theory that renders explicit how cognitive reflection can throw light on systemic distortions, whether individual or social, and through that illumination allow some emancipatory action." Tracy, *Plurality and Ambiguity*, 80.

43. The use of a hermeneutics of suspicion has been described by David Tracy: "In a post-Freudian culture the need for a hermeneutics of suspicion—and the need for critical theories (such as psychoanalytic theory and Marxist ideology critique) to spot and possibly heal systematic distortions in our personal and, beyond that, our cultural and social lives—has become an indispensable aspect of many modern interpreters' preunderstandings, including several hermeneutical theorists (such as Habermas). . . . For any interpreter who suspects that there may be systematic distortions in a particular tradition, a hermeneutics of suspicion can be a helpful correlate to a hermeneutics of recovery. At any such points of recognition of systematic distortions (e.g., by a cultural anthropologist) the hermeneutic model of conversation becomes inadequate to describe the full process of interpretation." David Tracy, "Interpretation (Hermeneutics)," in *International Encyclopedia of Communications*, ed. Erik Barnouw et al. (New York: Oxford University Press, 1989), 2:343–48. Elsewhere Tracy notes: "[A]ll experience and all understanding is hermeneutical. To interpret well must now mean that we attend to and use the hermeneutics of both retrieval and suspicion." Tracy, *Plurality and Ambiguity*, 77.

44. Ibid.

45. Schneiders, *Proceedings*, 58. Ricoeur explores the meaning of ideology and ideology critique in *Hermeneutics and the Human Sciences*, esp. chapter 9. He traces the concept of ideology from its relatively neutral connotation to what he considers its natural development as a statement about authority structures and relationships: "All ideology is simplifying and schematic. It is a grid or code for giving an overall view, not only of the group, but also of history and, ultimately, of the world. . . . [T]he interpretative code of an ideology is something *in which* men live and think, rather than a conception *that* they pose. . . . [A]n ideology is operative and not thematic. . . . What ideology interprets and justifies is, above all, the relation to the system of authority. . . . Ideology is defined both by its function and its content" (ibid., 228–30).

46. Schneiders, *The Revelatory Text*, 120.

47. Ibid.

48. Ibid., 157. Schneiders draws here on Ricoeur, *Interpretation Theory*, 71–88, and Ricoeur, *Hermeneutics and the Human Sciences*, 145–64.

49. In *Plurality and Ambiguity*, David Tracy demonstrates the variety of meanings that may be attached to a single event. He uses the example of the

French Revolution, indicating the variety of meanings or interpretations that
are offered for this event, each held by a different constituency or person with
a distinct pre-understanding and perspective of the events leading up to the
French Revolution and the revolution itself. Interpretation, and especially relevant for the purposes of this book, *meaning* is not something that accrues primarily or only to texts, but to events. And just as there are a variety of meanings
(often competing meanings) offered for a text, a variety of meanings may be
offered for an event.

50. Schneiders, *The Revelatory Text*, 158.

51. For feminist hermeneutics this is a particularly important point. Paul
Ricoeur advises that "[t]he sense is the ideal object which the proposition intends, and hence is purely immanent in discourse. The reference is the truth
value of the proposition, its claim to reach reality. Reference thus distinguishes
discourse from language [*langue*]; the latter has no relation with reality, its
words returning to other words in the endless circle of the dictionary. Only
discourse, we shall say, intends things, applies itself to reality, expresses the
world" (Ricoeur, *Hermeneutics and the Human Sciences*, 140). If the assumptions underlying the reference of a text are shown to be invalid (untruthful),
then the meaning of the text is also compromised.

52. Schneiders, *The Revelatory Text*, 163.

53. Ibid., 165.

54. Ibid.

55. Schneiders, "Feminist Ideology Criticism," 8. See Paul Ricoeur, *Conflict of Interpretations* (Chicago: Northwestern University Press, 1954), 21.

56. Schneiders, *The Revelatory Text*, 173.

57. Ibid., 196.

58. Ibid., 174.

59. Ibid., 173.

60. Lisa Sowle Cahill identified Ruether as "perhaps the most prominent
Catholic feminist ethicist," in Cahill, "Notes on Moral Theology: 1989, Feminist Ethics," *Theological Studies* 51, no. 1 (1990): 50.

61. Several feminist authors (including Ruether) pursue extrabiblical
sources (Gnostic gospels, noncanonical materials, sources from other disciplines such as philosophy and literature) to develop a corpus of material which
is able to contribute to a norming perspective. Kathryn Allen Rabuzzi writes of
Ruether: "Looking for sources for the theology that emerges from her particular feminism, Ruether pans the gold of usable tradition from the dross of patriarchy to include Hebrew and Christian scriptures; various 'heretical' Christian
traditions; the major theological themes of Christian theology; ancient Near
Eastern and Greco-Roman religions and philosophies; and such post-Christian
views as liberalism and Marxism." Kathryn Allen Rabuzzi, "The Socialist Feminist Vision of Rosemary Radford Ruether: A Challenge to Liberal Feminism,"
Religious Studies Review 15, no. 1 (1989): 5.

62. Rosemary Radford Ruether, "Feminist Interpretation: A Method of Correlation," *Feminist Interpretation of the Bible*, ed. Letty M. Russell (Philadelphia: Westminster Press, 1985), 111. In this regard Werner Jeanrond notes: "Christian theology . . . needs to engage in hermeneutical reflection because it is concerned (among other things) with the interpretation of the biblical texts and of other religious texts, such as creeds, liturgies, theological writings and spiritual expressions. . . . Even more so than in most interpretations of literary texts, the theological interpretation of the texts of the Christian church has immediate social consequences, namely for the self-understanding of the Christian church, since these texts are seen to provide a major foundation of the church. Thus, the continuous reinterpretation of these texts must affect our understanding of the identity of the church in some way." Jeanrond, *Theological Hermeneutics*, 4.

63. "Criterion of adequacy" is a term used by David Tracy to indicate the need for a sufficient degree of coherence between human experience and the language, concepts, and symbols used to explain and extrapolate theologically from the experience: "[T]he final appeal to our experience is an appeal not so much to what we may verify through our senses as to what we may validate as meaningful to the experience of the self as an authentic self, to what phenomenologists call our 'lived experience'. . . . When we state that an appeal to experience is meaningful, we often mean no more and no less than the fact that the appeal 'resonates' to our own immediate experience as a self." David Tracy, *Blessed Rage for Order: The New Pluralism in Theology* (Minneapolis, Minn.: Winston Seabury Press, 1975), 66. Tracy notes further: "A particular experience or language is meaningful when it discloses an authentic dimension of our experiences as selves. It has 'meaning' when its cognitive claims can be expressed conceptually with internal coherence. It is 'true' when transcendental or metaphysical analysis shows its 'adequacy to experience' by explicating how a particular concept (e.g., time, space, self, or God) functions as a fundamental 'belief' or 'condition of possibility' of all our experience" (ibid., 71).

64. Rosemary Radford Ruether, "The Development of My Theology," *Religious Studies Review* 15, no. 1 (1989): 1.

65. Rosemary Radford Ruether, *New Woman, New Earth: Sexist Ideologies and Human Liberation* (San Francisco: Harper & Row Publishers, 1975), 167.

66. Ibid., 182.

67. Ruether, "The Development of My Theology," 1.

68. Katie Geneva Cannon offers a powerful analysis of the dependence of ideologies of domination on construals of dualism in "Slave Ideology and Biblical Interpretation," *Semia* 47 (1989), 9–23. Her focus is on the use of a dualistic anthropology to produce interpretations of scripture that endorsed the domination of blacks by whites. Her argument, however, is equally applicable to interpretations of scripture to justify the domination of women by men. She identifies ideological myths that promoted biblical interpretations sustaining ra-

cial slavery: (1) Black people were not members of the human race; (2) Africans were by nature framed and designed for subjection and obedience; and (3) Slavery was not a sin because there was no specific biblical prohibition of it.

69. Rosemary Radford Ruether, *Liberation Theology: Human Hope Confronts Christian History and American Power* (New York: Paulist Press, 1972), 17.

70. Ruether also refers to the "prophetic-messianic tradition" as "the critical principle by which biblical thought critiques itself and reviews its vision as the authentic Word of God over against corrupting and sinful deformations." Ruether, "Feminist Interpretation," 117.

71. Rosemary Radford Ruether, *Sexism and God-Talk: Toward a Feminist Theology* (Boston: Beacon Press, 1983), 22–23.

72. Ibid., 24.

73. Ruether, "The Development of My Theology," 3.

74. Edward Schillebeeckx proposes that salvation cannot accurately be understood primarily as a spiritual reality, or reality limited to the eschatological dimensions of existence: "Christian salvation, in order to be salvational, must be *universal* and *total*. Consequently, salvation, in the sense of that which makes whole, should entail as a minimum requirement that no one group be whole at the expense of another one. This does not imply that Christian salvation can be reduced to making of a universally human just society. It does imply, however, that the making of such a society is a minimum ingredient of Christian salvation. This suggests that whole-making, salvation of and for man, is also an *experiential* concept. The Christian concept of salvation would lose its rational meaning (i.e., rationally speaking it would not be a concept of salvation) if there were no *positive* relationship between the 'justification by faith alone' and the construction of a more just, integrated world. Salvation must be at least a partial and fragmentary reflection of that which is experienced by man as whole-making. Salvation that is merely 'promised' loses all reasonableness. Therefore, Christian salvation must satisfy minimum requirements if we wish to prevent this term 'salvation,' and, with it, *Christian* salvation, from dying the death of a thousand qualifications. By introducing salvation as an experiential concept, we are able, on the one hand, to safeguard God's freedom 'to be God,' i.e., a reality which cannot be pinned down to our human concepts of salvation, while, on the other hand, man receives the freedom 'to be human,' i.e., a living creature with his own say in the matter whether a certain type of salvation will or will not take place." Edward Schillebeeckx, O.P., "Questions on Christian Salvation of and for Man," in *Toward Vatican III: The Work That Needs to Be Done*, ed. David Tracy, Hans Küng, and Johannes B. Metz (New York: Seabury Press, 1978), 41 (emphasis in original).

75. Ruether, *Liberation Theology*, 16.

76. Ruether, *Sexism and God-Talk*, 256.

77. Ruether references the two poles of the covenant in the Hebrew scriptures: the covenantal promise of God to be the faithful God of the Hebrew

people, and the correlative covenantal promise of the people to be faithful to God. Part of the promise of God, Ruether contends, is the promise to make the Hebrew people a mighty nation, a this-world reality, not a promise of spiritual salvation. Therefore, the apocalyptic vision Ruether suggests has its origins in the ancient Covenant between God and the people, which includes living out and enjoying the benefits of the Covenant in this life.

78. Ruether, "Feminist Interpretation," 118.

79. I have addressed the meaning of the term "postmodern" in note 1 of the Introduction. The term is most commonly associated in its origins with Jean-Francois Lyotard, who in 1934 used the term to point to the end of the master narratives of modernity. In general terms, "postliberal theologians approach the biblical narratives as narratives, rather than as historical sources or as symbolic expressions of truths which could be expressed non-narratively. . . . [P]ostliberals do not let the stories of *our* lives set the primary context for theology. They insist that the *biblical* narratives provide the framework within which Christians understand the world." William C. Placher, "Postliberal Theology," *The Modern Theologians, Volume 2*, ed. David Ford (New York: Basil Blackwell, 1989), 117. There is a relationship between the terms "postmodern" and "postliberal" inasmuch as both reject universal, ostensibly normative truth claims. Instead, they emphasize the particularity and uniqueness of communities organized around different phenomena or characteristics (religious belief, ethnicity, gender, etc.). Paul Lakeland offers the useful term "countermodern" for those who "celebrate the demise of modernity as an opportunity to return to the securities of an earlier age." Paul Lakeland, *Postmodernity: Christian Identity in a Fragmented Age* (Minneapolis: Fortress Press, 1997), 12–13. This is an inclusive category that could refer to a variety of ideological positions, but identifies this "postmodern" group by their conviction that a return to a much earlier age is desirable. Those whom William Placher identifies as postliberal could be seen as countermodern. Lakeland also describes those (such as David Tracy) who continue to believe that the project of modernity is not yet finished and who wish to prudentially carry it forward in the dramatically changed circumstances that exist today.

80. For an excellent analysis of the debate within theology between the postliberal and hermeneutical positions, see Placher, "Postliberal Theology," 115–128, and William C. Placher, *Unapologetic Theology: A Christian Voice in a Pluralistic Conversation* (Louisville, Ky.: Westminster/John Knox Press, 1989).

81. Other theologians who are frequently associated with the postliberal approach to theology are Karl Barth and Stanley Hauerwas.

82. Representatives of the liberal, hermeneutical approach to theology are Paul Knitter, Schubert Ogden, and John Hick, who suggest the most full engagement with society and who view Christian doctrinal formulations as impediments to this engagement. David Tracy is usually identified as the preeminent

representative of the revisionist, correlational approach between the Christian tradition and the larger society. Tracy would not suggest suppressing doctrinal claims of the Christian community, but he would require that such claims be judged as to whether the warrants for them are presented in a manner that is reasonable to intelligent, rational members of society at large. Postliberal theologians reject this requirement.

83. Stanley Hauerwas has championed this position.

84. For example, feminist theologian Sheila Greeve Devaney argues for the radical historicity of all knowledge and rejects the project of distinguishing any universal anthropological elements. See her "Problems with Feminist Theory: Historicity and the Search for Sure Foundations," in *Embodied Love: Sensuality and Relationship as Feminist Values*, ed. Paula M. Cooey, Sharon A. Farmer, and Mary Ellen Ross (San Francisco: Harper and Row, 1987).

85. Some scholars who hold for a minimal set of anthropological constants include Lisa Sowle Cahill, Margaret Farley, Seyla Benhabib, Susan Moller Okin, Martha Nussbaum, and Ruth Anna Putnam.

86. Mary Ann Hinsdale, "Heeding the Voices: An Historical Overview," in *In the Embrace of God: Feminist Approaches to Theological Anthropology*, ed. Ann O'Hara Graff (Maryknoll, N.Y.: Orbis Books, 1995), 25. Hinsdale advises in a footnote: "The term *kyriarchal* has been coined by Elisabeth Schüssler Fiorenza to highlight that Western patriarchy is 'ruling power . . . in the hands of elite, propertied, educated, freeborn men'" (n. 23, p. 39). Elisabeth Schüssler Fiorenza, "Introduction," in *Violence against Women*, ed. Elisabeth Schüssler Fiorenza and Mary Shawn Copeland (Maryknoll, N.Y.: Orbis Books, 1994), xxi–xxii, n. 1.

87. As noted earlier, this term is associated with Edward Schillebeeckx, who offers a set of "anthropological constants" that he suggests constitute the fundamental reality of the human person. He also describes these as "coordinates," the focus of which is the *personal identity* within *social culture*: (1) the relationship of human beings to their bodies and the environment; (2) the relationship of a person to other people; (3) the relationship of people to social structures and institutions; (4) the situatedness of human beings in time and space—their historical reality; (5) the dialectical relationship between theory and praxis; (6) the utopian or religious consciousness of human beings; (7) the combination and interplay of the first six constants. See Edward Schillebeeckx, *Christ: The Experience of Jesus as Lord*, trans. John Bowden (New York: Crossroad Publishing Company, 1990), 734–43. The term "anthropological constants" is used in this book not to refer to Schillebeeckx's precise list of constants, but to refer to his suggestion that such anthropological constants or markers exist, and are important to identify for the purpose of ethics and the identification of those situations that destroy the human person and thereby stand as occasions of injustice.

88. The work of Michel Foucault is important in this regard.

89. There are numerous classic texts which demonstrate the accusatory and misogynist attitudes toward women that existed in patristic times and continue in contemporary attitudes invoking scriptural/theological justifications for according women a different status in the human community than men. One of the most frequently cited and most harsh condemnations of women was made by the Latin Church Father Tertullian: "*You* are the Devil's gateway. *You* are the unsealer of that forbidden tree. *You* are the first deserter of the divine law. *You* are she who persuaded him whom the Devil was not valiant enough to attack. *You* destroyed so easily God's image in man. On account of *your* dessert, that is death, even the Son of God had to die." Tertullian, *de Cult. Fem* 1. 1, quoted in Ruether, *Sexism and God-Talk*, 167 (emphasis in original).

90. Ruether, *Sexism and God-Talk*, 93.

91. Margaret Farley, "Feminism and Universal Morality," in *Prospects for a Common Morality*, ed. Gene Outka and John P. Reeder, Jr. (Princeton, N.J.: Princeton University Press, 1993), 171. In this same vein Martha Nussbaum comments: "Many essentialist conceptions have been insular in an arrogant way and neglectful of differences among cultures and ways of life. Some have been neglectful of choice and autonomy. And some have been prejudicially applied—sometimes even by their inventors (as in the cases of Aristotle and Rousseau). But none of this, it seems to me, shows that all essentialism *must* fail in one or more of these ways." Martha Nussbaum, "Human Functioning and Social Justice: In Defense of Aristotelian Essentialism," *Political Theory* 20, no. 2 (1992): 214.

92. Farley, "Feminism and Universal Morality," 178.

93. Nussbaum offers particularly apt examples of extremes of postmodern admiration of cultural difference to the detriment of women and others in a culture when she describes a United Nations–sponsored conference she attended where an American (male) economist lamented the inroads Western values were making in the Indian culture. In Western culture, the speaker suggested, a sharp split is experienced between the values of the workplace and the values of the home. In rural India there still exists an "embedded way of life," a situation in which there is coherence between practices and customs observed in the home and in the workplace. As an example, he pointed to the custom in rural India of prohibiting a menstruating woman from entering the kitchen because she is thought to be a polluting presence, and also prohibiting her from entering the workplace where looms are kept for similar reasons. When the speaker's perspective was challenged by an Indian economist, the challenge was angrily rebuffed by other delegates who rejected his right to speak to the situation he described as "repellant," charging him with denying the "radical otherness" of the rural people. At the same conference, a French anthropologist regretted the introduction of smallpox vaccination to India by the British for its eradication of the cult of Sittala Devi, the goddess to whom people used to pray in order to avert smallpox. The anthropologist pointed to

this as one more example of Western binary opposition (life/death) and neglect of difference. See Nussbaum, "Human Functioning and Social Justice," 202–46.

94. Lisa Sowle Cahill, "Presidential Address: Feminist Ethics and the Challenge of Cultures," *Proceedings, Catholic Theological Society of America* 48 (1993), ed. Paul Crowley (Santa Clara, Calif.: Catholic Theological Society of America, 1993), 72.

95. Martha Nussbaum, "Non-Relative Virtues: An Aristotelian Approach," in *The Quality of Life*, ed. Martha C. Nussbaum and Amartya Sen (Oxford: Clarendon Press), 261. This article was also published in *Midwest Studies in Philosophy*, 1988.

96. Cahill, "Presidential Address," 71.

97. Nussbaum, "Human Functioning and Social Justice," 212.

98. Natural law is a distinctively Roman Catholic orientation to moral theology. Tracing its origins to the philosophy of Aristotle and Aquinas, natural law has been interpreted in a wide variety of ways over the centuries. (See chapter 2, note 85.) Catholic natural law theory is a valuable moral resource in its use of reason and experience as significantly determinative elements in discerning the good, elements which are not limited to a particular faith tradition and to which an appeal may be made in dialogue with those outside the tradition. Natural law, therefore, demands a careful attention to the ways in which we understand the good for the human person. An excellent retrieval of natural law from a feminist perspective is Christina L. H. Traina, *Feminist Ethics and Natural Law: The End of the Anathemas* (Washington, D.C.: Georgetown University Press, 1999).

99. Margaret Farley offers a good summary of the role of experience in moral reasoning generally in "The Role of Experience in Moral Discernment," in *Christian Ethics: Problems and Prospects*, ed. Lisa Sowle Cahill and James F. Childress (Cleveland, Ohio: Pilgrim Press, 1996), 134–51. The end of her essay particularly suggests the appropriate function of experience as a norming principle that holds important possibilities for the role of the experience of women as a component of moral discernment.

100. I use the word "suffering" deliberately because it is inclusive. The phenomenon being pointed to is more than just poverty, or just high maternal mortality rates or any one particular social practice that disadvantages women. Suffering is broadly inclusive of the multiple and overlapping forms of injustice and distress women experience, and is a word that allows for different interpretations and specifications in particular situations.

101. In this regard, a 1992 UNICEF report noted: "The enjoyment of human rights and fundamental freedom is likely to depend on the one cruel chromosome." UNICEF document, State of the World's Children, in *Ours by Right: Women's Rights as Human Rights*, ed. Joanna Kerr (Ottawa: North-South Institute, 1993), 3.

102. This is similar to the methodology of liberation theology, which takes the reality of suffering of a particular people as the starting point from which to pursue any theological development. David Tracy affirmed this orientation in his address to the Catholic Theological Society of America in 1995: "All thought must be interpreted by the great counterexperience whose echoes no serious thinker can avoid. To develop a *logos* on *theos*—a theology—today is to start by facing evil and suffering." David Tracy, "Evil, Suffering, Hope: The Search for New Forms of Contemporary Theodicy," *Proceedings of the Fiftieth Annual Convention, Catholic Theological Society of America* 50 (1995): 16.

103. Maria Pilar Aquino, "Women's Contribution to Theology in Latin America," in *Feminist Ethics and the Catholic Moral Tradition: Readings in Moral Theology No. 9*, eds. Charles E. Curran, Margaret A. Farley, and Richard A. McCormick (New York: Paulist Press, 1996), 91. This essay first appeared in Maria Pilar Aquino, *Our Cry for Life: Feminist Theology from Latin America* (Maryknoll, N.Y.: Orbis Books, 1993).

104. Feminist sociologist Dorothy Smith addresses this topic extensively in her books.

105. Lisa Sowle Cahill, *Sex, Gender, and Christian Ethics* (New York: Cambridge University Press, 1996), 54.

106. She outlines this in detail in "Non-Relative Virtues: An Aristotelian Approach." This examination of Aristotle's conception of virtues forms the basis of her suggestions regarding human functioning capabilities as cross-cultural characteristics of human beings.

107. Martha Nussbaum, "Human Capabilities, Female Human Beings," in *Women, Culture, and Development: A Study of Human Capabilities*, ed. Martha Nussbaum and Jonathan Glover (Oxford: Clarendon Press, 1995), 76–80.

108. Ibid., 74.

109. In the sense of a static, achieved characteristic or quality.

110. The description and significance of human functioning capabilities is a repeated element of Nussbaum's writing. She offers slightly amended descriptions of human functioning capabilities in several places.

111. Nussbaum, "Human Capabilities, Female Human Beings," 83–85.

112. Cahill, *Sex, Gender, and Christian Ethics*, 59–61.

113. These five elements repeatedly raised by feminist scholars regarding anthropology are summarized by Jane Kopas, "Transforming Theological Anthropology," in *Women and Theology, The Annual Publication of the College Theology Society*, vol. 40, ed. Mary Ann Hinsdale and Phyllis H. Kaminski (Maryknoll, N.Y.: Orbis Books, 1995), 224–28. Kopas emphasizes that feminists are indeed wary of the anthropological project, out of a concern that the attempt to describe the human inevitably results in a form of exclusion. Those feminists who do consider the theological anthropological issue insist that, to the extent that a set of anthropological markers are described, they must be understood to be open to revision as necessary.

114. Nussbaum, "Human Capabilities, Female Human Beings," 88.

115. The idea that salvation must include the social and political dimensions of life is one which Edward Schillebeeckx develops in his writings: "[I]t must be experienced as saving by 'historical men of flesh and blood who are referred to their natural environment and one another to build up a living world in which they can exist as people.' If we call this 'earthly salvation', that means making *real people* whole. . . . [T]he consequence is that as a minimal presupposition, 'salvation in the sense of that which makes 'whole' needs social, economic and political institutions which do not make one group whole at the expense of others, but make all 'whole'." Edward Schillebeeckx, *Christ: The Experience of Jesus as Lord*, 756–57. In this section Schillebeeckx draws on the work of H. Kuitert, "De vrede van God en de vrede van de wereld," in *Kerk en Verde* (In honor of Prof. J. de Graaf) (Baarn, 1976), 66–84.

116. This design of implementation must be developed collaboratively with those who have the most immediate stake in the situation. A repeating pattern of listening, reflection, strategizing, implementation, and review of the action is crucial to a liberationist response to suffering. This process draws together the intellectual, theological, sociological, pastoral, and "pragmatic" disciplines. This design is basically the strategy recommended by Joe Holland and Peter Henriot, S.J., in *Social Analysis: Linking Faith and Justice*, revised and enlarged edition (Maryknoll, N.Y.: Orbis Books in collaboration with the Center of Concern, Washington, D.C., 1983).

CHAPTER 2. THE COMMON GOOD IN THE THOUGHT OF THOMAS AQUINAS

1. Katherine Archibald, "The Concept of Social Hierarchy in the Writings of St. Thomas Aquinas," in *St. Thomas Aquinas on Politics and Ethics*, ed. and trans. Paul E. Sigmund (New York: W. W. Norton & Company, 1988), 136.

2. Etienne Gilson, *The Christian Philosophy of St. Thomas Aquinas* (New York: Random House, 1956). Gilson suggests that for Aquinas, God is "the personal God who acts by intelligence and will, and who freely places outside himself that real universe which his wisdom chose from an infinity of possible universes" (ibid., 35).

3. Lisa Sowle Cahill, *Love Your Enemies: Discipleship, Pacifism, and Just War Theory* (Minneapolis: Fortress Press, 1994), 84. Cahill quotes Thomas Gilby, *The Political Thought of Thomas Aquinas* (Chicago: University of Chicago Press, 1958), xxiii. In the same vein, A. P. D'Entreves comments: "[T]he art of politics is anything but mere technique. It cannot and must not be measured solely by its achievements, by standards of efficiency and success. And the reason for this is that politics always imply a moral responsibility, a deliberation,

a willing, a choice. They are not a purely pragmatic science. . . . [Politics] deals with the choice of means, but the means are dependent on the end, and the end is a moral one. This end is the common good, an end which is higher in value than that of the individual and that of the family, and which constitutes the proper object of politics." A. P. D'Entreves, *Aquinas: Selected Political Writings*, trans. J. G. Dawson (Oxford: Basil Blackwell, 1959), xii. While one may contest D'Entreves's suggestion that the common good is higher in value than the person, this represents a classically Thomistic/Aristotelian point of view. His point that the end that is chosen has a moral "valence" should not be lost in the midst of disagreement over the valuing of the communal versus the person.

4. This is not to say that the "definition" of a person and the variables that are used to describe fundamental personhood are not highly debated even now. Many feminist theologians resist the very presumption that a "definition" of the human person is possible, to the extent that definition is understood as a closed set of identifying characteristics. To work toward a "symbolic presentation" of the person suggests a more tentative, dynamic, and open set of human markers.

5. Linda M. Maloney, "The Argument for Women's Difference in Classical Philosophy and Early Christianity," in *The Special Nature of Women*, ed. Anne Carr and Elisabeth Schüssler Fiorenza, *Concilium* 6 (1991).

6. "Lower" functioning beings would have been understood as those who do not possess reason for intellectual activity. Their raison d'être was contained in their physicality. "Higher" functioning would have been understood as the capacity for intellectual activity, reasoning, and free choice. The destiny of higher functioning beings is not coterminous with their physicality.

7. Aristotle, *Generation of Animals* I, 728a, quoted in Susan Moller Okin, *Women in Western Political Thought* (Princeton: Princeton University Press, 1979), note 7, Part II: Aristotle, 82.

8. Thomas Aquinas, *Summa Theologica* (hereafter *ST*), trans. Fathers of the English Dominican Province (Westminster, Md.: Christian Classics, 1981), I.92.2.c.

9. *ST* Ia.92.1 ad 2.

10. *ST* Ia.93.4.

11. *ST* I.93.6 ad 2.

12. *ST* I.92.1.1.

13. *ST* I.94.1–4.

14. Similarly, Aquinas (*ST* II-II.47.12) emphasizes that all people are capable of exercising the virtue of prudence in a manner appropriate to their responsibilities: "Since every man, for as much as he is rational, has a share in ruling according to the judgment of reason, he is proportionately competent to have prudence. Wherefore it is manifest that prudence *is in the ruler after the manner of a mastercraft* (*Eth.* vi.8), but in subjects, *after the manner of a handicraft*." (The parenthetical reference is to Aristotle's *Ethics*.)

15. *ST* I.94.3 ad 1.

16. Cahill, *Love Your Enemies*, 83.

17. Jean Porter, *The Recovery of Virtue: The Relevance of Aquinas for Christian Ethics* (Louisville, Ky.: Westminster/John Knox Press, 1990), 34.

18. Thomas Aquinas, *Quaestiones Disputate De Veritate*, Q. 21, a. 2 *corpus* as found in *Truth*, vol. 3, p. 10, a translation of the *De Veritate* by Robert W. Schmidt (Chicago: Henry Regnery, 1954), as quoted in Ronald Duska, "Aquinas' Definition of Good: Ethical-Theoretical Notes on *De Veritate*, Q. 21," *The Monist* 58, no. 1 (1974): 152. Duska comments further: "Something can be called 'good' if it is not the cause of the good state in the primary sense but merely useful (instrumental) in achieving the good state" (ibid., 153).

19. Thomas Aquinas, *Summa Contra Gentiles* (hereafter *SCG*), ed. Anton C. Pegis (New York: McGraw Hill, 1948), I.37.307.

20. Thomas Aquinas, *Compendium of Theology* (hereafter *CT*), trans. Cyril Vollert (St. Louis, Mo.: B. Herder Book Company, 1947 and 1958), chapter 103.

21. *CT* CXIV.223.

22. James F. Keenan, S.J., *Goodness and Rightness in Thomas Aquinas' Summa Theologiae* (Washington, D.C.: Georgetown University Press, 1992), 96–97.

23. *CT*, First Treatise on Faith, chapter 109.

24. *CT*, Part Two on Hope, chapter 9.

25. *ST* I.5.1–3.

26. *ST* I.65.2: "Hence, any creature's having existence reflects the divine existence and goodness."

27. *ST* I.1a 6, 4. Similar citations can be found in *ST* I.46.2 ad 3; III.65.3 ad 1; *SCG* III.17; 4 *Sentences* 49, 1, 1, 1, ad 3; *Quod lib.* 1, 4, 8; *ST* I-II.60.5 ad 5; I-II.100.8; *De Perf. Vitae Spirit.* 13.

28. Aquinas discusses human nature in *ST* I.76–83.

29. *ST* I-II.1.2.7.

30. *ST* I-II.3.2.

31. Porter, *The Recovery of Virtue*, 70. Aquinas also writes: "If we speak of the ultimate end with respect to the thing itself, then human and all other beings share in it together, for God is the ultimate end for all things without exception. But if with respect to the act of gaining it, then the final end of man is not that of non-rational creatures. For men and other rational creatures lay hold of it in knowing and loving God, which non-rational creatures are not capable of doing, for they come to their final end through sharing in some likeness of God, inasmuch as they actually exist or live and even know after their fashion" (*ST* I-II.1.8).

32. Jean Porter, "Desire for God: Ground of the Moral Life in Aquinas," *Theological Studies* 47 (1986): 53–55. Porter notes that Aquinas understands the cardinal and moral virtues to direct the person to the happiness that is pro-

portionate to human nature. These virtues have as their arena of functioning the powers that are constitutive of human nature, i.e., rationality, intellect, and free choice. The theological virtues (faith, hope, and charity) are gifts of God to the person which enable her "to attain the true happiness of direct communion with God." There is a fine point at issue here concerning the relationship between the cardinal and moral/theological virtues. The cardinal and moral virtues, no matter how fully they are exercised, do not bring a person to the beatific vision of God; however, they do orient the person to a goodness, sensitivity, and availability to the guidance of God; that is, they establish her in a posture of "right order" as far as that is possible for her to attain through the use of her natural powers, so they are not discontinuous.

33. *ST* I.62.1.

34. Porter, *The Recovery of Virtue*, 63.

35. Kevin M. Staley, "Happiness: The Natural End of Man?" *The Thomist* 53, no. 2 (April 1989): 226.

36. *ST* I-II.1.8.

37. *SCG* III.48.1: "If then ultimate human felicity does not consist in the knowledge of God whereby he is known in general by all or by most men by a sort of confused appraisal, and again if it does not consist in the knowledge of God which is known by way of demonstration in the speculative sciences, nor in the cognition of God whereby he is known by faith as has been shown in the foregoing, and if it is not possible in this life to reach the higher knowledge of God so as to know him through his essence or even in such a way that when the other separate substances are known God might be known through the knowledge of them as if from a closer vantage point as we showed, and if it is necessary to identify ultimate felicity with some sort of knowledge of God as we proved above, then it is not possible for man's ultimate felicity to come in this life."

38. *SCG* III.37.1. In this regard Michael Sherwin writes: "Thomas holds, however, that even though this fulfillment is not perfect, it provides the means for acquiring perfect fulfillment. It is in and through the life of virtue that we advance toward perfect beatitude. God gave the human person a nature which is perfected through virtuous living and he elevates this nature with his gift of grace. We cannot attain the vision of God without his grace, but neither do we attain it apart from the nature God has given us. Specifically, the human person acquires wisdom and the freedom to love what is truly good by growing—with the help of grace—in the speculative and practical virtues. Thus, God's plan for us is that by acquiring these virtues (by acquiring temporal fulfillment) we acquire the freedom to choose God's offer of salvation (*ST* I-II 5.5. ad 1; 5.7)." Michael Sherwin, O.P., *St. Thomas and the Common Good: The Theological Perspective: An Invitation to Dialogue* (Rome: Pontificia Universita San Tommaso, 1993), 315. Sherwin's position that this fulfillment "provides the means for acquiring perfect fulfillment" might seem to propose a quasi-Pelagian stance.

If this is what Sherwin intends by this statement, it runs counter to orthodox Christian teaching in which, while the response of the creature to the action of God's grace is genuine and important, it is not something that in and of itself achieves perfection for the person apart from the first action of God on the human person.

39. *ST* I-II.5.5.

40. Porter, *The Recovery of Virtue*, 100. Aquinas understood virtue, most basically, as "a good quality of the mind." But: "The end of virtue, since it is an operative habit, is operation" (*ST* I-II.55.4).

41. Porter, *The Recovery of Virtue*, 67.

42. Ibid.

43. *ST* I-II.82.1.2.3.4; I-II.83.3.4.

44. Ralph McInerny, *Ethica Thomistica: The Moral Philosophy of Thomas Aquinas* (Washington, D.C.: Catholic University of America Press, 1982), 1.

45. Porter, *The Recovery of Virtue*, 70.

46. Ibid., 71–72.

47. *ST* I.4.5: "Accordingly, since complete happiness is the vision of divine essence, it does not hinge on the body. . . . Note however, that something may be part of a thing's perfection in two ways. First as constituting its nature, thus soul is part of man's perfection. Secondly, as required for its full development. Thus good looks and swift wit are parts of his perfection. Now the body enters into happiness in the second way, not in the first. For since a thing's activity depends on its nature, the more perfect its condition so much more perfectly will the soul enjoy its characteristic activity in which happiness lies."

48. *SCG* IV.50.

49. *SCG* IV.50.

50. *ST* I-II.109.3. Aquinas writes similarly in *ST* III.46.2 ad 3; III.65.3 ad 1; *SCG* III.17.6: "Now the highest good, which is God, is the common good, since the good of all things taken together depend upon him; and the good whereby each thing is good is its own particular good, and also is the good of the other things that depend on this thing. Therefore, all things are ordered to one good as their end, and that is God." *Sentences* 49, 1,1,1, ad 3; *Quod lib.* 1, 4, 8; *ST* I-II.60.5 ad 5; I-II.100.8; *De Perf. Vitae Spirit.* 13.

51. Charles de Koninck, "In Defence of Saint Thomas," *Laval Théologique et Philosophique* 2 (1945), 42, as quoted by Sherwin in *St. Thomas and the Common Good*, 310.

52. *ST* I.96.4; II-II.47.10. This is but one of the many places in which Aquinas describes the human person as social, or in some instances "political and social," and again in other places he calls the person a "political animal." See also *On Kingship*: "Yet it is natural for man, more than for any other animal, to be a social and political animal, to live in a group. This is clearly a necessity of man's nature." Thomas Aquinas, *On Kingship: To the King of Cyprus*, trans. Gerald B. Phelan, revised with introduction and notes by I. Th. Eschmann (To-

ronto, Ontario: The Pontifical Institute of Medieval Studies, 1949). Hereafter this will be referred to as *On Kingship*. This description of the person Aquinas inherited from Aristotle, such as is found in Aristotle's *Politics*, I, 2; 1255a2: "Hence it is evident that the state is a creation of nature, and that man is by nature a political animal." The use of the terms "political" and "social" individually and together in the work of Aquinas is discussed at length in Edgar Scully, "The Place of the State in Society According to Thomas Aquinas," *The Thomist* 45, no. 3 (1981): 407–29.

53. *ST* II-II.109.3.

54. For all this, Aquinas is indebted to Augustine for his conception of the common good as the ordination of all things to God. Augustine, however, did not see that it was the responsibility of the state to enhance its citizens' opportunities for acquiring the earthly benefits of health, security, and human fellowship, even though he spoke of these as gifts of God. He did, however, understand peace as the earthly common good, which the state had the responsibility to pursue. See A. Nemetz, "The Common Good," in *The New Catholic Encyclopedia*, vol. 4 (Washington, D.C.: Catholic University of America, 1967), 15.

55. Augustine, *The City of God (De Civitate Dei)*, vols. I and II (New York: E. P. Dutton, 1947), 17.2.

56. *ST* Ia.96.4.

57. The one exception to this might be seen in *On Kingship*. Even in this work, however, Aquinas's intention is not to offer political advice as much as it is to offer wisdom regarding how one might govern in a manner so that one's governance and the resulting society offer the best opportunity for a created reality—people living in society—to give glory to God and to fulfill their purpose of existence—union with God.

58. Sherwin, *St. Thomas and the Common Good*, 316.

59. *On Kingship*, Book One, chapter 1.8.

60. Richard A. Crofts, "The Common Good in the Political Theory of Thomas Aquinas," *The Thomist* 37 (1973), 156.

61. Ibid., 158.

62. *On Kingship*, chapter 3.103, 106, 107.

63. Ibid., Book Two, chapter 4.118.

64. Ibid. (emphasis added).

65. Crofts, "The Common Good in the Political Theory of Thomas Aquinas," 158.

66. *SCG* III.37.

67. *ST* I-II.105.1.

68. Jacques Maritain, *The Person and the Common Good* (South Bend, Ind.: University of Notre Dame Press, 1947), 41–42 (emphasis in original).

69. Ibid., 47–48.

70. Porter, *The Recovery of Virtue*, 126. She references *ST* I.84–88.

71. Porter, *The Recovery of Virtue*, 126.

72. Sherwin, *St. Thomas and the Common Good*, 319.

73. *SCG* III.85; see also *On Kingship*, Book One, 1.14: "Now since man must live in a group, because he is not sufficient unto himself to procure the necessities of life were he to remain solitary, it follows that a society will be the more perfect the more it is sufficient unto itself to procure the necessities of life."

74. On peace, see *SCG* IV.76; *ST* I-II.96.3; *On Kingship*, Book One, 1.5; *ST* I-II.98.1. On goods of the heart and soul, see *ST* II-II.114.2 ad 1.

75. *ST* I-II.109.3 ad 1; II-II.114.2 ad 1; *SCG* III.147.

76. *ST* I-II.100.8.

77. *ST* I-II.92.1; 96.3 ad 2; 100.8.

78. Maritain, *The Person and the Common Good*, 48.

79. *SCG* III.128.

80. Aquinas, *Com. Ethics* 1, 1, 4.

81. *On Kingship*, Book Two, chapter 3.106.

82. *On Kingship*, 1.12; *SCG* III.117.

83. Maritain, *The Person and the Common Good*, 51 (emphasis in original).

84. *ST* I.96.4.

85. Aquinas is usually referenced as a source of the natural law tradition (*ST* I-II.91.2). Natural law is a principle found in Roman Catholic moral theology based on a belief in the possibility of created reality and the human person functioning as vehicles of revelation. "The natural law he [Aquinas] defined as humans' innate inclination toward what promotes human fulfillment; it has been instilled in the creature by God and is knowable by reason. By reflecting on experience itself, the human person can understand what sort of personal and political life will be most fulfilling for humans and, with a somewhat lesser degree of certitude, what specific actions best fulfill in the concrete the universal moral values that can be generalized from human behavior." Lisa Sowle Cahill, "Feminism and Christian Ethics," in *Freeing Theology: The Essentials of Theology in Feminist Perspective*, ed. Catherine Mowry LaCugna (San Francisco: HarperSanFrancisco, 1993), 214.

86. *On Kingship*, Book One, chapter 1.5.

87. Porter, *The Recovery of Virtue*, 49. Porter here references Aquinas, *ST* I.65.2.

88. Porter, *The Recovery of Virtue*, 50.

89. This issue, of whether it is possible to move from what *is* to a judgment about what *ought to be*, is one that Porter has contested with theologians Germain Grisez and John Finnis, who refute this as a possibility. They contend, contrary to the interpretation of Aquinas offered by Porter and others, that it is not possible to extrapolate moral obligation from a metaphysical or anthropological theory of the good and the human good. They offer a case for recognition of seven self-evident, basic goods as a moral point of reference. For further

discussion of this, see John Finnis, *Natural Law and Natural Rights* (Oxford: Clarendon Press, 1989); Germain Grisez, *The Way of the Lord Jesus, Volume One: Christian Moral Principles* (Chicago: Franciscan Herald Press, 1983); Germain Grisez, Joseph Boyle, and John Finnis, "Practical Principles, Moral Truth, and Ultimate Ends," *The American Journal of Jurisprudence* 32 (1987), 99–151; Janice L. Schultz, "Thomistic Metaethics and a Present Controversy," *The Thomist* 52, no. 1 (1988): 40–62; Jean Porter, "The Dreadful Chasm: Deriving Ought from Is," in Porter, *The Recovery of Virtue*, 43–48; and Jean Porter, "Basic Goods and the Human Good in Recent Catholic Moral Theology," *The Thomist* 57, no. 1 (1993): 27–49.

90. Porter, *The Recovery of Virtue*, 44. Aquinas's conception of both good and evil operates from an analogical perspective; i.e., his natural law theory allows him to propose that all goodness is analogical of the ultimate goodness of God, as well as seeing evil as a "privation" of a good that rightly should be a part of something. Some Protestant theologians have challenged this conception of the good, and particularly of evil, maintaining that creation (including human nature) is too damaged to be able to trust as an analogue of ultimate goodness. Further, critical theorists and liberation theologians such as Edward Schillebeeckx have maintained that considering evil simply as a privation of a good is too benign an interpretation for many of the destructive realities that exist. They suggest that while Aquinas attempts to explain the pursuit of destruction by a person as a misguided attempt to achieve a presumed good, in fact we are faced with the blatant reality of people deliberately choosing evil and destruction, for what it is. This will be discussed further in the next chapter.

91. Michael Sherwin notes: "The Thomistic conception of the common good is therefore relational. We cannot properly understand the common good except in relation to a Lover (God) and the beloved, the rational creature who is drawn into God's love. From the outset, therefore, Thomas places the common good in the context of a love relationship." Sherwin, *St. Thomas and the Common Good*, 313. Sherwin's observations point to the fundamentally relational quality to anything understood as the common good.

92. Ibid., 315.

93. *ST* I-II.1.2.

94. *ST* I-II.90.1 sed contra.

95. *ST* I-II.96.4 sed contra (emphasis added).

96. *ST* I-II.95.1.

97. Aquinas, *De Perf. Vitae Spirit.* 14.

98. Walter Farrell, *A Companion to the Summa, Vol. 2* (New York: Sheed and Ward, 1945), 369. Commenting on this changing content but enduring quality of the common good of a community, Farrell notes: "The immediate common good of the state might be summed up in one word, 'peace,' or in the phrase, 'the preservation of unity.' It is an end constituted by the assurance of the necessities of life to the subjects, by the establishment of internal harmony

through just distribution of rewards and penalties and by giving security against external enemies. . . . In plain language, it means no more than the assurance to all the subjects of the opportunity to follow the law of reason to individual perfection, the opportunity to live a successful human life."

99. I. T. Eschmann, "In Defense of Jacques Maritain," *The Modern Schoolman* (St. Louis, Mo.: St. Louis University Press, 1945), 192.

100. *On Kingship*, Book One, chapter 1.10.

101. *ST* II-II.58.7 ad 2.

102. *ST* II-II.58.9 ad 3.

103. *ST* I-II.19.10.

104. *ST* II-II.47.10.

105. Porter, *The Recovery of Virtue*, 127.

106. *ST* II-II.10 ad 2.

107. *ST* II-II.141.8.

108. *ST* II-II.26.4.

109. *ST* II-II.31.3. Aquinas speaks of the subordination of the private good to the public good in numerous places: *ST* I-II.90.3; II-II.47.10; II-II.68.1; II-II.117.6; II-II.185.2.

110. Maritain, *The Person and the Common Good*, 58.

111. Ibid., 47–89.

112. Ibid., 57–58.

113. *ST* II-II.175.

114. Sherwin, *St. Thomas and the Common Good*, 325–27.

115. Porter, *The Recovery of Virtue*, 125.

116. Ibid., 134–35.

117. *ST* I-II.94.2. In this section Aquinas outlines what constitute the fundamental elements of "natural law" in regard to the human person.

118. *ST* II-II.64.2–3.

119. *ST* II-II.31.3; II-II.32.9; II-II.66.7.

120. *ST* I-II.55.4.

121. *ST* I-II.55.1 ad 2.

122. Who is included among the beneficiaries of the common good? I suggest Aquinas would answer that all human persons are entitled to share in the benefits of the common good. However, the distribution of these goods would not result in the same benefits for everyone: i.e., as an issue of justice they would be appropriate to the person's needs which vary because of the difference in what Aquinas saw as the varying capacities with which people are endowed. For example, I believe Aquinas would hold that it would be an injustice to withhold from the free males of a family the type of intellectual formation and opportunities they require to carry out their roles in the family and in society.

123. Porter, *The Recovery of Virtue*, 134.

124. *ST* II-II.58.1.

125. *ST* II-II.57.6.

126. *ST* II-II.57.2. Aquinas notes further in Question 57: "[T]he other virtues are commendable in respect of the sole good of the virtuous person himself, whereas justice is praiseworthy in respect to the virtuous person being well disposed toward another, so that justice is somewhat the good of another person" (*ST* II-II.57.12).

127. Aquinas holds that justice "resides" in one part of the soul, the will, from which it moves and has influence on all other parts of the soul.

128. *ST* II-II.57.11.

129. *ST* II.61.1.

130. *ST* II.61.1.

131. *ST* II.61.1.

132. Porter, *The Recovery of Virtue*, 127.

133. Ibid., 128–32.

134. *ST* II-II.66.2 ad 1.

135. *ST* II-II.66.5, 8, esp. ad 3.

136. *ST* II-II.66.7.

137. *ST* II-II.57.1.

138. Porter, *The Recovery of Virtue*, 136.

139. *ST* II-II.72.1.

140. Porter, *The Recovery of Virtue*, 136. This refers to section II-II.72.1 in the *Summa Theologica*, in which Aquinas states: "Words uttered with the intention of taking away character constitute an insult or defamation in the strict sense and are sins no less fatal than theft or robbery, since a man prizes his character just as much as his material possessions. . . . [A] man should pick his words carefully, since uttered incautiously they might take away a person's character, and a fatal wrong might be done without even intending it."

141. *ST* I-II.94.4–6; II-II.47.12.

142. Porter, *The Recovery of Virtue*, 137–38.

143. Ibid., 124.

144. *ST* I-II.94.2.

145. *ST* II-II.64.6.

146. *ST* II-II.64.7.

147. *ST* II-II.64.3.

148. Porter, *The Recovery of Virtue*, 129.

149. Cahill, *Love Your Enemies*, 85.

150. The criteria for a "just war" (both *jus ad bello* and *jus in bello*) required by Aquinas (building on the thought of Augustine) to justify the killing of war highlight the role of the sovereign, who is permitted to declare a situation of war and place a claim on the citizens to fight the enemy. In order for a war to be just, three things are necessary: "First the authority of the sovereign by whose command the war is waged. For it is not the business of a private individual to declare war, because he can seek for redress of his rights from the tribunal of his superior. Moreover, it is not the business of the private individual to sum-

mon together the people, which has to be done in wartime. And as the care of the common good is committed to those who are in authority, it is their business to watch over the common good of the city, kingdom or province subject to them. And just as it is lawful for them to have recourse to the sword in defending that common good against internal disturbances when they punish evil doers . . . so too it is their business to have recourse to the sword of war in defending the common good against external enemies. For this reason Augustine says (*Contra Faust.* xxii.75) 'The natural order conducive to peace among mortals demands that the power to declare and counsel war should be in the hands of those who hold the supreme authority.' Secondly, a just cause is required, namely that those who are attacked should be attacked because they deserve it on account of some fault. Thirdly, it is necessary that the belligerents should have the right intention, so that they intend the advancement of good or the avoidance of evil" (*ST* II-II.40.1).

151. *ST* II-II.66.1; *ST* II-II.66.2.

152. *ST* II-II.66.3.

153. *ST* II-II.66.7.

154. *ST* II-II.66.7.

155. *ST* II-II.66.5.8.

156. Porter, *The Recovery of Virtue*, 132–33.

157. Aquinas describes grace as uncreated (God in God's self) and created (God's self as revealed or communicated). While uncreated grace is not mediated, created grace requires some vehicle of mediation, i.e., creation, reason, etc. Even when God communicates directly with the soul, it might be argued that this still constitutes a mediated grace because the vehicle of mediation is the person himself or herself.

158. As noted earlier in this chapter, Aquinas distinguishes between the theological virtues (faith, hope, charity), which he held were infused in the soul by God, and all other virtues, which he maintained required human cooperation and response for their development. Aquinas believed that no amount of human effort could result in an increase in the theological virtues, that they were a qualitatively different kind of virtue and were unavailable through human labor.

159. David Tracy points to this distinction in several places in his writing. In *The Analogical Imagination* he observes: "It is equally naive, and equally destructive of systematic theology's hermeneutical task, to assume with the traditionalist and fundamentalist that so autonomous in one's heteronymous obedience is the theologian that one can be faithful to the tradition to which one belongs by repeating its *tradita* rather than critically translating its *traditio*." Tracy uses *tradita* to refer to elements of a tradition that are repeated with technical accuracy but without interpretation. *Traditio* refers to the set of elements of a tradition which, while representing faithfully the tradition, are marked by the hermeneutical process of interpretation and some attempt at mutually criti-

cal correlation. David Tracy, *The Analogical Imagination: Christian Theology and the Culture of Pluralism* (New York: Crossroad Publishing Company, 1991), 100.

160. This is not to say that Aquinas adopted the Aristotelian philosophical conceptual framework uncritically, but he did clearly find great portions of it useful for the Christian theological project.

CHAPTER 3. A FEMINIST RETRIEVAL OF THE PRINCIPLE OF THE COMMON GOOD

1. These five presuppositions are discussed in the final section of chapter 1. They are: (1) The texts and traditions of the Christian community in themselves function from a conception of women that is erroneous and invalid. (2) The experience of women is virtually absent from the tradition. (3) The texts and traditions of the Christian community have been used to justify the oppression of women. (4) Neither the texts nor the tradition should be totally abandoned. (5) The distortions in themselves, when identified as such, bear witness to a purpose and capability of the texts to still function in a liberating manner on behalf of women.

2. Wendy Farley, *Tragic Vision and Divine Compassion: A Contemporary Theodicy* (Louisville, Ky.: Westminster/John Knox Press, 1990), 53–55, cited by Elizabeth Johnson, *She Who Is: The Mystery of God in Feminist Theological Discourse* (New York: Crossroad Publishing Company, 1992), 249.

3. Elson is on the Faculty of Economic and Social Studies, University of Manchester, United Kingdom.

4. Kabeer is a member of the Institute of Development Studies, University of Sussex, United Kingdom.

5. *World Bank Development Report on Poverty, 1990,* 2; cited in *Women 2000*, Vol. 1, 1994 (New York: United Nations Division for the Advancement of Women, 1994), 9.

6. *United Nations Human Development Report, 1990,* 22; cited in *Women 2000*, Vol. 1, 1994, 9.

7. Diane Elson, "Public Action, Poverty, and Development: A Gender Aware Analysis," paper prepared for a seminar on "Women in Extreme Poverty: Integration of Women's Concerns into National Development Planning," Vienna, November 1992; cited in *Women 2000*, Vol. 1, 1994, 10.

8. Naila Kabeer, "Women in Poverty: A Review of Concepts and Findings," paper prepared for a seminar on "Women in Extreme Poverty: Integration of Women's Concerns into National Development Planning," Vienna, November 1992; cited in *Women 2000*, Vol. 1, 1994, 11.

9. Statement presented by the United Nations Development Programme to the Commission on the Status of Women, 37th session, 17–26 March 1993; cited in *Women 2000*, Vol. 1, 1994, 15.

10. *Women: Challenge to the Year 2000* (New York: United Nations, 1991).

11. The final report of the Fourth World Conference on Women, sponsored by the United Nations in September 1995 in Beijing, used similar categories to identify situations requiring urgent attention because they are related to fundamental needs of women which are ignored: women and poverty, education and training of women, women and health, violence against women, women and armed conflict, women and the economy, women in power and decision making, human rights of women, women and the media, women and the environment, the girl child.

12. Michael E. Beasley and Dorothy Q. Thomas, "Domestic Violence as a Human Rights Issue," in *The Public Nature of Private Violence: The Discovery of Domestic Abuse*, ed. Martha Albertson Fineman, Michael E. Beasley, and Roxanne Mykitiuk (New York and London: Routledge, 1994), 324.

13. Julie Peters and Andrea Wolper, "Introduction," in *Women's Rights, Human Rights: International Feminist Perspectives*, ed. Julie Peters and Andrea Wolper (New York and London: Routledge, 1995), 2–3.

14. United Nations Convention on the Elimination of All Forms of Discrimination Against Women, Article 28, 1979.

15. Elissavet Stamatopoulou, "Women's Rights and the United Nations," in Peters and Wolper, eds., *Women's Rights, Human Rights*, 36.

16. This is a generally accepted (although probably conservative) estimate of the number of the world's refugees. Susan Forbes-Martin, *Refugee Women* (London: Zed, 1992), as cited in Sima Wali, "Human Rights for Refugee and Displaced Women," in Peters and Wolper, eds., *Women's Rights, Human Rights*, 336.

17. Wali, "Human Rights for Refugee and Displaced Women," *Women's Rights, Human Rights*, 336–37. Wali further notes: "The distribution of refugee food rations is handled by the UNHRC [United Nations Human Rights Commission] and its implementing partners (host governments, international NGOs) usually in public places easily accessible to men who have ration cards. Ration cards are issued to male family members; this of course is a problem for widowed women and a woman who cannot appear in public places. Furthermore, male family members make decisions about food distribution, an additional problem for widowed women who have to rely on male members of the extended family."

18. Dorothy Smith, *The Conceptual Practices of Power: A Feminist Sociology of Knowledge* (Toronto: University of Toronto Press, 1990); Dorothy Smith, *The Everyday World as Problematic: A Feminist Sociology* (Boston: Northeastern University Press, 1987), esp. chapters 1 and 5; Dorothy Smith, *Texts, Facts, and Femininity: Exploring the Relations of Ruling* (New York and London: Routledge, Chapman and Hall, Inc., 1990), esp. chapter 6.

19. An acquaintance who worked in the poorest section of a Mexican barrio remembered an elderly woman who, when asked what she thought heaven

would be like, responded that it would be the place where she would be filled by one tortilla. The woman was simply unable to imagine two tortillas. The capacity of the imagination to even conceive of a different lot is frequently deeply crippled where people have known only misery and suffering.

20. Johnson, *She Who Is*, 26.

21. John W. O'Malley, "Reform, Historical Consciousness, and Vatican II's Aggiornamento," in O'Malley, *Tradition and Transition: Historical Perspectives on Vatican II* (Wilmington, Del.: Michael Glazier, 1989), 75.

22. Ibid., 76.

23. Ibid., 73.

24. Critiques of Pope John Paul II's encyclical *Mulieris Dignitatem* address this point. In the encyclical, maternity is held up as the natural and properly defining role/function of women. This view is rejected by many women, both by those who have given birth and do not feel that their "nature" is encompassed or adequately described by the phenomenon of motherhood/parenting, as well as by women who have not given birth and who reject the implication that their incarnation of female personhood is acceptable but not complete. John Paul II, *Mulieris Dignitatem*, in *Origins* 18, no. 17 (October 6, 1988): 262–83.

25. Beverly Harrison raises an interesting point in this regard. "The value accorded female 'being' varies somewhat from society to society, but all existing societies are in some degree male supremacist, so male nature is held to be expressive of full humanity, while female nature is held to be different from and of less value than male human nature. . . . One stigma of homosexuality, then, was that it 'reduced' some men to the role of females. . . . The depth of the hatred toward women is clearly reflected in this projection of female stigma onto any male who needs to be distanced from dominant norms of 'real manhood' for purposes of social control." Beverly Wildung Harrison, "Misogyny and Homophobia: The Unexplored Connections," in *Making the Connections: Essays in Feminist Social Ethics*, ed. Carol S. Robb (Boston: Beacon Press, 1985), 139–40. To the extent that a society denigrates women and creates or allows situations of injustice that particularly impact women, to that extent also that society will penalize men who fail to meet some standard of masculinity by treating them "no better than women." Attention, therefore, to the forms of oppression and injustice that are particular to the lives and experience of women produces benefits for both women and men in the society. Obviously it is not good that the way to penalize a man is to make his lot "no better than that of a woman"; but the fact that it is a form of social punishment to reduce a man to the status of a woman points to the acceptability in current society of valuing women so much less than men.

26. Rosemary Radford Ruether has presented a sustained challenge to dualistic conceptions of the person as a matter of justice. Her works addressing dualism are too numerous to cite, but her *Sexism and God-Talk: Toward a Fem-*

inist Theology (Boston: Beacon, 1983) and *To Change the World: Christology and Cultural Criticism* (New York: Crossroad Publishing Company, 1983) are particularly fine developments of this issue. Her *Gaia and God: An Ecofeminist Theology of Earth Healing* (San Francisco: Harper and Row, 1992) moves into cosmic concerns around materiality, embodiment, and the destructive patterns of dualism in the wider environment.

27. Evidence of this can be seen in recent Vatican documents. For example, *Familiaris Consortio* (the 1980 apostolic exhortation *On the Family*) lauds mutual self-giving both sexually and interpersonally between two spouses, which results in children and a strengthening of their relationship. However, the document also observes that "the true advancement of women requires that clear recognition be given to the value of their maternal and family role, by comparison with all other public roles and professions." John Paul II, *On the Family* (Washington, D.C.: United States Catholic Conference, 1982), no. 1. This identification of woman with maternity is even stronger in the 1988 pastoral letter *Mulieris Dignitatem* (*On the Dignity and Vocation of Women*): "Motherhood is linked to the personal structure of the woman." John Paul II, *Mulieris Dignitatem* (1988), no. 18.

28. Much discussion has occurred around whether there is in fact some fundamental distinction between male and female. Apart from the biological differences (differences in reproductive functioning; men generally having more muscle mass than women), how are we to understand the realities of male and female? Is there, as some suggest, no difference at all apart from these biological differences? Is there such difference between female and male (over and above biological differences) that it actually is a case of men and women existing as two vastly different and incommensurable expressions of the same species? To what degree are the differences we observe between male and female inherent, and to what degree are they the product of socialization? We must be very cautious about definitive claims about gender differences. A conclusive determination of the nature/nurture conundrum regarding gender characteristics is impossible. There is no such creature as a completely unsocialized example of male or female humanity from which to come to a conclusion. Psychologists Eleanor Maccoby and Carol N. Jacklin offer the modest suggestion that at best we can tentatively identify four gender-related characteristics based on statistical data: verbal ability in girls and mathematical ability, visual-spatial ability, and aggression in boys. They point out, however, that the differences *within* each gender are greater than the differences *between* the genders. Eleanor Maccoby and Carol N. Jacklin, *The Psychology of Sex Differences* (Stanford, Calif.: Stanford University Press, 1974).

29. Thomas Aquinas, *Summa Theologica* (hereafter *ST*), trans. Fathers of the English Dominican Province (Westminster, Md.: Christian Classics, 1981), I.93.3–4.

30. The work of Maureen D. Kemeza has been useful in this section, highlighting the embodied conception of the person that is found in Aquinas's an-

thropology. See Maureen Kemeza, "The Developing Tradition: A Feminist Reading of Thomas Aquinas on Embodied Relationality," unpublished dissertation, Boston College, 1993.

31. Irish ethicist Enda McDonagh employs relationality as an ethical criterion which maintains that the presence of the other exerts a moral obligation on me, which I must fulfill through recognition, respect, and response to them in their specific reality as an adequate acknowledgment of their otherness. See Enda McDonagh, "Structure and Basis of Moral Experience," *The Irish Theological Quarterly* 38 (1971): 4–20.

32. *ST* I-II.19.5.

33. This is the position taken by theologians endorsing a "virtue ethic." This is a diverse group, but would be represented by scholars such as James Keenan, William Spohn, and Stanley Hauerwas. The emphasis here is on the development of the character of a person, so they grow as persons with a particular type of habitual orientation and behavior shaped by the classically named virtues, such as prudence, justice, temperance, and fortitude.

34. Johnson, *She Who Is*, 36 (emphasis added). In this excerpt, Johnson references Clifford Geertz, "Religion as a Cultural System," in *The Interpretation of Cultures* (New York: Basic Books, 1973), 90.

35. *ST* Ia.3, prologue.

36. F. C. Copleston, *Aquinas* (London: Penguin Books, 1955, 1991), 132.

37. *ST* Ia.13.2.

38. *ST* Ia.13.5.

39. *ST* Ia.13.4.

40. *ST* Ia.13.12.

41. Copleston, *Aquinas*, 135.

42. Johnson, *She Who Is*, 252–53.

43. Ibid., 147.

44. James F. Keenan and Thomas R. Kopfensteiner, "Moral Theology Out of Western Europe," *Theological Studies* 59, no. 1 (1998): 107.

45. David Tracy, "Approaching the Christian Understanding of God," in *Systematic Theology: Roman Catholic Perspectives, Vol. 1*, ed. Francis Schüssler Fiorenza and John P. Galvin (Minneapolis: Fortress Press, 1991), 145.

46. Catherine LaCugna, *God for Us: The Trinity and Christian Life* (San Francisco: HarperSanFrancisco, 1991).

47. Ibid., 2 (emphasis in original).

48. Ibid., 148.

49. Ibid., 149. "*Exitus-reditus*" is used to refer to the dynamic of the human person coming from God and returning to God in Christ.

50. Ibid.

51. Ibid., 168.

52. Elizabeth Schüssler Fiorenza's work as a scripture scholar explores the synoptic Jesus and the Jesus movement from a feminist reading; see especially

In Memory of Her: A Feminist Reconstruction of Christian Origins (New York: Crossroad Publishing Company, 1989); *But She Said: Feminist Practices of Biblical Interpretation* (Boston: Beacon Press, 1992); and *Jesus: Miriam's Child, Sophia's Prophet—Critical Issues in Feminist Christology* (New York: Continuum, 1994). Here, however, I am referring more to feminist theologians who appeal to the Jesus of the synoptic gospels as a resource for feminist systematic theology and ethics. Certainly preeminent among such feminist theologians is Elizabeth Johnson; see her *Consider Jesus: Waves of Renewal in Christology* (New York: Crossroad Publishing Company, 1991), and *She Who Is*. Rosemary Ruether also appeals to the synoptic Jesus in her feminist theology, particularly in *Sexism and God-Talk*. Ethicist Lisa Sowle Cahill's work makes strong appeal to the scripture and the Jesus of the synoptic gospels; see her *Between the Sexes: Foundations for a Christian Ethics of Sexuality* (Philadelphia: Fortress Press, 1983), and *Sex, Gender, and Christian Ethics* (New York: Cambridge University Press, 1996).

53. Ann O'Hara Graff, "The Struggle to Name Women's Experience," in *In the Embrace of God: Feminist Approaches to Theological Anthropology*, ed. Ann O'Hara Graff (Maryknoll, N.Y.: Orbis Books, 1995), 73–74.

54. Valerie Goldstein Saiving, "The Human Situation: A Feminine View," *Journal of Religion* 40 (1960): 100–112.

55. See chapter 2, note 85, for a description of natural law. In what follows, what is being invoked as natural law tradition is not the biologically defined conception of the human person, but what has come to be seen as a "revised natural law" position that understands that the human person can only be described with appreciation for the complex and dynamic reality of the human, involving body, mind, relationships, transcendent orientations, spirit, psyche, etc.

56. *ST*.I-II.7.1.

57. *ST*.I-II.4.7. Aquinas refers here to Aristotle's *Nichomachean Ethics*.

58. Cahill, *Sex, Gender, and Christian Ethics*, 47.

59. See Edward Schillebeeckx, "Church, Sacrament of Dialogue," in *God the Future of Man*, trans. N. D. Smith (New York: Sheed and Ward, 1968), 136.

60. "Food is not always distributed equally among family members. In some regions, and especially in South Asia, men and boys eat first; whatever is left is then distributed among the women and girls. Invariably, the latter eat less food which is of inferior quality and nutritive value. As a result, girls in the developing world are more than four times as likely to be malnourished as boys." The United Nations, *Women: Challenges to the Year 2000* (New York: United Nations, 1991), 23. The picture accompanying the article captures the plight of girl children in developing countries regarding food and survival. In the picture, a Pakistani mother breast-feeds a plump boy of nine months. His twin sister lies in her mother's other arm, tiny, wizened, drinking from a bottle.

The woman had been told that since she did not have enough milk for both children, only the boy should be breast-fed. The girl died the day after the picture was taken.

61. The principle of the "option for the poor" originated with the Latin American liberation theologians in the 1960s (although it could be argued that it is a gospel principle expressed in contemporary idiom). It came into prominence in the Medellín documents of 1968, prepared by the Latin American bishops at the conclusion of a regional synod. It was echoed in the 1971 Apostolic Letter, *Octogesima Adveniens*, particularly in paragraph 23.

62. The option for the poor is incorporated strongly in the 1986 document of the U.S. Bishops, *Economic Justice for All: Pastoral Letter on Catholic Social Teaching and the U.S. Economy*, particularly chapter 2, section B. In addition, this document repeatedly invokes the principle of the common good as the most adequate guide for public policy and economic and social-welfare choices.

63. A discussion of versions of the option for the poor and a set of recommendations for including it as an element in ethical theory is found in Stephen J. Pope, "Proper and Improper Partiality and the Preferential Option for the Poor," *Theological Studies* 54 (1993): 242–71.

64. Ibid., 265.

65. Ibid., 266.

66. Ibid.

67. Ibid., 266–67.

68. Particularly *On Kingship*, Book Two, chapter 4.118: "The first and most important is to act in accordance with virtue since virtue is what make one live well. The second—and it is secondary and a means to the first—is sufficiency of the material goods that are necessary for virtuous action." And: "A third requirement is that the king work to see that there is a sufficient supply of the necessities required to live well."

69. Amartya Sen, Nobel prize winner in economics, draws attention to the phenomenon of "missing women": the fact that in many developing countries, demographic data show that given the number of girl children born and the ratio of girls to boys, by the time these children reach adulthood (where one would expect to find a roughly similar ratio of women to men) what is found is a shocking reduction in the number of women in the population in proportion to the men who survive. Sen suggests that there are a variety of reasons for this reduction in the number of women, but that ultimately it points to a pattern of life that so specifically disadvantageous women that it shifts the population's demographics through a disproportionate number of women's deaths. See Amartya Sen, "Missing Women," *British Medical Journal* 304 (1992), 588. See also J. Dreze and Amartya Sen, *Hunger and Public Action* (Oxford: Clarendon Press, 1989), 52.

70. *ST* II-II.47.1.3 (emphasis added).

71. *ST* II-II.47.2.1.

72. *ST* II-II.47.3 sed contra (emphasis added).
73. *ST* II-II.47.3 ad 2.
74. *ST* II-II.47.6 sed contra.
75. *ST* II-II.47.8 sed contra.
76. *ST* II-II.47.10 sed contra. Here, again, Aquinas refers to Aristotle's *Ethics*. When he uses the phrase "According to the Philosopher" in his writing, it is Aristotle to whom he refers.
77. *ST* II-II.47.10.1 (emphasis in original).
78. *ST* II-II.47.10.2.
79. *ST* II-II.47.11 sed contra (emphasis added).
80. *ST* II-II.47.12 sed contra.
81. *ST* II-II.47.11 sed contra.
82. Justice is being discussed here as a comprehensive reality rather than the particular expressions of distributive, commutative, and communicative justice.
83. John Rawls, *A Theory of Justice* (Cambridge, Mass.: The Belknap Press of Harvard University Press, 1971), 136–42.
84. Rebecca Chopp offers provocative considerations on the phenomenon and function of testimony in theories of justice. See Chopp, "Theology and the Poetics of Testimony," 1997 Alumna of the Year Address, Chicago Divinity School, October 13, 1997. Published in *Criterion: A Publication of the Divinity School of the University of Chicago*, winter 1998, 2–12.
85. Chopp writes: "The poetics of testimony is my way of naming the discursive practices and various voices that seek to describe or name that which rational discourse will not or cannot reveal" (ibid., 2).
86. Ibid., 2.
87. Ibid., 8.
88. Ibid., 12 n. 21.

CHAPTER 4. THE RETRIEVED PRINCIPLE OF THE COMMON GOOD AND HEALTH CARE IN THE UNITED STATES

1. Hans-Georg Gadamer, *Truth and Method* (New York: Seabury Press, 1975), 308.
2. Ibid., 341. For an idea analogous to Gadamer's notion of "application," see Ricoeur's discussion of "appropriation" in Paul Ricoeur, "Appropriation," in Ricoeur, *Hermeneutics and the Human Sciences*, ed. and trans. John B. Thompson (New York: Cambridge University Press, 1981), 182–93.
3. I am grateful for the assistance of Brian Berry in articulating this insight.
4. The idea of a "hermeneutic circle" is often associated with the work of liberation theologians Juan Luis Segundo, Gustavo Gutiérrez, and José Míguez

Bonino. See for example Juan Luis Segundo, *The Liberation of Theology*, trans. John Drury (Maryknoll, N.Y.: Orbis Books, 1976), 179. In its various forms, a hermeneutic circle is a dialectical interaction and exchange between a specific social context or situation (generally a situation of injustice and/or suffering), ideology critique and social analysis of the situation, and consideration of biblical texts and faith tradition in light of the situation of suffering, all of which gives rise to an imperative for liberating action.

5. José Míguez Bonino, *Towards a Christian Political Ethics* (Philadelphia: Fortress Press, 1983), 83.

6. Ibid., 107.

7. Thomas L. Schubeck, S.J., *Liberation Ethics: Sources, Models, and Norms* (Minneapolis: Fortress Press, 1993), 221.

8. For example, in the late 1790s many local hospitals did not want to provide care to seamen from other towns. The United States government began taxing seamen's wages to fund a system of merchant marine hospitals, which evolved into the United States Public Health Service.

9. Janet O'Keefe, "The Right to Health Care and Health Care Reform," in *Health Care Reform: A Human Rights Approach*, ed. Audrey Chapman (Washington, D.C.: Georgetown University Press, 1994), 45.

10. John K. Iglehart, "The American Health Care System—Medicare," *New England Journal of Medicine* (November 12, 1992): 1467–72.

11. Commonwealth Fund Commission on Elderly People Living Alone, *Medicare's Poor: Filling the Gaps in Medical Coverage for Low-Income Elderly Americans* (November 20, 1987). Cited in O'Keefe, "The Right to Health Care and Health Care Reform," 38.

12. O'Keefe, "The Right to Health Care and Health Care Reform," 44.

13. Daniel Callahan, *The Troubled Dream of Life: In Search of a Peaceful Death* (New York: Simon and Schuster, 1993), 43–44.

14. Albert R. Jonsen, "Ethical Issues in Organ Transplantation," in *Medical Ethics*, 2d ed., ed. Robert M. Veatch (Boston: Jones & Bartlett Publishers, 1997), 267.

15. Charles J. Dougherty, Ph.D., "Ethical Values at Stake in Health Care Reform," *Journal of the American Medical Association* 268, no. 17 (1992): 2409–10.

16. The Universal Declaration of Human Rights, Article 25 states: "Everyone has the right to a standard of living adequate for health and well-being of himself and his family, including food, clothing, housing and medical care and necessary social services, and the right to security in the event of unemployment, sickness, disability, widowhood, old age or other lack of livelihood in circumstances beyond his control."

17. World Health Organization, Preamble to the Constitution, in *The First Ten Years of the World Health Organization* (Geneva: WHO, 1958), 459.

18. Ibid.

19. Pat Milmoe McCarrick, *A Right to Health Care: Scope Note 20*, Kennedy Institute of Ethics, National Reference Center for Bioethics Literature, Georgetown University, December, 1992, 1.

20. President's Commission for the Study of Ethical Problems in Medicine and Biomedical and Behavioral Research, Alexander M. Capron, Executive Director, *Securing Access to Health Care, A Report on the Ethical Implications of Differences in the Availability of Health Services, Volume One* (Washington, D.C., 1983). The commission, in its report, explicitly did not use the conceptual framework or language of moral or human rights of individuals to health care, but instead spoke in terms of a societal obligation to insure adequate health care for all. This option has been critiqued as conceding to the political climate in the United States at the time (the Reagan administration). See Dan W. Brock, "The President's Commission on the Right to Health Care," in *Health Care Reform: A Human Rights Approach*, ed. Audrey Chapman (Washington, D.C.: Georgetown University Press, 1994), 65–83.

21. Audrey Chapman, "Introduction," in *Health Care Reform: A Human Rights Approach*, 6.

22. See chapter 1.

23. Clarke E. Cochran, "The Common Good and Healthcare Policy," *Health Progress: Official Journal of the Catholic Health Association of the United States* 80, no. 3 (1999): 43.

24. Daniel Callahan, "Minimalist Ethics," *Hastings Center Report* 11, no. 5 (1981): 20.

25. Marion Danis and Larry R. Churchill, "Autonomy and the Common Weal," *Hastings Center Report* 21, no. 1 (1991): 25.

26. Thomas H. Murray, "Individualism and Community: The Contested Terrain of Autonomy," *Hastings Center Report* 24, no. 3 (1994): 32.

27. The phrase "relatively speaking" is inserted here to indicate several things: The definition of good health means different things in different societies, in different parts of the world; even in the same society, the "good health" of a twelve-year-old probably means something different than the health of an eighty-year-old. Here it is helpful to refer to Martha Nussbaum's use of the human functioning capabilities. She suggests that these represent universal human goods, no one of which in itself completely defines the person. She also notes that these goods will be embodied differently in different times and in different cultural settings. This is not to foster a colonial mentality, in which "civilized" societies expect more and better for themselves in terms of health than what might be expected for indigenous peoples, but it is to prevent the discussion from lapsing into whose definition of good health is applicable.

28. This is particularly Dan Brock's criticism of the report of the President's Commission. The report uses unambiguous, emphatic language in establishing the obligation of government to guarantee adequate care for all:

"Because . . . other means of securing care have failed to ensure adequate care for all, the Commission argued that 'the ultimate responsibility for ensuring this obligation is met rests with the Federal government' (30). The Federal government 'has a major responsibility for making sure that certain basic social goods, such as health care . . . are available to all' (31)." Yet the commission refrained from using the language of a *right* to health care for all citizens, which establishes an explicit legal obligation for the government to guarantee this right. Brock, "The President's Commission on the Right to Health Care," 67–68.

29. Mary Ann Baily, Ph.D., "Defining the Decent Minimum," in Chapman, ed., *Health Care Reform: A Human Rights Approach*, 169–70 (italics in original). The issue of what would constitute a basic minimum of health care guaranteed to all people is a strongly argued one. See Gene Outka, "Social Justice and Equal Access to Health Care," *The Journal of Religious Ethics* 2, no. 1 (Spring 1974): 11–32; Philip S. Keene, *Health Care Reform: A Catholic View* (New York: Paulist Press, 1993), 122–150; James Lindemann Nelson, "Public Participation and the Adequate Standard of Care," in Chapman, ed., *Health Care Reform: A Human Rights Approach*, 186–96; and Janet Weiner, "Towards a Uniform Health Benefit Package," in Chapman, ed., *Health Care Reform: A Human Rights Approach*, 197–210.

30. This contribution recalls the perspective of virtue ethics, emphasizing the shaping of the character of members of the community to become certain kinds of persons who subsequently make choices guided by corporately shared values and ethos. At the same time, I maintain that the securing of human rights is too crucial to be left to the voluntaristic instincts of the community.

31. Ron Hamel, Ph.D., "Of What Good Is the 'Common Good'?" *Health Progress: Official Journal of the Catholic Health Association of the United States* 80, no. 3 (1999): 46–47 (emphasis added).

32. Cochran, "The Common Good and Healthcare Policy," 42.

33. Chapman, "Introduction," 1.

34. Ibid., 2.

35. Dougherty, "Ethical Values at Stake in Health Care Reform," 2411.

36. Kenneth E. Thorpe, *The Rising Number of Uninsured Workers: An Approaching Crisis in Health Care Financing*, Institute for Health Services Research, Tulane University Medical Center, 1 October 1997.

37. Chapman, "Introduction," 2.

38. O'Keefe, "The Right to Health Care and Health Care Reform," 45–46.

39. Christopher F. Koller, "Money and Medical Care: Where Resources and Needs Conflict," *Commonweal* 126, no. 12 (June 18, 1999): 11.

40. Ibid.

41. Ibid., 12.

42. The point of this chapter is not to maintain that women alone are frequently ill served by the health care system in the United States. It is to claim

the validity of examining a social reality from the perspective of a historically marginalized constituency and to insist on a response to the fact that a great many women have distinct, serious, and overlooked problems in achieving health care services for themselves and for their dependents.

43. Institute for Women's Policy Research, *Women's Access to Health Insurance* (Washington, D.C., 1994), ii.

44. P. J. Farley, "Who Are the Underinsured?" *Milbank Quarterly* 63 (1985): 476–503.

45. Employee Benefit Research Institute, *Update: Americans Without Health Insurance*, Washington, D.C., Issue Brief No. 104, 1990.

46. M. L. Berk and A. K. Taylor, "Women and Divorce: Health Insurance Coverage, Utilization, and Health Care Expenditures," *American Journal of Public Health* 74 (1984): 1276–78.

47. B. A. Harvey, "A Proposal to Provide Health Insurance to All Children and All Pregnant Women," *New England Journal of Medicine* 323 (1990): 1216–20.

48. S. Sofaer and E. Abel, "Older Women's Health and Financial Vulnerability: Implications for the Medicare Benefit Structure," *Women Health* 16 (1990): 47–67.

49. Institute for Women's Policy Research, *Women's Access to Health Insurance*, 11.

50. Special Committee on Aging, U.S. Senate, *Aging America: Trends and Projections, 1987–88*, U.S. Department of Health and Human Services, 1988. Publication GPO 003–001–91543–0.

51. Nancy S. Jecker, Ph.D., "Age-Based Rationing and Women," *Journal of the American Medical Association* 266, no. 21 (1991): 3012–15.

52. M. E. Lutz, "Women, Work, and Preventive Health Care: An Exploratory Study of the Efficacy of HMO Membership," *Women Health* 15 (1989): 21–33; in Carolyn M. Clancy, M.D., and Charles T. Massion, M.D., "American Women's Health Care: A Patchwork Quilt with Gaps," *Journal of the American Medical Association* 268, no. 14 (1992): 1918–20.

53. A very small percentage of men do develop breast cancer, and their treatment options are similar to those for women.

54. Regina Griffin, RSCJ, "Black Women and Breast Cancer," *America* 179, no. 12 (October 24, 1998): 20.

55. National Cancer Institute statistics.

56. National Cancer Institute, Surveillance, Epidemiology, and End Result (SEER) database, 1999. Website: www-seer.ims.nci.nih.gov (accessed July 13, 2003).

57. This data was presented on February 5, 1997, by Dr. Ann Leitch, a surgeon from the University of Texas, at a hearing of the Senate Health and Human Services Subcommittee on the subject of mammography.

58. National Cancer Institute.

59. Young-Hee Yoon, *Briefing Paper: Women of Color and Access to Health Care* (Washington, D.C.: Institute for Women's Policy Research, 1994), 1. The term "women of color" is used to refer to more than just African-American women. It includes the very large population of women who are *not* Caucasian.

60. Dr. Jon Kerner, associate director of the Cancer Prevention and Control Program at the Lombardi Cancer Center of Georgetown University, quoted in Griffin, "Black Women and Breast Cancer." "In this now infamous project, the U.S. Government for four decades neither informed nor adequately treated a group of black men suffering from syphilis who were being used as human guinea pigs" (ibid., 21). The men were left untreated in order for the researchers to observe the disease progression if left untreated.

61. Ronald Bayer, Daniel Callahan, Arthur L. Caplan, and Bruce Jennings, "Toward Justice in Health Care," *American Journal of Public Health* 78, no. 5 (1988): 583.

62. Ibid., 583–84.

63. Audrey Chapman, "Policy Recommendations for Health Care Reform," in Chapman, ed., *Health Care Reform: A Human Rights Approach*, 312.

❧

Bibliography

BOOKS

Aquinas, Thomas. *Compendium of Theology.* Translated by Cyril Vollert, S.J. St. Louis, Mo.: B. Herder Book Company, 1947.

———. *The Summa Contra Gentiles.* Edited by Anton C. Pegis. New York: McGraw Hill, 1948.

———. *On Kingship.* Translated by Gerald B. Phelan. Toronto: Pontifical Institute of Medieval Studies, 1949.

———. *The Summa Theologica,* I-II, II-II. Translated by Fathers of the English Dominican Province. Westminster, Md.: Christian Classics, 1981.

Aquino, Maria Pilar. *Our Cry for Life: Feminist Theology from Latin America.* Maryknoll, N.Y.: Orbis Books, 1993.

Augustine. *The City of God (De Civitate Dei).* Volumes I and II. New York: E. P. Dutton, 1947.

Baumgarth, William, and Richard Regan, S.J., eds. *Saint Thomas Aquinas on Law, Morality, and Politics.* Indianapolis and Cambridge: Hackett Publishing Company, 1988.

Bequaert Holmes, Helen, and Laura M. Purdy, eds. *Feminist Perspectives in Medical Ethics.* Bloomington: Indiana University Press, 1992.

Borreson, Kari E. *Subordination and Equivalence: The Nature and Role of Women in Augustine and Thomas Aquinas.* Oslo, Norway: Universitetsforlaget, 1968. Washington, D.C.: University Press of America, 1981.

Brubaker, Pamela. *Women Don't Count: The Challenge of Women's Poverty to Christian Ethics.* AAR Academy Series No. 87. Atlanta, Ga.: Scholars Press, 1994.

Cahill, Lisa Sowle. *Between the Sexes: Foundations for a Christian Ethics of Sexuality.* Philadelphia: Fortress Press. 1983.

———. *Love Your Enemies: Discipleship, Pacifism, and Just War Theory*. Minneapolis: Fortress Press, 1994.

———. *Sex, Gender, and Christian Ethics*. New York: Press Syndicate of the University of Cambridge, 1996.

Callahan, Daniel. *What Kind of Life?* New York: Simon and Schuster, 1990.

———. *The Troubled Dream of Life: In Search of a Peaceful Death*. New York: Simon and Schuster, 1993.

Christ, Carol. *Womanspirit Rising: A Feminist Reader in Religion*. San Francisco: HarperSanFrancisco, 1992.

———. *Rebirth of the Goddess: Finding Meaning in Feminist Spirituality*. Cambridge, Mass.: Perseus Publishing, 1997.

Commonwealth Fund Commission on Elderly People Living Alone. *Medicare's Poor: Filling the Gaps in Medical Coverage for Low-Income Elderly Americans*. Commonwealth Fund, November 20, 1987.

Copleston, Frederick, S.J. *A History of Philosophy, Volume 2, Medieval Philosophy*. New York: Doubleday Books, 1948.

Daly, Mary. *Gyn/Ecology: The Metaethics of Radical Feminism*. Boston: Beacon Press, 1978.

———. *Beyond God the Father: Toward a Philosophy of Women's Liberation*. 2d ed. London: Women's Press, 1986.

———. *The Church and the Second Sex*. Boston: Beacon Press, 1986.

D'Entreves, A. P. *The Medieval Contribution to Political Thought*. Oxford: Oxford University Press, 1939.

———. *Aquinas: Selected Political Writings*. Translated by J. G. Dawson. Oxford: Basil Blackwell, 1959.

Dreze, J., and Amartya Sen. *Hunger and Public Action*. Oxford: Clarendon Press, 1989.

DuBose, Edwin R., Ronald P. Hamel, and Laurence J. O'Connell, eds. *A Matter of Principles? Ferment in U.S. Bioethics*. Valley Forge, Pa.: Trinity Press International, 1994.

Ehrenreich, Barbara, and Deidre English. *The Sexual Politics of Sickness*. Old Westbury, N.Y.: Feminist Press, 1973.

Farrell, Walter. *A Companion to the Summa, Volume 2*. New York: Sheed and Ward, 1945.

Finnis, John. *Natural Law and Natural Rights*. Oxford: Clarendon Press, 1989.

Fiorenza, Elisabeth Schüssler. *In Memory of Her: A Feminist Reconstruction of Christian Origins*. New York: Crossroad Publishing Company, 1989.

———. *But She Said: Feminist Practices of Biblical Interpretation*. Boston: Beacon Press, 1992.

———. *Jesus: Miriam's Child, Sophia's Prophet—Critical Issues in Feminist Christology*. New York: Continuum, 1994.

Forbes-Martin, Susan. *Refugee Women*. London: Zed, 1992.

Gadamer, Hans-Georg. *Truth and Method*. New York: Seabury Press, 1975.

Gilby, Thomas. *The Political Thought of Thomas Aquinas*. Chicago: University of Chicago Press, 1958.

Gilson, Etienne. *The Christian Philosophy of St. Thomas Aquinas*. New York: Random House, 1956.

Gonzalez, Justo L. *The Story of Christianity, Volume 1: The Early Church to the Dawn of the Reformation*. San Francisco: HarperSanFrancisco, 1984.

Grisez, Germain. *The Way of the Lord Jesus, Volume 1: Christian Moral Principles*. Chicago: Franciscan Herald Press, 1983.

Haight, Roger. *Dynamics of Theology*. Mahwah, N.J.: Paulist Press, 1990.

Haraway, Donna J. *Simians, Cyborgs, and Women: The Reinvention of Nature*. New York: Routledge, 1991.

Hauerwas, Stanley. *The Peaceable Kingdom: A Primer in Christian Ethics*. South Bend, Ind.: University of Notre Dame Press, 1984.

———. *A Community of Character: Toward a Constructive Christian Social Ethic*. South Bend, Ind.: University of Notre Dame Press, 1988.

———. *After Christendom? How the Church Is to Behave If Freedom, Justice, and a Christian Nation Are Bad Ideas*. Nashville: Abingdon Press, 1991.

Holland, Joe, and Peter Henriot, S.J. *Social Analysis: Linking Faith and Justice*. Maryknoll, N.Y.: Orbis Books, 1983.

Institute for Women's Policy Research. *Women's Access to Health Insurance*. Washington, D.C.: Institute for Women's Policy Research, 1994.

Jeanrond, Werner G. *Text and Interpretation as Categories of Theological Thinking*. New York: Crossroad Publishing Company, 1988.

———. *Theological Hermeneutics: Development and Significance*. New York: Crossroad Publishing Company, 1991.

Johnson, Elizabeth. *Consider Jesus: Waves of Renewal in Christology*. New York: Crossroad Publishing Company, 1991.

———. *She Who Is: The Mystery of God in Feminist Theological Discourse*. New York: Crossroad Publishing Company, 1995.

Kaiser Commission on the Future of Medicaid. *Medicaid at the Crossroads*. Baltimore, Md.: Kaiser Commission, 1992.

Keenan, James. *Goodness and Rightness in Thomas Aquinas' Summa Theologiae*. Washington, D.C.: Georgetown University Press, 1992.

Keene, Philip S. *Health Care Reform: A Catholic View*. New York: Paulist Press, 1993.

Küng, Hans, and David Tracy, eds. *Paradigm Change in Theology: A Symposium for the Future*. New York: Crossroad Publishing Company, 1991.

LaCugna, Catherine Mowry. *God for Us: The Trinity and Christian Life*. San Francisco: HarperSanFrancisco, 1991.

Lakeland, Paul. *Postmodernity: Christian Identity in a Fragmented Age*. Minneapolis, Minn.: Fortress Press, 1997.

Lindbeck, George. *The Nature of Doctrine: Religion and Theology in a Postliberal Age*. Louisville, Ky.: Westminster/John Knox Press, 1984.

Maccoby, Eleanor, and Carol N. Jacklin. *The Psychology of Sex Differences.* Stanford, Calif.: Stanford University Press, 1974.

Maritain, Jacques. *The Person and the Common Good.* New York: Charles Scribner's Sons, 1947.

McInerny, Ralph. *Ethica Thomistica: The Moral Philosophy of Thomas Aquinas.* Washington, D.C.: Catholic University of America Press, 1982.

McKnight, Edgar V. *Post-Modern Use of the Bible: The Emergence of Reader-Oriented Criticism.* Nashville: Abingdon Press, 1988.

Míguez Bonino, José. *Towards a Christian Political Ethics.* Philadelphia: Fortress Press, 1983.

National Cancer Institute. "Surveillance, Epidemiology, and End Result" (SEER) data base. 1999.

Nicholas, David. *The Evolution of the Medieval World: Society, Government, and Thought in Europe, 312–1500.* New York: Longman Publishing, 1992.

Noddings, Nel. *A Feminine Approach to Ethics and Moral Education.* Berkeley: University of California Press, 1984.

Nussbaum, Martha, and Jonathan Glover, eds. *Women, Culture, and Development: A Study of Human Capabilities.* Oxford: Clarendon Press, 1995.

Nussbaum, Martha, and Amartya Sen, eds. *The Quality of Life.* New York: Oxford University Press, 1992.

Okin, Susan Moller. *Women in Western Political Thought.* Princeton: Princeton University Press, 1979.

———. *Justice, Gender, and the Family.* New York: Basic Books, 1989.

O'Malley, John W. *Tradition and Transition: Historical Perspectives on Vatican II.* Wilmington, Del.: Michael Glazier, 1989.

Outka, Gene, and John P. Reeder, Jr., eds. *Prospectus for a Common Morality.* Princeton, N.J.: Princeton University Press, 1993.

Pegis, Anton C. *At the Origins of the Thomistic Notion of Man.* New York: The MacMillan Company, 1963.

Placher, William C. *Unapologetic Theology: A Christian Voice in a Pluralistic Conversation.* Louisville, Ky.: Westminster/John Knox Press, 1989.

Porter, Jean. *The Recovery of Virtue: The Relevance of Aquinas for Christian Ethics.* Louisville, Ky.: Westminster/John Knox Press, 1990.

Rawls, John. *A Theory of Justice.* Cambridge, Mass.: The Belknap Press of Harvard University Press, 1971.

Ricoeur, Paul. *Interpretation Theory: Discourse and the Surplus of Meaning.* Fort Worth: Texas Christian University Press, 1976.

———. *Hermeneutics and the Human Sciences: Essays on Language, Action, and Interpretation.* Edited and translated by J. B. Thompson. Cambridge: Cambridge University Press, 1981.

Ruether, Rosemary Radford. *Liberation Theology: Human Hope Confronts Christian History and American Power.* New York: Paulist Press, 1972.

———. *New Woman, New Earth: Sexist Ideologies and Human Liberation.* San Francisco: Harper & Row Publishers, 1975.

————. *Sexism and God-Talk: Toward a Feminist Theology.* Boston: Beacon Press, 1983.

————. *To Change the World: Christology and Cultural Criticism.* New York: Crossroad Publishing Company, 1983.

————. *Gaia and God: An Ecofeminist Theology of Earth Healing.* San Francisco: Harper and Row, 1992.

Schillebeeckx, Edward. *God the Future of Man.* New York: Sheed and Ward, 1968.

————. *Christ: The Experience of Jesus as Lord.* Translated by John Bowden. New York: Crossroad Publishing Company, 1990.

Schneiders, Sandra. *The Revelatory Text: Interpreting the New Testament as Sacred Scripture.* San Francisco: HarperSanFrancisco, 1991.

————. *Beyond Patching: Faith and Feminism in the Catholic Church.* New York: Paulist Press, 1991.

Schubeck, Thomas L. *Liberation Ethics: Sources, Models, and Norms.* Minneapolis, Minn.: Fortress Press, 1993.

Segundo, Juan Luis. *The Liberation of Theology.* Translated by John Drury (Maryknoll, N.Y.: Orbis Books, 1976.

Sherwin, Michael, O.P. *St. Thomas and the Common Good: The Theological Perspective: An Invitation to Dialogue.* Rome: Pontificia Universita San Tommaso, 1993.

Sherwin, Susan. *No Longer Patient: Feminist Ethics and Health Care.* Philadelphia: Temple University Press, 1992.

Sigmund, Paul. *St. Thomas Aquinas on Politics and Ethics.* New York and London: W. W. Norton & Company, 1988.

Smith, Dorothy. *The Everyday World as Problematic: A Feminist Sociology.* Boston: Northeastern University Press, 1987.

————. *The Conceptual Practices of Power: A Feminist Sociology of Knowledge.* Toronto: University of Toronto Press, 1990.

————. *Texts, Facts, and Femininity: Exploring the Relations of Ruling.* New York and London: Routledge, Chapman, and Hall, 1990.

Stumpf, Samuel E. *Socrates to Sartre: A History of Philosophy.* 4th ed. New York: McGraw Hill, 1988.

Tracy, David. *Blessed Rage for Order: The New Pluralism in Theology.* Minneapolis, Minn.: Winston Seabury Press, 1975.

————. *Plurality and Ambiguity: Hermeneutics, Religion, Hope.* San Francisco: Harper & Row Publishers, 1987.

————. *Dialogue with the Other: The Inter-Religions Dialogue.* Grand Rapids, Mich.: William B. Eerdmans Publishing Company, 1990.

————. *The Analogical Imagination: Christian Theology and the Culture of Pluralism.* New York: Crossroad Publishing Company, 1991.

United Nations. *Woman 2000, Vol. I, 1994.* New York: United Nations for the Advancement of Women, 1994.

Wheelwright, Philip. *Metaphor and Reality*. Bloomington: Indiana University Press, 1968.

Wolf, Susan M., ed. *Feminism and Bioethics: Beyond Reproduction*. New York: Oxford University Press, 1996.

World Health Organization. *Preamble to the Constitution, The First Ten Years of the World Health Organization*. Geneva: World Health Organization, 1958.

Yoon, Young-Hee. *Briefing Paper: Women of Color and Access to Health Care*. Washington, D.C.: Institute for Women's Policy Research, 1994.

ARTICLES

Aquino, Maria Pilar. "Women's Contribution to Theology in Latin America." In *Feminist Ethics and the Catholic Moral Tradition: Readings in Moral Theology No. 9*, edited by Charles E. Curran, Margaret A. Farley, and Richard A. McCormick, 90–119. New York: Paulist Press, 1996.

Archibald, Katherine. "The Concept of Social Hierarchy in the Writings of St. Thomas Aquinas." In *St. Thomas Aquinas on Politics and Ethics*, edited and translated by Paul E. Sigmund, 136–42. New York: W. W. Norton & Company, 1988.

Baily, Mary Ann. "Defining the Decent Minimum." In *Health Care Reform: A Human Rights Approach*, edited by Audrey Chapman, 167–85. Washington, D.C.: Georgetown University Press, 1994.

Baum, Gregory. "Modernity: A Sociological Perspective." *Concilium* 179, no. 5 (December 1992).

Bayer, Ronald, Daniel Callahan, Arthur L. Caplan, and Bruce Jennings. "Toward Justice in Health Care." *American Journal of Public Health* 78, no. 5 (1988): 583–88.

Beasley, Michael E., and Dorothy Q. Thomas. "Domestic Violence as a Human Rights Issue." In *The Public Nature of Private Violence: The Discovery of Domestic Abuse*, edited by Martha Albertson Fineman, Michael E. Beasley, and Roxanne Mykitiuk, 323–46. New York and London: Routledge, 1994.

Berk, M. L., and A. K. Taylor. "Women and Divorce: Health Insurance Coverage, Utilization, and Health Care Expenditures." *American Journal of Public Health* 74, no. 11 (1984): 1276–78.

Bovbjerg, Randall R., Charles C. Griffin, and Caitlin E. Carroll. "U.S. Health Care Coverage and Costs: Historical Development and Choices for the 1990's." *The Journal of Law, Medicine, and Ethics* (summer 1993): 141.

Brock, Dan W. "The President's Commission on the Right to Health Care." In *Health Care Reform: A Human Rights Approach*, edited by Audrey Chapman, 65–83. Washington, D.C.: Georgetown University Press, 1994.

Cahill, Lisa Sowle. "Presidential Address: Feminist Ethics and the Challenge of Cultures." In *Proceedings, Catholic Theological Society of America* 48

(1993), edited by Paul Crowley, 65–85. Santa Clara, Calif.: Catholic Theological Society of America, 1993.

————."Feminism and Christian Ethics." In *Freeing Theology: The Essentials of Theology in Feminist Perspective*, edited by Catherine Mowry LaCugna, 211–34. San Francisco: HarperSanFrancisco, 1993.

————. "Notes on Moral Theology, 1989: Feminist Ethics," *Theological Studies* 51, no. 1 (1990): 49–65.

Callahan, Daniel. "Minimalist Ethics." *Hastings Center Report* 11, no. 5 (1981): 19–25.

Cannon, Katie Geneva. "Slave Ideology and Biblical Interpretation." *Semia* 47 (1989): 9–23.

Chapman, Audrey. "Introduction." In *Health Care Reform: A Human Rights Approach*, edited by Audrey Chapman, 1–32. Washington, D.C.: Georgetown University Press, 1994.

————."Policy Recommendations for Health Care Reform." In *Health Care Reform: A Human Rights Approach*, edited by Audrey Chapman, 149–63. Washington, D.C.: Georgetown University Press., 1994.

Childress, James. "The Normative Principles of Medical Ethics." In *Medical Ethics*, 2d ed., edited by Robert M. Veatch, 29–55. Boston: Jones and Bartlett Publishers, 1997.

Chopp, Rebecca. "Practical Theology and Liberation." In *Formation and Reflection: The Promise of Practical Theology*, edited by Lewis S. Mudge and James N. Poling, 120–38. Philadelphia: Fortress Press, 1987.

————. "Theology and the Poetics of Testimony." 1997 Alumna of the Year Address, Chicago Divinity School. *Criterion: A Publication of the Divinity School of the University of Chicago* (winter 1998): 2–12.

Clancy, Carolyn M., and Charles T. Massion. "American Women's Health Care: A Patchwork Quilt with Gaps." *Journal of the American Medical Association* 268, no. 14 (1992): 1918–20.

Cochran, Clarke E. "The Common Good and Healthcare Policy." *Health Progress: Official Journal of the Catholic Health Association of the United States* 80, no. 3 (1999): 41–44, 47.

Crofts, R. "The Common Good in the Political Theory of Thomas Aquinas." *The Thomist* 37 (1973): 155–73.

Danis, Marion, and Larry R. Churchill. "Autonomy and the Common Weal." *Hastings Center Report* 21, no. 1 (1991): 25–31.

de Koninck, Charles. "In Defence of Saint Thomas." *Laval Théologique et Philosophique* 2 (1945): 9–100.

Devaney, Shelia Greeve. "Problems with Feminist Theory: Historicity and the Search for Sure Foundations." In *Embodied Love: Sensuality and Relationship as Feminist Values*, edited by Paula M. Cooey, Sharon A. Farmer, and Mary Ellen Ross. San Francisco: Harper and Row, 1987.

Dougherty, Charles J. "Ethical Values at Stake in Health Care Reform." *Journal of the American Medical Association* 268, no. 17 (1992): 2409–10.

Duska, Ronald. "Aquinas' Definition of Good: Ethical-Theoretical Notes on *De Veritate*, Q. 21." *The Monist* 58, no. 1 (1974): 151–62.

Elson, Diane. "Public Action, Poverty, and Development: A Gender Aware Analysis." Paper presented at the seminar *Women in Extreme Poverty: Integration of Women's Concerns into National Development Planning*. Vienna. November 1992.

Employee Benefit Research Institute. *Update: Americans without Health Insurance*. Issue Brief No. 104. Washington, D.C. 1990.

Eschmann, I. T. "A Thomistic Glossary on the Principle of the Preeminence of a Common Good." *Mediaeval Studies* 5 (1943): 123–65.

———. "In Defense of Jacques Maritain." In *The Modern Schoolman*, 192. St. Louis, Mo.: St. Louis University Press, 1945.

Farley, Edward. "Toward a Contemporary Theology of Human Being." In *Images of Man: Studies in Religion and Anthropology*, edited by J. William Angell and E. Pendleton Banks, 56–78. Macon, Ga.: Mercer University Press, 1984.

Farley, Margaret. "Feminist Consciousness and the Interpretation of Scripture." In *Feminist Interpretation of the Bible*, edited by Letty M. Russell, 41–54. Philadelphia: Westminster Press, 1985.

———. "Feminism and Universal Morality." In *Prospectus for a Common Morality*, edited by Gene Outka and John P. Reeder, Jr., 170–90. Princeton, N.J.: Princeton University Press, 1993.

———. "The Role of Experience in Moral Discernment." In *Christian Ethics: Problems and Prospects*, edited by Lisa Sowle Cahill and James F. Childress, 134–51. Cleveland, Ohio: Pilgrim Press, 1996.

Farley, P. J. "Who Are the Underinsured?" *Milbank Quarterly* 63 (1985): 476–503.

Fox, Renee C. "The Evolution of American Bioethics: A Sociological Perspective." In *Social Science Perspectives on Medical Ethics*, edited by George Weisz, 201–17. Philadelphia: University of Pennsylvania Press, 1990.

Griffin, Regina. "Black Women and Breast Cancer." *America* 24 (October 1998): 20–22.

Grisez, Germain, Joseph Boyle, and John Finnis. "Practical Principles, Moral Truth, and Ultimate Ends." *The American Journal of Jurisprudence* 32 (1987): 99–151.

Gudorf, Christine. "A Feminist Critique of Biomedical Principlism." In *A Matter of Principles? Ferment in U.S. Bioethics*, edited by Edwin Dubose, Ronald Hamel, and Laurence J. O'Connell. Valley Forge, Pa.: Trinity Press International, 1994.

Hamel, Ron. "Of What Good Is the 'Common Good'?" *Health Progress: Official Journal of the Catholic Health Association of the United States* 80, no. 3 (1999): 46–47.

Harrison, Beverly. "Misogyny and Homophobia: The Unexplored Connections." In *Making the Connections: Essays in Feminist Social Ethics.* Edited by Carol S. Robb. Boston: Beacon Press, 1985.

Harvey, B. A. "Proposal to Provide Health Insurance to All Children and All Pregnant Women." *New England Journal of Medicine* 323 (1990): 1216–20.

Hinsdale, Mary Ann. "Heeding the Voices: An Historical Overview." In *In the Embrace of God: Feminist Approaches to Theological Anthropology,* edited by Ann O'Hara Graff, 22–48. Maryknoll, N.Y.: Orbis Books, 1995.

Iglehart, John K. "The American Health Care System—Medicare." *New England Journal of Medicine* 327 (November 12, 1992): 1467–72.

Jecker, Nancy S. "Age-Based Rationing and Women." *Journal of the American Medical Association* 266, no. 21 (1991): 3012–15.

John Paul II, Pope. *Mulieris Dignitatem. Origins* (October 6, 1988): 262–83.

Jonsen, Albert R. "Ethical Issues in Organ Transplantation." In *Medical Ethics,* 2d ed., edited by Robert M. Veatch, 239–74. Boston: Jones & Bartlett Publishers, 1997.

Kabeer, Naila. "Women in Poverty: A Review of Concepts and Findings." Paper presented at the seminar *Women in Extreme Poverty: Integration of Women's Concerns into National Development Planning.* Vienna. November 1992.

Kass, Leon R. "Practicing Ethics: Where's the Action?" *Hastings Center Report* 20, no. 1 (1990): 5–12.

Keenan, James F., and Thomas R. Kopfensteiner. "Moral Theology Out of Western Europe." *Theological Studies* 59, no. 1 (1998): 107–35.

Koller, Christopher F. "Money and Medical Care: Where Resources and Needs Conflict." *Commonweal* (June 18, 1999): 11.

Kopas, Jane. "Transforming Theological Anthropology." In *Women and Theology, The Annual Publication of the College Theology Society,* vol. 40, edited by Mary Ann Hinsdale and Phyllis H. Kaminski, 216–33. Maryknoll, N.Y.: Orbis Books, 1995.

Little, David. "The Nature and Basis of Human Rights." In *Prospectus for a Common Morality,* edited by Gene Outka and John P. Reeder, Jr., 72–92. Princeton, N.J.: Princeton University Press, 1992.

Lutz, M. E. "Women, Work, and Preventive Health Care: An Exploratory Study of the Efficacy of HMO Membership." *Women Health* 15 (1989): 21–33.

MacDonald, Scott. "Theory of Knowledge." In *The Cambridge Companion to Aquinas,* edited by Norman Kretzmann and Eleonore Stump, 160–95. New York: Cambridge University Press, 1993.

Mahowald, Mary B. "On Treatment of Myopia: Feminist Standpoint Theory and Bioethics." In *Feminism and Bioethics: Beyond Reproduction,* edited by Susan M. Wolf, 95–115. New York: Oxford University Press, 1996.

Maloney, Linda M. "The Argument for Women's Difference in Classical Philosophy and Early Christianity." *Concilium* 6 (1991): 41–49.

Mariner, Wendy K. "Business vs. Medical Ethics: Conflicting Standards for Managed Care." *Journal of Law, Medicine, and Ethics* 23 (1995): 236–46.

McCarrick, Pat Milmoe. "A Right to Health Care: Scope Note 20." Kennedy Institute of Ethics, Georgetown University, Washington, D.C. December 1992.

McDonagh, Enda. "Structure and Basis of Moral Experience." *The Irish Theological Quarterly* 38 (1971): 4–20.

Murray, Thomas H. "Individualism and Community: The Contested Terrain of Autonomy." *Hastings Center Report* 24, no. 3 (1994): 32–33.

Nelson, Hilde Lindemann, and James Lindemann Nelson. "Justice in the Allocation of Health Care Resources: A Feminist Account." In *Feminism and Bioethics: Beyond Reproduction*, edited by Susan M. Wolf, 351–67. New York: Oxford University Press in conjunction with the Hastings Center, 1996.

Nelson, James Lindemann. "Public Participation and the Adequate Standard of Care." In *Health Care Reform: A Human Rights Approach*, edited by Audrey Chapman, 186–96. Washington, D.C.: Georgetown University Press, 1994.

Nemetz, A. "The Common Good." In *The New Catholic Encyclopedia*, vol. 4. Washington, D.C.: Catholic University of America, 1967.

Nussbaum, Martha. "Human Functioning and Social Justice: In Defense of Aristotelian Essentialism." *Political Theory* 20, no. 2 (1992): 202–46.

———. "Non-Relative Virtues: An Aristotelian Approach." In *The Quality of Life*, edited by Martha C. Nussbaum and Amartya Sen, 242–69. Oxford: Clarendon Press, 1993.

O'Hara Graff, Ann. "The Struggle to Name Women's Experience." In *In the Embrace of God: Feminist Approaches to Theological Anthropology*, edited by Ann O'Hara Graff, 71–89. Maryknoll, N.Y.: Orbis Books, 1995.

O'Keefe, Janet. "The Right to Health Care and Health Care Reform." In *Health Care Reform: A Human Rights Approach*, edited by Audrey R. Chapman, 35–64. Washington, D.C.: Georgetown University Press, 1994.

Outka, Gene. "Social Justice and Equal Access to Health Care." *The Journal of Religious Ethics* 2, no. 1 (1974): 11–32.

Peters, Julie, and Andrea Wolper. "Introduction." In *Women's Rights, Human Rights: International Feminist Perspectives*, edited by Julie Peters and Andrea Wolper, 2–3. New York and London: Routledge, 1995.

Placher, William C. "Postliberal Theology." In *The Modern Theologians: An Introduction to Christian Theology in the Twentieth Century*, vol. 2, edited by David Ford, 115–28. New York: Basil Blackwell, 1989.

Pope, Stephen J. "Proper and Improper Partiality and the Preferential Option for the Poor." *Theological Studies* 54 (1993): 242–71.

Porter, Jean. "Desire for God: Ground of the Moral Life in Aquinas." *Theological Studies* 47 (1986): 53–55.

———."Basic Goods and the Human Good in Recent Catholic Moral Theology." *The Thomist* 57, no. 1 (1993): 27–49.

———. "At the Limits of Liberalism: Thomas Aquinas and the Prospects for a Catholic Feminism." *Theology Digest* 41, no. 4 (1994): 315–30.

Rabuzzi, Kathryn Allen. "The Socialist Feminist Vision of Rosemary Radford Ruether." *Religious Studies Review* 15, no. 1 (1989): 4–8.

Ruether, Rosemary Radford. "Feminist Interpretation: A Method of Correlation." In *Feminist Interpretation of the Bible*, ed. Letty M. Russell, 111–24. Philadelphia: Westminster Press, 1985.

———. "The Development of My Theology." *Religious Studies Review* 15, no. 1 (1989): 2–4.

Saiving, Valerie. "The Human Situation: A Feminine View." *Journal of Religion* 40 (1960): 100–112.

Schillebeeckx, Edward. "Questions on Christian Salvation of and for Man." In *Toward Vatican III: The Work That Needs to Be Done*, edited by David Tracy, Hans Küng, and Johannes B. Metz, 27–44. New York: Seabury Press. 1978.

Schneiders, Sandra. "Feminist Ideology Criticism." *Biblical Theology Bulletin* 19, no. 1 (1989): 3–10.

———. "Living Word or Deadly Letter: The Encounter between the New Testament and Contemporary Experience." *Proceedings, Catholic Theological Society of America* 47 (1992): 45–60.

Schultz, Janice L. "Thomistic Metaethics and a Present Controversy." *The Thomist* 52, no. 1 (1988): 40–62.

Scully, Edgar. "The Place of the State in Society According to Thomas Aquinas." *The Thomist* 45, no. 3 (1981): 407–29.

Sen, Amartya. "Missing Women." *British Medical Journal* 304 (1992): 587–88.

Sofaer, S., and E. Abel. "Older Women's Health and Financial Vulnerability: Implications for the Medicare Benefit Structure." *Women Health* 16 (1990): 47–67.

Staley, Kevin M. "Happiness: The Natural End of Man?" *The Thomist* 53, no. 2 (1989): 215–34.

Stamatopoulou, Elissavet. "Women's Rights and the United Nations." In *Women's Rights, Human Rights: International Feminist Perspectives*, edited by Julie Peters and Andrea Wolper, 36–48. New York and London: Routledge, 1995.

Tolbert, Mary Ann. "Social, Sociological, and Anthropological Methods." In *Searching the Scriptures: A Feminist Introduction*, edited by Elisabeth Schüssler Fiorenza, 255–71. New York: Crossroad Publishing Company, 1993.

Tracy, David. "Particular Questions within General Consensus." In *Consensus in Theology? A Dialogue with Hans Küng and Edward Schillebeeckx*, edited by Leonard Swidler, 33–39. Philadelphia: Westminster Press, 1980.

———. "Theological Interpretation of the Bible Today." In *A Short History of the Interpretation of the Bible*, edited by David Tracy and Robert Grant, 151–87. Philadelphia: Fortress Press, 1984.

———. "Interpretation (Hermeneutics)." In *International Encyclopedia of Communications*, vol. 2, edited by Erik Barnouw et al., 343–48. New York: Oxford University Press, 1989.

———. "Approaching the Christian Understanding of God." In *Systematic Theology: Roman Catholic Perspectives, Vol. 1*, edited by Francis Schüssler Fiorenza and John P. Galvin, 131–48. Minneapolis: Fortress Press, 1991.

———. "God, Dialogue, and Solidarity: A Theologian's Refrain," In *How My Mind Has Changed*, edited by James M. Wall and David Heim, 88–99. Grand Rapids, Mich.: William B. Eerdmans Publishing Company, 1991.

———. "Evil, Suffering, and Hope: The Search for New Forms of Contemporary Theodicy." *Proceedings of the Fiftieth Annual Convention, Catholic Theological Society of America*, vol. 50 (1995): 15–36.

UNICEF. "State of the World's Children." In *Ours by Right: Women's Rights as Human Rights*, edited by Joanna Kerr. Ottawa: North-South Institute, 1993.

United Nations. *Convention on the Elimination of All Forms of Discrimination against Women.* 1979.

United States Senate, Special Committee on Aging. *Aging in America: Trends and Projections, 1987–88.* Washington, D.C.: U.S. Department of Health and Human Services, 1988. Publication GPO 003–001–91543–0.

Wali, Sima. "Human Rights for Refugee and Displaced Women." In *Women's Rights, Human Rights: International Feminist Perspectives*, edited by Julie Peters and Andrea Wolper, 336–37. New York and London: Routledge, 1995.

Weiner, Janet. "Towards a Uniform Health Benefit Package." In *Health Care Reform: A Human Rights Approach*, edited by Audrey Chapman, 197–210. Washington, D.C.: Georgetown University Press, 1994.

Index

"anthropological constants," 4, 27–28, 160n8, 168nn84, 85, 87
anthropology. *See* anthropology of Thomas Aquinas; feminist theological hermeneutics and anthropology; human functioning capabilities
anthropology of Thomas Aquinas, 45–49, 82–84, 96–100; and Aristotle's hierarchical order of creation, 47–48, 82–83; and central importance of the common good, 59–60, 71; creation and humanity in, 47–49; and dualistic methodology, 97–98; and embodiment, 98–99; feminist retrieval of, 46, 86, 96–100; and free will/agency, 99; and literal use of scripture, 98; and participation in government, 99–100; relationality and extreme individualism, 99, 187n31; and the transcendent, 100; women, men, and reason, 48–49, 84, 173n14; women and, 46–49,

83–84, 97–98; women and hierarchical order of creation, 47–48; women and men in God's image, 48–49, 84; and women's biological roles and "special nature," 97–98, 186nn27, 28
apocalypticism, 22–23, 24, 166n77
Aquino, Maria Pilar, 33
Archibald, Katherine, 44
Aristotle: anthropology of, 4, 66, 82–83; and Aquinas, 43–45, 52, 66, 82–83, 84, 183n160; and Christian relation to natural world/creation, 43–45; on goodness and the highest good, 52; on hierarchy, 44–45, 47, 173n6; on human functioning capabilities and virtues, 4, 35
Augustine: and Neoplatonic view of creation, 43; on peace and just war, 181n150; on society and the state, 60, 177n54; and Western presumptions about women, 29

209

God/humanity, 107–9, 114; and tradition theory/experience split, 125–26; and the transcendent, 100; and women's biology and "special nature," 97–98, 186nn27, 28; and women's experiences of suffering, 114–19, 124–25, 153–54, 189n69; and women's self-abnegation, 110–11. *See also* health care and the retrieved common good

feminist theological hermeneutics, 1–41; basic premises of, 1–3; and classic texts, 1–2; critical retrieval, presuppositions of, 39–40, 86, 183n1; critical retrieval, proposed method for, 39–41, 85–96, 155, 172n116, 183n1; critical retrieval and mutually critical correlation, 3, 18–19, 23–24; and hermeneutics of suspicion, 2, 3, 11–12, 17, 163n43; and human functioning capabilities, 34–39, 40, 92–93, 111, 171n113; and liberation theology, 2–3; and Nussbaum's anthropology, 3–4, 24–39; and principle of analogy, 1, 159n5; and Ruether's feminist critical retrieval, 3, 18–24, 39–40, 85–86; and Schneiders's textual hermeneutics, 3, 4–17, 39–40, 85–86; and tools of critical analysis, 40–41; and women's experiences, 33–34, 39–40. *See also* feminist theological hermeneutics and anthropology; Nussbaum, Martha; Ruether, Rosemary Radford, and feminist critical retrieval; Schneiders, San-

dra, textual hermeneutics of; scripture

feminist theological hermeneutics and anthropology, 3–4, 24–39; and "anthropological constants," 4, 27–28, 160n8, 168nn84, 85, 87; and anthropological markers, 35–39, 40, 92–93, 111, 114–16, 171n113; and anthropological universals, 28–32, 34; and anthropology as methodological issue, 26–28, 168nn84, 85, 171n113; historical consciousness and universal truth claims, 28–29; the human good and Nussbaum's human functioning capabilities, 34–39, 92–93, 111, 171n113; and inductive anthropological method, 28; and normative presumptions about human nature, 29–32, 169nn89, 91, 93; postmodern and hermeneutical methodologies, 24–26, 167n82, 169n93; and the Roman Catholic moral tradition, 32–33; and women's experience of suffering, 33–34, 170nn100, 101, 171n102. *See also* human functioning capabilities

Finnis, John, 178n89
Fiorenza, Elisabeth Schüssler, 158n3, 168n86
Frankfurt philosophical school, 11
Frei, Hans, 25
Freud, Sigmund, 2, 11
Freudian psychoanalysis, 19–20

Gadamer, Hans-Georg, xii, 128; criticism of work of, 11, 162n40;

131–33, 142, 145; the poor and near-poor elderly, 132, 145–46; and supplemental coverage/policies, 132, 145–46; tradition of coverage for vulnerable groups, 131, 191n8; the uninsured/underinsured, 141–43, 145; and women, 143–50, 153; and women as caregivers, 146; and women's coverage/treatment issues, 144–46, 193n42

hermeneutical theology, 1–2; and classic texts, 1–2; defining, 1; and hermeneutics of suspicion, 2, 3, 11–12, 17, 163n43. *See also* feminist theological hermeneutics

"hermeneutic circles," 128–29, 190n4

hermeneutics of suspicion, 2, 3, 11–12, 17, 163n43

hermeneutics of transformation, 12–16, 17; and appropriation, 14–16, 17; and criteria for assessing validity of an interpretation, 13–14, 17; and goal of textual meaning, 13; and interpretation, 12–16, 17; and Ricoeur's theory of text and interpretation, 6, 12–14; steps in, 12–13, 17

Hick, John, 167n82

Hinsdale, Mary Ann, 27, 168n86

Holocaust Memorial/Museum (Washington, D.C.), 153

human functioning capabilities: as anthropological markers, 35–39, 40, 92–93, 111, 114–16, 171n113; and Aquinas's virtue of prudence, 124; and Aristotle,

4, 35; and feminist theological hermeneutics, 34–39, 40, 92–93, 111, 171n113; and the good life, 35–37; kinship and religion, 37; meaningful work, 37; the minimally human life and basic capabilities, 35–36; Nussbaum and, 34–39, 92–93, 111, 116, 136–37, 192n27; as open to revision, 38–39, 171n113; and universal right to health care, 136–37, 192n27; wonder and the transcendent, 37

human good: and acting well, 56–57; Aquinas and perfection as, 52–58, 109–16; and balance between action and contemplation, 55–56; and the body, 57, 112–13, 176n47; and contemplation of truth, 54–55; and embodiment, 110, 113; feminist retrieval of Aquinas's, 109–16; and free choice/free will, 52–54, 56–57; and happiness, 53, 57, 112–13, 176n47; the natural law tradition of Aquinas, 111, 188n55; pursued within society/community, 57–58; scriptural images of, 114; and traditional Christian conceptions of human nature, 109–10; and union with God, 53, 54, 174n31, 175nn37, 38; and virtues, 53–54, 55, 120–24, 174n32, 175n38, 176n40; and women's experiences of suffering, 114–16; and women's self-abnegation, 110–11. *See also* good